MOBSTER FOR HIRE

MOBSTER FOR HIRE

by

R. J. MATTHEWS

MOBSTER FOR HIRE

ISBN: 978-0-9980965-9-9

Cover design: CjBell Photomation

MOBSTER FOR HIRE

Place your bets

"I'll take State over the visiting team, and I'll give you five points," Marty shouts out to Vinny, one of the normal bettors on such college football games.

"Eight points would be more fair," Vinny says, trying to bump up the odds to his favor.

"It doesn't matter. At the end of the day, I'll still take your money anyway," he says, laughing at Vinny before sliding his hand in front of him and shaking his punter's sweaty hand. "Deal."

Vinny is skeptical of this back-alley oddsmaker—Mickey had recently given him permission to operate in the area. Granted, the bookie does give more points than the last oddsmaker, but this guy has unmatched skill in that he usually picks the winners over 90 percent of the time, even with the point spread added in. It's like this Marty fellow knows all bettors are going to lose no matter what, but he tries to coax them into thinking they have a shot at a winner with the point spread. Next time, Vinny is going to listen to the previous bettor and then bet the opposite.

"You think your so clever, eh, Marty?" Vinny says with a smirk, studying the bookie.

Marty only shrugs his shoulders, playing it off. "Naw. I just trying to earn a living, that's all."

"Then if you know the outcomes all the time, why aren't you putting more money down at the casinos, like Vegas or Atlantic City?"

Marty chuckles as he's taking the betting slip from the next customer, then replies, "What makes you think I'm not?"

Vinny is surprised by this response. He hadn't considered that Marty would be betting in the big-time casinos while still running a back-alley betting pool. Seconds later, a police siren pierces the sounds of the day, echoing louder in the alleyway the closer it gets. Marty has time to take one more bet and fills in the slip, hastily taking the cash in exchange.

"All righty, folks, that's all for now. I have to be going, and I would strongly suggest you do the same."

The police siren continues getting even louder, and most of the bettors start to bolt. Marty turns around and knocks on a door. The door opens, a man grabs Marty as he quickly enters the back of the restaurant. The door closes behind him with a thud. Vinny watches the entire sequence unfold and then realizes he needs to move quickly. His long strides shortly become a full sprint, and he turns a corner down another alleyway just before the police car pulls into the alley behind him. He never glances back.

Phew. That was too close, Vinny thinks as he blends into the crowds of people on the city streets. *Damn. How did Marty know when to disappear? Wait a minute—how did he know where to disappear to?*

Marty has done this action on many occasions that it's practically second nature to him. He then locks the door and adjusts the nearby boxes, adding the final touches to cover his tracks.

Geno Rossi, the owner of Romano's Eatery yells at Marty in the back. "My boy, what the hell are you doing?"

"Sorry, I was just adjusting these boxes," Marty answers, knowing it's all a ruse for anyone who might happen to be listening in.

"Well, don't make a mess—you hear me?"

2

"I understand completely," Marty says, giving a perfunctory reply as though he is following a well-rehearsed script.

"Good. I don't want people to think I'm running something illegal or such." Geno Rossi, smiles at Marty before resuming his operations at the restaurant.

A young man named Marty, still in his dashing thirties, with fair hair, yet tall and brawny, strolls down the alley. He spies the other gang members, the punters, who come here to gamble away their hard-earned money in hopes of gaining more and joins the group.

Too bad, guys. Though I have no remorse in taking your money, Marty thinks when it's his turn to roll. As the game continues, he wins again and again, thanks to his loaded dice.

"Damn, man. Why you always win?" one of the patrons who donates his income to Marty's windfall pot demands of the guy he is handing his hard-earned money over to.

"I dunno. I have no woman in my life. So it must be unlucky in love, lucky in everything else." Marty rolls again and throws a double five.

Fewer people had thrown money down to bet against Marty's double five. Noticing this, he wonders, *Should I throw something to lose in order to keep them in the game or throw something to take all their money now?*

"Well, what are you calling now?" a street gambler demands.

"I'll throw at hard seven."

"Then I'm putting twenty down says you crap out."

Damn, I only got one taker on this throw? Marty shakes the dice in his hand, hoping to attract more suckers. He gives up and lets go of the dice, watching them fall to the ground. One comes up as a three, and the other comes up as a four. He looks up, staring at this round's loser.

"That's fucked up. How are you doing that?" The gambler throws down a twenty in disgust. "Shit ain't right. It just ain't right." He walks away, continuing to mutter to himself.

Marty scoops up the cash. "Anyone else? Place your bets. Come on. My lucky streak's gotta end at some point. I can't go on taking all your money." He smiles as he grabs the dice, hoping to attract more bettors.

"You gotta lose at some point. I'll take your offer," a new gambler to the game says as he pushes his way forward and plops two twenties down on the street.

Staring at the money thrown before him, Marty shouts out, "Anyone else? Anyone want me to throw a lucky ten? Come on, a ten! You know how hard it is to throw a ten!"

Another bettor caves into the temptation. He slaps a twenty on top of the money in the pot. "I want to see this."

With a quick motion, Marty picks up the dice and lets them roll back and forth in his hand before releasing them to the ground. They roll over the three twenties before stopping on a four and a six. He never looks down at the dice, but based on the facial expressions of the gamblers, he can tell that they lost and he won.

"Thank you, gentleman. It is always a pleasure." Marty takes the pot, hoping it has built up to more but realizing that it grows more slowly after each win. People start to see a winning streak and tend to bet less. A few of the gamblers leave. He knows it's time and packs up his game for the day. "All righty, fellas. I love taking ya'll money, but I must run. See ya here tomorrow. I gotta lose at some point." Marty takes his dice, hoping no one thinks about the dice being loaded, and saunters down the alley. The crowd disperses with him and he smiles, knowing he scammed these guys for over five hundred in less than an hour. Not bad for a half a day's work. He now wonders what he should do with the other half of the day.

As Marty enters a convenience store, Mickey, out of nowhere, knocks into his shoulder, nearly causing Marty to fall over, but he catches himself before making an embarrassing mistake.

"You know, you should start thinking of your future," Mickey says, grabbing Marty and pushing him forward, through the entrance to the store and back onto the streets. "A man of your talents can go far in this business—that is, if you have the right mentorship." Mickey smiles at him.

"Oh, I guess it will only cost me, what, twenty percent?"

"Hey, I was only gonna charge you ten percent, but if you want to pay more, I'm not gonna argue with ya." Mickey grabs Marty by the shoulder.

Marty lets out a snort. "Pretty soon, you'll want a cut in my action on the sports betting, too, I reckon."

"Naw. I'll leave you to make your money for now. But once you start getting greedy, then you can pay me my cut. Fair is fair." Mickey pulls out a smoke, flicks his Zippo, and lights the cigarette all in one fluid motion. He dangles the lit cigarette while still saying, "Now, you look like a smart lad. Surely you have no issues with our arrangement?"

Marty waves the smoke away from him. "Meaning I make all the money and you profit from it—that's what you call fair?" Marty continues to wave his hand and even blows the smoke in another direction. "I do the work, and you take your generous cut. What a deal!"

"Hey, you're lucky I'm not taking more." He guides Marty down the street, eventually slowing as they come to a dive bar, one with no windows. It's predictably dimly lit on the inside.

Mickey looks back over his shoulder to see that his car is still parked down the street.

"Yeah. I feel so lucky. You can buy me a drink with the money I just paid you," he says, engaging in ribbing with Mickey, his soon-to-be mentor, for the moment but looking around at the dark and bleak bar they have ended up at.

"Oh, you have so much to learn from me . . . Where do I begin?" Mickey then walks up to the bartender and orders a round, throwing down enough cash to pay for this round and the next couple of rounds.

The bartender takes the money and pours a couple of house beers in some pint-size glasses. It's debatable if the glasses are clean or semi clean. Mickey grabs the two full glasses of beer and heads over to the table Marty secured in the dingy bar.

"Here," he says, planting the beers on the table.

Marty grabs the glass and starts to take a pull from the freshly poured beer but waits as Mickey sits down and grabs the other beer.

"Cheers, bro."

"Cheers to ya," Marty joins in. He then slams the beer.

Mickey takes a drink and sets the glass back on the table. "You shouldn't drink so fast. It comes with age." Mickey reaches for the glass and takes a longer pull this time.

Marty finishes his beer and taps the glass, signaling for another as he looks around for the waitress. He finally spies a waitress—maybe the one who should have served them so that they didn't have to go to the bar for a drink. He waves a hand to get the waitress's attention.

"Excuse me, miss. Hello?"

The waitress wanders over. "Yes, sir, what do you need?"

Moving his glass toward her, Marty says, "Another beer, if you'd be so kind."

The waitress smiles back at him. "Sure, love, anything for you." She then turns around and, swaying her hips, approaches the bar to give the order to the bartender to refill his glass.

Moments later, the waitress returns. "You know, you're my favorite customer tonight. Are you sure you don't want to be my favorite customer in the morning too?"

It takes Marty a few seconds to get the innuendo. He decides to look back at the fishing show on the TV screen rather than giving his attention to the flirtatious waitress.

"I hear ya, but all I really need is another beer. Sorry." He taps his empty glass in front of her, ignoring her pointed remark.

"Here ya go," the waitress says as she roughly slides the beer to him across the table, a curt response to the insipid dialogue and her failed attempt to woo him.

Mickey chuckles as he watches Marty mop up some of the spilled beer with a few napkins.

Marty throws the wet napkins off to the side. "If that's how it's gotta be, then so be it. I still got my beer. Though I'm probably not getting anything else tonight."

"Clearly, you're not in touch with the local scene. Maybe you should try it out sometime," Mickey says, offering some advice.

"Hey, look," Marty says, not paying attention to the conversation at the table but watching as the person on the screen reels in a large fish. "The fishing tournament is back on!"

Looking down at his now-empty beer glass, Mickey shakes his head. "I suppose it is . . ."

Watching fishing shows has always been one of Marty's dirty little secrets, although he's not attempting to hide it at the moment. When the show cuts off for commercial break, Marty looks back across the table, waiting for Mickey to say something. But he just sits there looking back at him, like he is trying to make a decision about whether to tell him something or maybe debating on whether to order another round.

Mickey sees the waitress heading in their direction. Finally, the silence is broken when she asks, "You want another one?"

"Why not?"

After ordering yet another round and watching the waitress depart, Mickey leans in toward the center of the table. He waves his hand to his companion, indicating that he should do the same—like he is going to reveal a secret or something.

"I've been thinking." A long pause follows.

"About what?" Marty says, unsure what he is getting at.

"Oh, about having you on my team," Mickey reveals.

"Sounds great. How's the pay?" he responds sarcastically.

Mickey stops to think this whole deal through. Granted, looking at this guy across the table, he clearly has a knack for sports betting and can handle himself when the situation dictates, but he's also a smartass wise guy. He weighs the options in his head for quite a while, wondering if he is making the right decision or a smart decision. In the end, he goes with his judgment and decides to invite Marty to the underground world.

"So, Marty, you ready to join us? You want the good life or not?" It's a heavy question, the kind that will mark a person's direction in life.

"Show me what you got—I suppose I can follow along," Marty says, sealing the deal with his characteristic sarcasm.

"That's good enough for me. Welcome to the club."

Mickey then begins talking about the mobster life and how it will affect him at some point, whether he's joining for amusement or employment. Marty continues to nods his head in agreement, knowing that what he is signing up for is beyond his imagination. He thinks it is even better and certainly worth the risk.

"So what do I have to do?"

"For starters, everything and anything I say. Then we can negotiate. How's that sound?"

"You're the boss, I reckon. You call the shots. I follow along. Easy enough."

Mickey laughs. "See? You're learning already. Now, if you remember that all the time, then we should have no future issues." He calls over the waitress again and orders two shots of some expensive alcohol.

When the waitress comes back, she gracefully places one the glasses in front of Marty. She raises her head, looking at him, and then grabs the other shot glass and drops it in front of the paying patron. She departs, hoping the first guy has some interest in her.

Mickey raises the glass in the traditional fashion and says, "Marty. Marty. Welcome to the club!"

Marty then raises his to match, deciding his fate in one fell swoop of a shot glass. "Cheers."

With that fateful shot of some brown-colored liquor, he has now joined forces with the path of the unrighteousness and claimed the career path of what he has haphazardly been trying to avoid. He accepts the ramifications of his permanent decision.

"OK. OK. I hear ya. Now, what is required of me?" Marty asks.

"Oh, you mean, when do you begin?" Mickey inquires sarcastically. "You can begin whenever, just not tonight."

"Fine, then."

Mickey leans back, relaxing. "This night is yours. After that, you just signed your eternal deal with the devil."

Slamming the glass down on the table after finishing it, Marty says, "Then the devil can pay for the next round as well."

"Fine. But come tomorrow, your life will change for the better."

"Or the worst," Marty adds,

"Or for the betterment of yourself," Mickey quickly responds. "It all depends on your perspective. And, of course, if you stay alive. Ha-ha."

"Well, then, my perspective is a little clouded—or a little drunk." He gestures the waitress to deliver another round. She does eventually, but she approaches with hesitation.

"I need to cut you boys off," the waitress says. "Last round."

"Do what you must," Marty replies, slurring slightly. "Me and my colleague were just about to leave anyway."

Mickey nods his head in affirmation. "Sure. Let's go where we are more appreciated. This should cover the tab." He stands up and throws a couple of twenties down on the table before heading toward the door.

Marty takes the same route as his mentor and finds Mickey in the parking lot.

"What do you want to do?" Marty asks.

Mickey smiles back and declares, "We need to show the competition what we're made of."

"So . . . you want to bust up some of their joints? Sounds risky, but what the hell, why not?"

"Good. We hit this one first," Mickey declares.

"I'm right behind ya," Marty says, affirming his loyalty.

Marty always could predict the winner. Well, about 90 percent of the time. The rest of the time he would guess, but he tended to favor the winning side. Even back in high school, he would take bets here and there. He'd win somebody's lunch money, which he'd eventually use to buy smokes or beer. After a while, he realized he never lost or very rarely did, but he kept it a secret—although he did draft a paper for English class about it, for which he earned an A, and discussed it with the statistics teacher many times after class. Eventually, the statistics teacher bet on a few of the games Marty predicted. When he started winning a lot of money, he decided he had "enough evidence" to prove Marty's ability.

"Hey, Mr. Stubbs," Marty called out one day after class. He then asked the teacher if he could get a cut of the prize money.

"Marty, my boy, it would not be ethical for me to share the winnings with you. I could lose my job."

Marty saw through this excuse—Mr. Stubbs was trying to bullshit him and not share any of the prize money.

"Wait a minute. You're profiting for my advice," Marty declared.

"It's all for research, of course," he said, giving another excuse.

"Well, then, at the very least, I reckon you buy me a case of beer, and we'll call it even."

"You know I can't do that."

"Fine. And you know I won't be giving you any more picks. How's that sound?" Marty grinned.

"How 'bout I fail you? How would you like that?" Mr. Stubbs threw back, playing hardball.

"Go ahead. Then you'll have to explain the sudden windfall to the IRS when I call them—anonymously, of course—about your taxable winnings. I assume they can audit your recent bank deposits."

"OK, then, what brand of beer you say you wanted?"

Marty paused to think about his choices. "Oh, something Canadian will do. Throw in a bottle of whisky as well. No cheap shit."

"Sure, kid. Whatever. Now, who's gonna win this week?" He wanted the latest predictions.

Glumly, Marty picked up the newspaper, turned to the sports section, and rifled through the pages until he reached the column containing the games for that coming Saturday. Laughing at the odds, he began to circle the correct winners for the week. There were times when he thought about circling the opposites, just to watch Mr. Stubbs lose a bucket of money, but he didn't want to be too vindictive—plus, it was a good deal to have this guy buy alcohol for him. How else was he going to score some beer and whisky at the age of seventeen?

Marty finished circling the correct winners and flipped the paper back to the teacher. Mr. Stubbs grabbed the paper carefully like he was holding the original Declaration of Independence document. Looking over the marks, he began to comment on the picks.

"Are you sure about this one?" he asked, pointing to an upset pick.

"Bet what you want, for all I care. I won't say I told you so."

Mr. Stubbs shakes his head. "I just don't know. Are you sure?"

"It's your money—bet how you want to. You're the adult. Make a decision. Just drop off the beer by Friday. Part of our deal."

"Yeah, sure. Whatever, kid."

A week later, Mr. Stubbs stopped Marty in the hall. He grabbed him and pulled him to the side, then waited for the other students to walk by before accosting him.

"What the hell, kid? How did you know two of the games would be upsets?"

Marty laughed to himself. "I told you who would win. And yet you still bet against what I said? Dude, don't be pissed at me."

Mr. Stubbs started to raise a hand before realizing his action, then grabbed Marty by both shoulders and shook him. "How do you know? What's your secret?"

"Shit, man, I dunno. I just do it. Now are you gonna listen to me next time?"

"Yeah. I believe ya. I really do."

"Good. Because the deal has changed. I now get fifty percent of the winnings, or you don't get shit."

"Why, you little motherfucker!"

Marty jacked the statistics teacher in the chest, hard. "Sorry. That doesn't sound very nice to your new business partner. I should demand a hell of a lot more, but I can't get too greedy now, can I?"

Sweat rolled down Mr. Stubbs's face as he decided on what course of action to take—whether profiting, at a reduced amount, was worth it or whether he should save face and walk away.

"Fine. Give me seven winners and throw in three losers so that it doesn't look too suspicious. I figure we'll win about seven hundred bucks, and we'll split it fifty-fifty. Happy now?"

Marty put out a hand in good faith. The teacher hesitated reluctantly but then grabbed Marty's outstretched hand and shook it.

"This is it. We do this week, and that's it."

Withdrawing his hand, Marty stared back at his teacher.

Two more weeks went by until the teacher decided to call it quits, for good. No problem for Marty, as he had already saved up over two grand—plus, he was slowly building a taste for Canadian beer and whisky.

It happened one night

Marty stands outside of the bar with Mickey. Both are amped up from a little too much alcohol in such a short time—or just for the hell of it. Either way, both are looking for some action.

Mickey walks down the street and stops next to his car. Unlocking the door, he leans over and says, "Now, Marty, are you positive you're ready for what happens next?"

Marty stumbles up and stops in front of him, exhaling a breath of booze. "Sure. Why the fuck not?"

"Then tonight's your test, my friend. Let's see how well you do." He then proceeds to climb behind the wheel. Marty opens the passenger door on the third attempt and falls into the seat, closing the door and pulling his jacket up before it gets caught.

Mickey shifts the car into drive and peels out of the parking lot and onto the streets. He reaches over to turn on the radio. Some classic rock band is screeching away. They both roll down their windows, and Mickey reaches for a smoke, lighting it. Thinking he should do the same, Marty grabs the pack from the dashboard, punches the cigarette lighter in, and waits for the coils to heat up before lighting a smoke. He takes two puffs and starts coughing like a fiend. Mickey looks over as Marty waves him off.

"So I take it you're not a smoker," Mickey says over the loud radio song in the background.

"Yeah." Cough. Cough. "No shit. You've guessed it." Marty decides to abandon the ruse and throws the cigarette out the window.

"I should call you Smokey. Just because." He laughs hysterically and starts to cough himself.

Marty flips him off through choking coughs, trying to rid himself of the toxic smoke. Mickey chuckles at Marty's misfortune and takes a drag from his own cigarette, exhaling in Marty's direction. He then slams on the brakes for a yellow light and leans toward Marty.

"You really want to do this?" he asks, staring sternly at his passenger.

"I'd be in better spirits if you played a different station." He then reaches forward and fiddles with the dial to find a better song. "Sometimes, it's all about the right song before doing a job properly."

"Well, then, you just might be able to handle this after all."

"Don't worry about me—I got this. Now, what are gonna do?"

"Fine. For starters, we're going to collect on this business. You know, for protection."

"That's ironic. They should be protected from guys like us," Marty remarks.

"You're learning this business real fast. I may have to sleep with a gun under my pillow for the day you try to take me down."

"Don't worry. I'll shoot you long before you have a remote chance of firing back."

"Until then, funny guy, just listen and learn. You got that?" he says to his passenger.

Mickey explains the many facets of being a mobster in this town, including but not limited to protection, money laundering, prostitution, gambling and booking, drug running, drug selling, and above all, eliminating the competition. Marty takes it all in, listening and trying to prioritize all the different enterprises and thinking about what he should specialize in.

"So. We control a lot and have to manage a lot," Mickey says, summing up.

Marty tries to listen intently to every word.

As Mickey drives the Buick, he slows down to point out various mob-related businesses. He cranks the radio as they pass an element of the vast money-making scheme and says, "Now, you see here. This is our territory. But you go two blocks up, and then it becomes another rival gang, or mob, if you like."

"I'll have to remember the borders."

"Yeah, unless you want your ass shot off," Mickey retorts. "Now pay attention to this cross street because there are three different, uh . . . what's the word I'm looking for . . . ah, yes, factions." He points to different areas, noting the specific gangs and what corners they control.

Still riding shotgun, Marty wonders how he can possibly remember whose territory is whose. And does it even make a difference? If he strays a block north across the line, is he likely to be shot at immediately? To be killed because he couldn't find a parking spot in his territory—now, that would be crazy.

"What happens if we stray across the line?" Marty asks after his last thought.

Mickey's head rolls back in a fit of laughter. "Marty. Marty. Why are you trying to buck the system? There are rules, and they have to be abided by all at every moment. For everyone's sake."

"Bullshit. Utter and useless BS, I say," Marty replies.

"Wait. What? No. What the hell are you going on about? You've got it all wrong."

"I don't think so. Besides. What proof do you have?"

"Why, none. But it doesn't matter. You must never underestimate the balance that we have been trying to maintain between us and the competition."

Marty chuckles this time. "So it's all about saving your own private hide and nobody else's. Got it!"

Mickey shakes his head. "No. No. No. Shut the hell up. I want to preserve the natural order. Not destroy it."

"Well, then, you're doing a shitty job because territory is constantly changing, and normal people are being killed in the crossfire. It's always on the news. Shit ain't right—that's all I'm saying. Normal folk shouldn't die. We need them so we can collect from them each week," he replies with a smirk on his face.

"What do you think you can do about it?" Mickey challenges him.

Marty doesn't hesitate one bit and responds, "Just wait and see. You never know."

"Until then, follow my orders and do your fucking job. You got that? Want me to repeat it for ya?" Mickey stops the car and parks. "Good. Here is your first test to see if you can hack it. We are gonna collect the weekly tribute."

"The what?"

"The protection payment. And I tell ya, these business owners don't like paying it."

Marty thinks about the last statement. He wouldn't want to pay it either.

Marty nods his head. "Sure. You're the boss."

"And don't ever forget it."

The evening air is slightly chilled as they step out of the car. They will be going door to door before the businesses close for the night. Both of them get out and check that their guns are ready to use.

Muscling the business

Marty begins his first test. This particular business began as a newsstand and expanded to operating inside a larger store. The owner, Mr. Robinson, has been here on this street for many years, from its beginnings with selling newspapers for a nickel to eventually having a roof over his head and offering cigarettes, beer and other alcoholic beverages, and an assortment of other goods, needed or not. He has survived and has been a mainstay in the neighborhood.

Mickey and Marty open the door to the store as the little bells chime to announce their presence. The store owner, an older gentleman with old-world ways, greets the two customers in a typical fashion until he notices that one of them is familiar, a mobster he immediately recognizes.

"Oh, hello, Mickey. What brings you by on this Tuesday evening?" Mr. Robinson eyes both of the men but focuses more on the one he does not recognize.

"I thought Marty and me would grab some beers and go hang down by the river," Mickey responds politely, which Marty interprets as a cover in case anyone else is in the store.

"Is that your friend's name? Marty, is it?" Mr. Robinson lowers his glasses to give the new guy a once-over.

Marty feels unnerved and stares back at him but sees nothing but an old guy just trying to run a store.

Mickey sees the exchange and changes the course of the conversation. "Say. How's business been for you? I assume pretty good, judging by the low levels of beer I see in stock."

Quick on the defense, Mr. Robinson negates any idea of his business doing well. "No. No. I'm barely surviving. People don't want the newspapers anymore. I guess they get their news online. And everyone wants to quit smoking. And who really buys beer anymore, with all these craft breweries everywhere. I'm telling you, boys, it ain't like the old days." He sighs.

Mickey reaches over the counter and grabs the old guy. "Still. You must be selling stuff all day."

Marty is appalled as he watches Mickey manhandle the shopkeeper, but he keeps his emotions back in lieu of maintaining his business face. Mickey starts to muscle the store owner and slams his face against the counter.

"What are you bringing in these days? What's your daily take? Come on—how much?" Mickey demands.

"I . . . I . . . I dunno," Mr. Robinson, in pain, stammers.

Mickey is frustrated with the store owner's lack of honesty. He pulls his gun and points it at the old man. Mr. Robinson is terrified and starts to shake, but he has been through this time and time again. He continues to play his part as the hapless victim to a T.

"I have nothing. You . . . you guys take everything I earn. What more do you want from me?"

Mickey looks down at the store owner and then back at Marty. Marty has a sympathetic expression as he silently questions his partner's motives. Mickey is holding the gun to Mr. Robinson's head but raises a finger from the other hand toward Marty's direction.

Marty is still trying to determine Mickey's intent until he watches Mickey open the register and lift the cash drawer, revealing several hundred-dollar bills. He grabs them and puts the cash drawer back. Releasing Mr. Robinson, Mickey stashes the cash in his front pocket.

"You're robbing me blind," Mr. Robinson says after taking a step back.

"And you are lying to me. We should raise the amount for your lying ass." Mickey stares at the store owner.

Marty watches the whole scene, hearing and viewing both perspectives in a nonbiased way. He wonders if he is cut out for this type of work and whether muscling store owners is his ultimate dream job in life. In the end, he sees it as a business operation and walks up to Mr. Robinson.

"Why are you holding out on us?" Marty asks as he walks around the counter and up to the store owner.

"You're really new to this, aren't you?" the owner says with a chuckle as he tidies up the area around the register.

Marty, insulted, grabs the owner and slams him against a wall. "You think you know me, don't ya?" Marty presses his gun to the store owner's head and cocks it.

"No. No. I mean no disrespect. I'm so sorry."

Marty looks deep into the store owner's eyes, showing his own fear of doing this terrible but necessary job. The store owner sees but doesn't utter a word.

Marty lets go of Mr. Robinson. "Fine. Another time."

"You are welcome to come by any time, Marty," Mr. Robinson says, shrugging it off.

Mickey doesn't understand the exchange that just transpired but grabs Marty. "Yo. We got to get going."

Marty acknowledges Mickey's pressure and steps back, but then he pushes the store owner one more time. "I'm looking forward to our next meeting."

"I know. Me too," Mr. Robinson replies.

Mickey pulls Marty toward the exit. "Come on. We're leaving." As they leave, the little chimes announce their departure from the store.

That first business collection Marty had to endure had been tough. But with Mickey showing him the ropes over the next few days, this protection-collection job soon became part of Marty's daily routine. Mickey showed him who would pay right away and those they had to play hardball with, like Mr. Robinson. Then there were certain ones who gave them perks. Like a fresh donut from Samuel's Café or hot pastrami sandwich at Lou's Deli, washed down with a cold draft at the Corner Tavern—even served in a clean stein. These and many more were always offered with a forced, fake friendly smile from the owners. It was like they were bribing the collectors, thinking that they wouldn't get muscled out of more protection money.

A couple of weeks later and no longer so fresh in the job, Marty walks toward a table in the corner of the bar where Mickey is watching TV. Marty knew he'd find him here. He puts his glass of beer down on the rickety table.

"Hey," Marty says.

"What? Can't you see I'm watching the highlights from the game?" Mickey shouts, still watching the TV screen.

"I told you who was going to win, didn't I?"

"Yeah. Yeah. Thanks for the tip. I won fifty bucks."

Marty stares across the table, trying to think of how to ask his question. As he reflects, the bartender comes over and asks if they need a round. They wave him off.

Standing up, Mickey announces, "We got to get going. Now that you finally decided to meet me here. I was wondering if you forgot to come."

Marty follows him out the door, and they get into Mickey's car. He sits back in the passenger seat and leans over to the left. He's had a burning question to ask his mentor for a few days now. He can't wait another moment and blurts out, "You never said what happens if we collect more than what's due."

Driving down the street and then making a right turn, Mickey tells him about what he is required to collect and bring back with him to turn in on a daily basis. "What is over and above is sorta like a tip," he further explains. "But there's a catch. If word gets out that someone is strong-arming more than they should, well, the boss doesn't like to hear about such things."

Mickey parks the car and motions to Marty to stay put because he wants to share a story.

"There was a guy a few years back who was profiting quite handsomely from many months of strong-arming store owners into paying a heck of a lot more than what was required," Mickey explains. "It got so bad, these people lived in fear every time this collector came by. Eventually, they'd had enough and came up with a plan. They actually went as far as to stage a fake robbery and beat up an owner, demanding justification for their so-called protection.

"The next day, the beaten-up owner complained to the big boss, wondering why he has paid so much more money for zero protection. He showed him the injuries. The boss was a lot more concerned about the additional amount that he hadn't authorized. He immediately called in the collector, and when he arrived, he saw the owner. The collector started to spill his guts and apologized, saying he would pay it all back, even the money he didn't extort. The boss got way more of a confession than he was originally expecting.

"The boss had the guy taken outside and then turned to the store owner, handing him a loaded gun. He led the owner outside and said, 'Go ahead—take a shot or two.' The store owner was confused at first but then turned toward the collector and shot him in the stomach. His hands were quivering, and he decided not to take another shot. The boss took the gun back and handed the owner a wad of cash, telling him the problem was taken care of and to spread the money to the other store owners."

"Bullshit," Marty exclaims.

"Nah, for real. I'm telling ya because I had to drive the guy to the mob doctor," Mickey responds. "You're taking a chance if you try something like that. That's all I'm advising you, but don't think you can get one over on the boss without paying the price. I mean, if you can stomach it!" He chuckles at his own joke.

Looking perplexed but still letting the story sink in, Marty asks a follow-up question: "So whatever happened to the guy?"

"Oh, the boss ordered him whacked once he paid back the money," Mickey says as they get out of the car. "I guess the amount was over ten grand. Can you believe that? Trying to rip off the boss?" He points a finger toward a business on the right. "We're going in here." He opens the door and enters, with Marty close behind.

Another store

Both men walk into CC's Florist and Gifts and are greeted right away by the owners, Chad and his wife, Cindy. Mickey walks up to Chad, says a few words, and then is led to the back of the store. Cindy finishes her bouquet before walking around from behind the counter, stopping in front of Marty.

"I take it you're the new guy." She extends her calloused hand toward him. He takes it, and she squeezes his hand, hard. She whispers, barely audibly, "Remember, we're the owners. This is our store." She then lets go of his hand.

"You wanna explain that?" Marty glares at her, ready to punch her out.

Her expression turns from seriousness to that of laughter in the blink of an eye. She leans over to him, placing her hand on his shoulder, still snickering away. She stops to take a breath before resuming normalcy.

"He must not have told you about us."

"I assume this is a collection for protection."

She snorts. "Well, you're half-right. It is a collection, but we don't pay in cash."

Getting frustrated by Cindy's beating around the bush, he starts to raise his hands but then stops. Instead, he demands that she explain herself.

"Fine, silly boy. We're a drug store." She laughs but sees that he is not laughing, obviously missing the obvious. "We sell weed. We're the distribution center. And we make and sell really nice bouquets too. Perhaps there's a young lady you want to buy flowers for?"

Ignoring her commentary, he moves his head around, sniffing the air. "I don't smell it. All I smell is flowers."

"Yeah, wise guy, a florist store is a good cover to mask the smell."

Marty's face turns a shade of red roses after the revelation of the front and this business's importance. He's willing to bet they help launder money for the mob too—although judging by the orders on the counter, this store looks to be doing pretty good business on its own. Or does one get an ounce of weed within each bouquet order? His thoughts are interrupted by the return of the other two. Chad is telling Mickey a joke, and Mickey nods his head until the punchline is delivered, and then they both laugh at the same time.

Seeing Marty standing in the center of the store, Mickey stops next to him. "Did Cindy tell you about our business?"

"Yes, she did. Pretty fucking brilliant, I might add."

"It is and thank you. No, let me tell you. Don't go ruining it for us. It took us a while to build the business. Yes, both businesses, in case you were gonna ask. Don't come in here trying to strong-arm us. Ever," Chad says, his temper rising as he speaks what's on his mind.

Mickey puts a hand on Chad. "Now, hold on. Marty's all right. He won't be messing around with you. I will personally see to it."

"In that case, then, how do you do, Marty? Pleasure to meet you." Chad extends an equally calloused hand, like his wife's, out toward Marty.

"I'm fine. Pleasure."

"Good to hear. Now if you'll excuse me, we have a big order to fill." Chad waves goodbye and turns around, heading over to where his wife is diligently working on a flower arrangement.

Exiting CC's Florist, Mickey turns to the left and walks up the block. Marty walks beside, remaining quiet until they reach the car and get in.

"That's some crazy shit," Marty says as soon as the doors shut.

"And let's keep it that way. Boss Mazoli loves this place and wants no one near it or going there any more than they have to, period. Except on business, like you will be doing on Thursday morning. You got it?"

"I'm cool with that. Just wondering who's the genius who came up with that idea. That's all I want to know, so I can meet him."

Slamming on the brakes for a red light, Mickey declares, "You're talking to the genius right now."

"That's brilliant. Really brilliant," he states aloud, thinking in his head to call Mickey a true wise guy.

Borrow a car

A couple of days later, an unfamiliar car pulls up to the corner café where Marty is sitting outside having lunch, reading the sports scores from the previous day. He sees that he predicted ten out of twelve winners, although he tries not to bet on the games too often. He just knows that he can usually pick the winners anytime, any sports match. Well, except curling or darts competitions. He reaches down to take the last two bites of a sandwich as a car horn beeps. Twice. Now three times in a row. Annoyed, he lifts his head up only to find a familiar face smiling at him. *What does he want?* Marty wonders. *I'm trying to enjoy my lunch.* He thinks it over and throws down a twenty for the waitress. He grabs the newspaper, chewing the last of his lunch, and walks over to the car.

"Say, nice wheels. What happened to the other car you were driving around a couple of days ago?"

"Dunno. I just picked this one up," Mickey says.

Marty grimaces. "You mean you stole it? You? I figured you would be stealing motorcycles, not cars."

"Just get in, wiseass." Marty gets in, and Mickey drives off in his recently acquired—otherwise as known as stolen—car.

"You know, I really liked the feel of the other one," Marty says as he moves his hand over the interior and starts to reach for the radio.

"Shut up for a sec, will ya? We got an assignment." He hands a folded piece of paper to Marty. "Here. Read this."

Marty takes the paper and unfolds it. He looks the list up and down twice before folding it up and handing it back.

"So can you do it or not?" Mickey demands, wanting an answer right away.

Marty rolls down the window and looks out as he says, "Of course. There's a dozen cars on this list. Stealing them is easy. Locating them to steal is a different ballgame."

"Well, I reckon if we get at least five today, the boss will be all right with that."

"That's mighty nice of him," Marty responds sarcastically.

"Hey, as the new guy you're still on thin ice with Boss Mazoli. I wouldn't be dogging him just yet. You never know who may be listening." Mickey looks up and down and around as though there is a hidden mic in the car.

"I hope at least you are giving me accolades," Marty says.

"Yeah, yeah. What—"

"Stop the car!" Marty interrupts.

Mickey slams on the brakes and turns toward his passenger, annoyed until he realizes the reason for the urgency. He now sees what Marty obviously saw. One of the cars on the list.

"Good eyes. Can you do it?" Mickey asks as he hits the gas and turns the corner, parking not far from the intended target.

"What tools you got?" Marty asks.

"Lucky for you, I brought you some. Since I just stole this baby hours ago."

"Well, open the trunk so I can get them and get going. Time's a wasting. Oh, one more thing. It might be helpful to tell me where the chop shop is located."

"Look who thinks they're the one in charge now." Mickey lets out a chuckle while opening the trunk. They both scan the different tools lying about in the trunk, and Marty grabs a slim-jim, some wire strippers, a screwdriver, and a fake license plate and places them all in a bag. Mickey tells him the address for where to take the car, and Marty acknowledges it.

"Are you gonna time me? See how fast I can take this? You know, for my weekly performance review?"

"Just don't get caught, cocky ass. Let's see how good you really are."

"I'm pretty fast even without the tools." He taps the bag. "I'll be at the place before you. Fifty bucks is backing me up."

"Shit. You still got to steal it first."

"Is that a no, then, chicken shit?"

"Let's see you walk the talk. And double the bet."

Marty raises a hand to salute him and turns about, walking briskly down the street, heading to the target car. Mickey heads back in his own stolen car, watching the new guy. In seconds flat, he watches him gain entry to the car, disable the alarm, and start it, peeling out from the spot. *Damn, this guy is good,* Mickey thinks, and then he remembers it's a race to the chop shop. He slams his own car into drive and takes off.

Twenty-seven minutes later, Mickey is cruising along, knowing he has won this bet and will teach the wise guy a lesson. He turns a corner and flashes his lights twice, heading to the warehouse where the chop shop is secretly located. The fence closes behind him as he heads over to bay number four, where the garage door starts to open up. He confidently cruises into the bay and parks, only to grasp right away that the car he watched get stolen a half an hour ago is sitting in bay number three.

As he gets out, Mickey whispers to himself, "What the hell?" An attendant holding a license plate walks past him to start switching out the license plate. Mickey looks over at Marty, who is leaning against the car in the next bay, waving at him.

"Hey, Mickey. Took you long enough. Did you stop for a bit to eat?"

Mickey flips him the bird and casually strolls over to the guy who just won the bet.

"How in the hell did you get here so fast?"

"Apparently, I drive fast. Well, let me rephrase that. I drive faster than you." Grinning from ear to ear, he relieves Mickey's hand of the crisp hundred-dollar bill it holds and pockets the money in seconds flat. Another attendant is already removing engine parts from the stolen car in bay three, so the two of them move through the garage to the waiting area. The door closes behind them, and the sounds are less deafening. Mickey heads to the coffee machine and pours himself a coffee, whereas Marty decides on a soft drink. They both take a seat at a table.

"I assume someone is going to pick us up and take us back out to get more cars?" Marty asks.

"Can't you see I'm making the call now?" Mickey holds the phone to his ear and lowers his hand to tell Marty to pipe down.

"Yes. I'm ordering two for pickup," he says.

Sipping his soda, Marty feels like he has found a family, well, a mob boss, that he can honestly, or dishonestly, work for. Despite his mentor Mickey, with his temperament and other quirks, Marty is relieved to find a place to work without too many problems to deal with. Mickey hangs up the phone.

"We got about a thirty-minute wait."

"No worries."

Mickey stumbles for the words while holding the hot coffee. "Hey. You did good out there. Let's see if you can keep it up. You're competing against me now, hotshot."

"Do I hear another bet coming up?" Marty laughs.

"You bet your ass you don't. I ain't losing twice today. Just focus on getting another one of the cars off the list."

Still reeling for the latest bet won, Marty picks up today's newspaper from the table next to him and reads the games for this evening. After making a couple of marks and circles, along with some other cryptic notes, he throws the newspaper in Mickey's direction.

"What's this?"

"Well, I feel bad. No wait, I really don't. But I guess I have to say that," Marty jeers triumphantly.

"Where are you going with this?"

"Oh, yeah. Right. I took your money fair and square. But here's a chance for you to win it back or a hell of a lot more." He points to the newspaper.

Picking it up, Mickey sees the winners Marty has picked for tonight's games. He cautiously eyes the column. "And what do you want me to do?"

As if already rehearsed, Marty tells him directly, "If you place bets for at least six of the games I circled, you should do all right. You'll win about fifty percent of the twelve games tonight. And if you bet conservatively, you should make about three hundred to five hundred. I, of course, ask for only twenty-five percent of the take."

Mickey thinks it over, realizing that he should bet a lot but that he'll still have to give some to Marty. In the end, he still profits, so why not?

"Sure. Let's see how good you are at sports betting."

"Seriously? If you are gutsy enough, I expect a payment of five hundred bucks in an envelope when you see me tomorrow morning."

"You have the delivery job to do tomorrow morning." Mickey is quick to point out the job assignments. He then looks at his phone and sees that their transportation is about to arrive sooner than expected. "You ready to go?"

"Absolutely. I love this. You know that."

"Then we need to do this twice. That will give them six cars, and we can push this assignment back to next week."

"Whatever you need. Remind me again on the job tomorrow?"

"You get to make deliveries for the florist business." Mickey laughs. "And try not to skim some of the bouquets."

Marty joins in the laugh. "Heck no. Not after you told me the story about the one dude trying to skim the boss. Hell no."

"See? You got this job. Too easy," Mickey affirms.

"I'd like to think so," Marty says as he hears the car horn announcing their ride' arrival.

Mickey declares, "Time to get back to work and steal some more cars."

"Easiest gig I've had all week."

"Then maybe you should try for the Camaro—that will be a challenge to find and steal."

"At least there are no pickup trucks," Marty responds. "I hate stealing those, especially if they have a gun rack. 'Cause you know the owner is probably carrying another gun and will shoot without hesitation."

"No pickup trucks this time."

Both guys get in the unmarked car, ready to go find another car to steal.

Delivery changes it all

The next day, Marty sits in the park, passing the time before he has to make his appointed delivery. Looking down at his watch, he realizes he needs to leave soon if he is going to make the scheduled time. He stands up and waves to the birds that he has been feeding for the better part of the last hour and slowly strolls back to his car—a car he had legitimately acquired rather than stolen, although he previously had four cars that would fall under the stolen description.

He drives to the florist parking lot and stops, shutting off the engine and just sits in the car. He begins to consider how easy this job is going to be. After all, all he has to do is pick up some bouquets, obviously concealing bags of marijuana, and deliver them to the various clients, most of whom he assumes are repeat customers. Pretty simple and basic in his mind. How could he possibly mess this up?

Out of the blue, he lets out a laugh. Thinking to himself, *What happens if they ever vote to legalize marijuana in this state?*

Cindy exits the shop and strolls up to the parked car Marty is sitting in and taps on the driver's side window. She speaks loudly through the glass. "Hey, you all right, buddy?"

Marty, startled from being lost in his own thoughts, rolls down the window and responds, "Ah . . . yeah . . . sure."

"OK. You just didn't look . . . well . . . OK."

"Naw . . . I got this. Just give me the goods and tell me where to make these deliveries."

"Ah . . . sure. Fine. You got this one here and the other one here." Cindy, still holding her tablet, points to the screen, showing the two destinations on Google Maps.

"I got it." Marty then waits for Cindy and Chad to return to load up the back of the car with the goods to be delivered.

With everything loaded and ready to go, Marty is about to put it in reverse and leave. Before he can go, Cindy reaches in her back pocket handing him some cards, "I almost forgot, you need to add these cards to the goods." She thrusts the cards into his hands. "It helps, you know, for the ruse." She steps away, allowing him room to back up.

Before shifting into drive, he scans the address of the first delivery. It's about ten miles away from his current location. He googles the other address, and it's even farther away. As he plans out the best route, he hears a tap on the glass, again.

His thoughts once again interrupted, he glares at the tapper, wondering what warrants the disturbance.

"What do you want?" he inquires.

Cindy motions for him to roll down the window.

He repeats himself, this time without sounding annoyed. "What do you need, Cindy?"

There's a long pause before Cindy says what's on her mind. "I'm just concerned for your safety. You're transporting a lot of, um, merchandise for the first time."

"I appreciate your concern, but I got this. It's cool."

"Oh, OK, then. Just making sure." She still sports a worried facial expression.

"It's good, trust me." Grinning, Marty shifts the engine into drive and flicks the evergreen-scented air freshener hanging from the rearview mirror. He waves goodbye to Cindy as he pulls away.

He maneuvers along the downtown streets rather slowly, seeming to get caught, unfortunately, at every traffic light. Marty stops at a light and fiddles with the radio. The light changes, and he moves forward. He notices that this neighborhood appears familiar. He gets stuck at another traffic light, and his eyes scan the block. Marty watches a beautiful blonde woman strutting down the street and sees her enter a newspaper store. Through the store window, he can still see her as she then hugs the store owner. The light may have changed, but Marty doesn't move. He stares at the store, realizing it belongs to Mr. Robinson, and makes the connection after a flurry of beeps and honks from numerous cars behind him. He drives forward but then decides to turn at the next corner and circle around the block.

Oh, Mr. Robinson. You have been holding out on me, he says to himself before parking, intending to pursue the matter further. He stops himself, though, remembering the job he must do first before scoping out the newspaper stand for the woman.

Another time, he thinks as he drives off, heading to the address for the first delivery. Meanwhile, he wonders about the woman who entered the store and hugged the owner. *Hmmm, it must be someone Mr. Robinson knows or is related to.* Either way, Marty has to formulate a plan on how he is going to have a chance to talk to this beautiful woman.

"I'll be back and be looking for you, Mr. Robinson. I guarantee it." Marty says aloud before speeding off to his first delivery.

Days went by with Marty bouncing between working the chop-shop list and making additional marijuana deliveries around town. When Marty finally found the last car on the list, he drove it to the chop shop a little bit too fast, even for his standards, and nearly got pulled over. As luck would have it, the police officer was tailing him but got a call and did a U-turn, heading in the opposite direction. *Phew, that was way too close, and I didn't even have time to change the license plate.*

Minutes later, he drops off the car and grabs a ride with another relatively new gangster who happens to be heading in the direction of Marty's apartment. He gets dropped off, goes up to his apartment, and thinks about what to fix for lunch and maybe taking a midafternoon nap.

It's not long before someone disrupts his planned relaxing afternoon. Hearing a hard knock on his door catches him off guard because he isn't usually at his apartment during the day. Marty stands up and walks over to the front door, grabbing his gun in the process, the one he keeps on a table behind the door. He looks through the peephole and then puts the gun down before opening the door.

"Jesus, Mickey! You scared the shit out of me."

"It's just Mickey, no Jesus, by the way," Mickey says, cracking a lame joke. "What? Did I disturb your afternoon nap?"

Marty grimaces back.

"I didn't stop by for lunch." He pauses. "But I do have a message to deliver to you. Top-secret level." Mickey reaches into his jacket. Marty freezes, thinking for a second that the message has *9 mm* written on it. He tenses up, only to relax after realizing Mickey has retrieved a plain envelope, which he hands to him.

"Boy, are you tense. Did ya think I was gonna pull out a gun and put a bullet to your brain?" He chuckles. "I didn't know I was so intimidating to you!"

Rolling his eyes, Marty sighs and flips him off and then opens the envelope. He pulls out the contents, rubbing his thumb across the large stack of cash.

While Marty is still staring down at his newly acquired bonus, Mickey mentions the other message he has to deliver. He tells Marty how pleased Boss Mazoli is with the acquisition of the cars on the list and, more importantly, not getting caught or arrested. He also reveals that the boss has big plans for him, starting with expanding his duties.

"Ha! It looks like I'm going after your job," he jests, giving Mickey a pat on the back.

"Over my cold, dead body is the only way you'll get my job."

"Is that a challenge?"

Mickey heads to the door. "You got a long way to go." He grabs the handle and pushes the door open slightly before stopping. "But you did good this week. Now go spend your money—you earned it!"

He watches Mickey turn around and close the door behind him, exiting the apartment. Going back to his plan of taking an afternoon siesta no longer sounds appealing after being handed a big wad of cash. He thinks about foolish purchases, and his mind wanders carelessly for a bit until he has a moment of happiness with his latest thought. As he formulates a plan, he shoves some of the cash into his pocket. He heads to the spare bedroom, moves a few boxes, and finds the fake panel in the closet. Opening it carefully, he places the remaining cash in the envelope in his personal safe before fixing the panel back up and arranging the boxes to camouflage it. Grabbing his keys off the table but leaving the gun, he sits on the sofa, taking a break to work out his plan to meet the woman he had seen at the newsstand the other day.

He reflects on seeing this beauty talking with the newsstand proprietor, Mr. Robinson. Her long, glistening blonde hair had only invited him to stare even longer as she swooshed it back when she turned her head toward him. Marty thought she must have been staring at him and felt that connection, the love connection, right away when their eyes met for that glimmering moment—oh, what a moment, forever etched in his mind.

She's gotta be a relative or something. Maybe a granddaughter? Naw, he ain't that old—or is he? Marty wonders. *If not her grandfather, then he must be her uncle, and she is dutifully helping out with the family business. Yeah, that sounds about right.* Marty thinks her nobleness and kindness in helping the family only add to the appeal of her beauty and killer body.

Marty snaps to attention, suddenly realizing he has been caught up in a daydream, and quickly looks around, instinctively making sure nobody witnessed him doing anything strange, even though he's alone. He gets up from the sofa and moves over to the kitchen, grabbing a cold soda from the fridge and slamming it until it is bone dry, crushing the can at the very end. He pitches the can toward the recycling bag and scores two points for the perfect throw.

After walking out of the apartment and remembering to lock it up, he turns down the hall and leaves the building. He has a job to do over the next few days, but when it's done, he will find a way and the gall to confront her, to ask her out, or to just plain speak to her.

Thinking out loud, he says, "But first I gotta deliver some drugs for my day job. Oh, maybe I shouldn't mention that to her until the third or fourth date." Marty bursts out laughing and then starts the car and drives off.

The next day, Mickey picks up Marty, and they drive over to the local gangster hangout. Mickey pulls Marty off to the side to have a few words with him. He informs Marty that he has a new assignment and says that because it's a risky one, this time, he will be partnered up.

"TJ, get over here," Mickey shouts across the noisy bar.

A man dressed in a slick dark-purple suit lifts his head just as he sinks the eight ball and starts to collect his money. His gold-capped front tooth glimmers as he struts over to where the two of them.

"What up, Mickey." He shakes hands with Mickey while glaring toward Marty. "Who's the newbie?"

"Your new partner for the next job."

"Shit. I thought I was riding along with Ben on this one."

Mickey shakes his head. "Nope. Marty here is accompanying you on the drive."

Marty studies TJ's reaction, sensing his apprehension and feeling a bit doubtful himself. Still, he's teamed up with him, so he might as well be friendly. It's not like he has a choice of whether to take the job.

TJ extends a hand, and Marty throws out a hand to shake it. Both grips are tight and hostile. TJ finally releases. "It's cool.

We got this." He looks back to the newbie a second time. "We cool?"

Shaking his head only slightly, Marty replies, "Yeah."

"OK, then, fella. Now that that's over with, usual route, TJ." Mickey turns to Marty. "Listen and learn. TJ here is a pro at this."

"You bet your sorry ass I am." He punches Mickey in the arm.

Not to be outdone, Marty says to TJ, "What are we waiting for? Christmas or something? Times a ticking." With that, he walks to the car.

TJ and Mickey smile at one another, shaking their heads and silently signaling an understanding of what it's like to be the inexperienced guy. They laugh out loud as TJ moves to follow Marty to the car. He gets in and instructs Marty where to drive. They are heading across town, about a thirty-minute drive, but neither says a word to the other, besides the instructions TJ voices for where and when to turn.

They arrive at the house, pass through a gate, and head up a long driveway. Marty looks around but can't remember if he has been to this house before. He parks, and they both get out. TJ tells Marty to wait by the car. Fifteen minutes later, TJ exits the house as a garage door opens. TJ signals to Marty to come over and points to the car in the garage.

TJ gets behind the wheel and looks to his right, still studying his new partner as Marty latches the safety belt. "Have you checked the shipment is in place? You want to be responsible for a quarter million and realize it's not back there?" Both men open their doors, jump out, and head to the trunk. After hitting the latch to open the trunk, TJ inspects the container holding a quarter of a million dollars' worth of cocaine, as he has done countless times in the past. He leans over to the new guy, reiterating the importance of always checking that the goods are on board before leaving the area.

"Would you want to try to explain where hundreds of thousands of dollars of coke went? I tell ya, once we leave those gates"—he points over to the right—"we're on our own. You better damn well make sure the goods are in the trunk at all times. It's your ass if they aren't. You hear me, newbie?"

"I hear ya. How can you tell this is a quarter of a million worth of coke? Just saying."

TJ cracks a smile before attempting to answer the question. "Ha. Youse smarter than you look." He then explains the tricks of the trade to Marty while en route for the weekly delivery.

The open road. Stretches of land from exit to exit. The car zooms along mile after mile before the silence is finally broken when Marty reaches over to turn on the radio and find some classic rock. TJ shakes his head in disagreement.

"No. No," TJ explains. "You got the wrong station."

"Oh. You think you can find something better?"

"Yup."

Marty waves his hands as though yielding control. "Be my guest, then. Let's see what ya got."

With a flick of his right hand, TJ switches from regional radio to satellite. He then tunes it to the 1950s station, which is playing some old-school rock 'n' roll. He then sinks back in the driver's seat, having proven himself the winner in this round of radio wars.

After about the ninth bebop song, Marty switches it off, deciding on a different way to pass the time. He notes that this is his first delivery of cocaine and talks about the feeling of risking a prison sentence for an above-par wage.

"Well, you could be sitting in some office cubicle, clicking away repeatedly for eight hours a day and never experiencing the freedom of the open road or taking any risks with your life."

"If you put it that way . . ."

"Shit, of course. You must be living on the edge right about now. And how does that feel? You scared shitless? Think the po-po is gonna bust us and throw us in the slammer for five to ten years? Yeah, feels pretty fuckin' awesome."

Marty nods his head; the thrill of it all is quickly sinking in.

TJ smacks Marty in the arm. "And how do you think I'm feeling? You know, the po-po don't take a liking to my kind these days. Added to the fact of all that coke in the back, well, the chances of me meeting a bullet to the brain and surviving . . . The odds are not in my favor. You? No offense, but you'll probably walk away with a ticket, and maybe the deputy will make you buy a round at the local bar."

"Aw, man, it ain't always like that," Marty says, trying to lessen TJ's vivid description of the consequences if they get busted.

TJ turns his head so quickly, Marty can actually hear the crack of the snap. "Say what?" TJ exclaims.

"Oh, I ain't disagreeing that I have a better chance of surviving or not going to jail."

"Then what are you saying?"

"I'm saying, if we are involved in a situation involving death or a prison sentence, I need to know beforehand, how well do you shoot?"

TJ is surprised by the question but realizes the gangsters' oath transcends the law. "Oh, I can shoot way better than you."

"Then start swerving so that we get pulled over, and we'll see who's the better shot. I'd really hate to embarrass you. So we can call it even, for now. I'm kidding about trying to get pulled over."

"Man. You crazy. No wonder they teamed me up with you. Anyway, it's about your time to drive. You know, lessen our chances of getting pulled over for a taillight out." TJ chuckles at the last statement.

Marty is too quick. "Hey, if you can't hack driving, no worries. I'll take care of it. I won't let them get ya!" he says in jest.

"You would be singing a different tune if you were driving in my old stomping grounds." TJ exits and heads over to the travel plaza to fill up on gas. "Go get us some drinks while I fill 'er up."

"Fair enough. I gotta hear this story about where you came from."

"Oh, don't worry. It will scare you straight."

"Too bad. I'm already a criminal."

"Join the club." TJ uses the laundered credit card to pay for gas as Marty heads inside to get the drinks.

Marty gets comfortable in the driver's seat, adjusting the mirrors, the seat, and more importantly, the radio. Meanwhile, TJ stretches back and grunts as he extends his legs. He looks at Marty and suggests they get a move on before the night is over.

Cranking the engine and throwing it into gear, Marty begins the final leg of their journey—the last step being getting rid of the vast amount of cocaine they are hauling in the trunk. Marty ponders the level of criminal charges, with possession of cocaine being a felony versus being caught with hundreds of thousands of dollars of cash possibly being a misdemeanor.

"OK, TJ. Tell me your story." If it had been daytime, Marty would have switched on the cruise control and let the car take over. Being it is night, he still has to concentrate on actual driving skills and avoiding being pulled over. Still, he wants to hear this story.

Marty tries again after no reply. "The mic is yours—tell me the story."

"Shit. You ain't bullshitting, are you? Well, here it goes. Being from the South Side of Chicago is like a badge of honor. And I mean a badge that says I survived. No joke. It was rough, I tell ya."

Marty is about to ask how rough was it but decides not to, despite TJ waiting for the very same question to come out. TJ smirks as if holding back from a smartass response and instead continues with his story.

"As I was saying, the South Side was a testament to one's life. You look at it now, and everyone is moving there, and there's this gentrification in many parts. Ha, I tell ya. Back in my day, the only way outta there was in a body bag. And I ain't lying either."

Sighing, Marty keeps the steering straight and the speed right at the limit. TJ finishes his reflective pause before continuing on.

"Oh yeah, crack was moving in faster than people were. You weren't whack unless you were on crack. And let me tell you, I seen some motherfuckers that were more than whacked even when they weren't smoking crack."

TJ takes a break, gathering his thoughts and thinking of how many people he knew who didn't even make it to adulthood. "Now, I ain't saying I never been on crack. No. I'm saying I was smart enough not to be hooked on it. It's some scary shit. It messes with people's minds. I'm tellin' ya, it's just bad news."

"Some say the government was to blame for introducing crack to the streets of a lot of communities," Marty interrupts.

Leaning back and exhaling a deep breath, TJ looks up to the car ceiling. "All I say is that if it was the government, then hats off to them because their plan nearly worked. It almost destroyed us all. But a lot of folks got rich off it too."

Marty sighs. "Somebody wins and somebody loses."

TJ looks over at him. "But we're still surviving. The government can't repress us. Only the rich folk can. Now, back to the days on the South Side. I quickly realized two factors. One, I wasn't gonna fall victim or be addicted to this crack sweeping the hoods. And two, I needed to survive and fight the ones who were addicted."

"Oh shit, that's messed up. Well, you're here alive, so I assume you picked the right path," Marty says optimistically.

"You bet your ass I'm still alive. Let me tell you, brother, it wasn't easy at all. But when you look out for numero uno, the odds tend to be in your favor." As Marty listens, TJ continues his exposé on what it was like living on the South Side streets.

After a while, Marty swerves, barely avoiding another car, as he readjusts the steering and reaches over for his water bottle, taking a swig to quench his thirst. The last hour has been filled with intense conversation between two people who really didn't know much about one another. Marty is deciding whether to push further or just pick a benign topic like sports.

"Say, TJ," Marty throws out there.

TJ, although exhausted from the monologue, still entertains Marty's query. "What? What is it?"

"Nothing . . . I was just thinking." Marty pauses. "I was just thinking—why are we doing this shipment anyway?"

Laughter ensues, and TJ continues the hysterics for almost two minutes. When it subsides, he gracefully begins the tale of the bosses.

"See here. This is how it is. The bosses like to fight with each other. But I swear on my momma's grave, bless her soul"—he makes the sign of the cross—"if another gang tries to impinge on one's territory, then they pool together."

"I'm seriously not following you at all."

"Marty," TJ declares, "they may fight each other, but lord help the poor gang that tries to take on both of them."

"Huh?"

"Exactly. Boss Mazoli may be at war with Boss Nunzio, but if someone else tries to cut in, they will form some alliance or partnership to fight against the folks trying to upset the status quo."

"And this shipment?"

"Ah yes, the shipment." TJ rolls his eyes and cracks a grin. "This shipment is a ruse, a cover to keep the status quo intact."

Surprised, Marty says, "You got to be kidding me."

"I wish I was, my friend. The bosses basically help each other when necessary. We all know of this, but it's kept hushed and not spoken of."

Looking back at TJ before deciding he is actually serious, Marty waves a hand to signal him to continue.

"As I was saying, the bosses help one another. Some big guys working for Boss Nunzio were on the wrong end of a drug raid three days ago, and their supplies were nearly depleted. Boss Mazoli pitched in, for a modest fee, of course, and here we are delivering the goods to keep the flow of drugs remaining constant. You and I should receive a medal for the service we provide."

"Yet a gang war could be declared, and the two bosses would be going to war against each other. That shit's messed up."

"Like politics but for gangsters. Crazy-ass shit," TJ responds. "Didn't someone say that art imitates life?"

"How much you think Boss Mazoli is making on this deal? How much in fees you think he is charging for helping out?"

"Aw, man, whatever he wants to." After remaining silent for a while, TJ then adds, "On a happy note, we do get to drive a different car back home. I'm hoping it's a new Caddy or something in style."

"No way, man. It's gonna be a Beamer."

"Shit. You got it all wrong. Boss Mazoli is old school. Caddy it is," TJ declares.

Marty shakes his head. "Twenty bucks says it will be a hot-off-the-assembly-line Beamer, fully loaded. Think about it—what a nice gift to give in return for the generous donation of a week's supply of coke."

TJ slaps him on the shoulder. "I tell you what. If I'm wrong, I'll give you a cool, crisp fifty. But if I'm right, why don't you lay down a few of them sports picks for me. What do ya say?"

Marty mulls it over. "Fine. Deal. But I'm getting hungry. Why don't ya buy us a snack after this drop as part of the deal?"

"Then you need to tell me your odds for the game on Monday night."

"Sure. I can do that." Marty doesn't feel like he has to give up too much in this deal.

"Well, shucks. I should have asked for more."

"Don't get too greedy. And I didn't say I was gonna tell you the actual winner of the game. I have a fifty-fifty shot of being right."

"Dude. Everyone knows you are rarely wrong."

TJ and Marty have dropped off the coke package and are now beginning their drive back in a shiny new BMW, fully loaded. The rest of the conversation sticks to the more basic topics of sports and women. TJ points out a restaurant at the next exit and Marty signals, exiting the highway.

Marty pulls up at an old diner and parks. "Fine," he says. "Take the fifty I was gonna win from you anyway and put it down on the visiting team to win with three points."

"That's what I'm talking about." TJ dials his bookie and starts talking, placing the sports bet.

"Can we eat now?"

TJ hangs up the phone. "Sure, man. Hell, I'll even cover lunch," he says they both enter the diner.

By the end of the drive, both exchange phone numbers and agree, in principle, to help one another when and if needed. They shake hands tightly while eyeballing each other.

"You all right, Marty."

"You ain't so bad yourself, TJ."

"Don't let that get out on the street. I still have a rep to protect." Laughing, they give each other a quick hug.

Marty then adds, "I may even send you a pick or bet from time to time. Sometimes I like to send a loser, just for laughs."

"I would gladly accept your advice. Most of the time."

"Well, see ya around."

"Stay alive, bro," TJ says as he departs.

Marty watches him leave and then whips out his phone to call an old acquaintance.

The voice on the other end of the phone declares, "Well, I was beginning to think you had forgotten about me."

"I couldn't do that to you. I'm low on cash and have to hustle another hundred or two off you."

"I know you're lying to me. I heard you did the Nunzio run."

"I guess there are no secrets in the underworld," Marty muses.

"Nope. Somebody always knows what you are doing. Which leads me to say, what are you doing right now—besides standing on a street corner all by yourself and talking to me? Why don't you get your ass down here to the bar on Thirty-Sixth Street and let me take some of that money you declare you don't possess, Marty!"

"You know I don't lose in pool. And I won't feel one iota sorry about taking your money. Besides, I need a new hat, and you're going to be paying for it!"

"Only if you think you can win. Which you obviously won't."

"Sure. I'll be there in twenty minutes. You might as well start practicing—not that it matters." Ending the call, Marty cracks a smile, ready to win some money off someone who obviously doesn't know how good he really is at pool and most leisure games.

Marty arrives at the bar and scans the joint quickly—first to see who is playing pool and, second, to locate an open spot at the bar to get himself a drink to catch up to a proper level of drunkenness. He achieves the second objective before the first by ordering a draft beer with a cheap whisky chaser. Or is it the other way around? It doesn't matter, as Marty downs them both before ordering another round and heading over to the area with the pool tables.

"I got fifty bucks that says I can beat the next winner." Staggering a bit due to the alcohol starting to hit his system, he plops a fifty-dollar bill on the table and is met by the cold gaze of the surrounding players.

One of the players, an older guy, acknowledging the money on the table, says, "All right there, sonny, put your money away—let me beat this guy fair and square."

The other player opposing the older man pipes up, "What the fuck?" as he watches the old man knock in the next three balls before sinking in the eight ball on a nearly impossible shot. "You SOB . . ." the loser says, throwing down a stack of twenties that the older man quickly scoops up.

"All right, who's the next sucker who wants to donate their money to me?"

Marty steps up and throws his money down again. "Are we shooting to see who goes first, or should the youngest shoot first?"

"We're shooting, jackass. You know, you got some brass balls throwing money around and not winning anything so far, youngster."

"No worries. I'll be taking your money. The only question tonight is how much you want to lose." Marty aligns the cue ball and shoots it down, placing the ball closest to the cushion.

"Oh, is that the best you can do? Well, my friend, watch and learn from the pros." Mickey shoots the ball, but it's inches away from where he anticipated and, more importantly, a farther distance than Marty's ball. "Lucky break. Fine. Go ahead. You win the break," Mickey says, resigning control to Marty. A mistake he would soon regret.

Having won the opening round, Marty places the cue ball while watching Mickey stack and rack the rest of the pool balls. Once he sees the balls racked, he lines up his opening shot.

The noise of the pool balls breaking and the plopping sound of two solid-color pool balls falling into the pockets starts this round with a perfect beginning. Marty then reaches over and knocks in an additional two balls before yielding the table back to Mickey. At this point, his opponent is flabbergasted.

"Shit. I don't even have a fuckin' shot."

"I know. That was the point." Marty laughs in the background.

Raising his head to look into the eyes of his opponent, Mickey still tries in vain to sink an impossible shot. He misses widely, and Marty seizes the moment when the turn returns to him, knocking in the next three balls, along with the called pocket on the eight ball. He throws the stick down on the table victoriously.

"Is that all you got, Mickey?" He grasps the winnings as Mickey throws the money down on the table.

Mickey nods his head in defeat. "We ain't done yet, though. Someday, my friend, mark my words. Your luck will change for the worse."

"Ha! Not in this lifetime."

"We shall see. We shall see."

Triumphally, Marty boasts, "Until that day, it is me collecting my winnings off you or any other joe I can hustle."

"You may have won this round. But what if I told you could make a lot more? Does that pique your interest?"

"It all depends how much further I go down the rabbit hole."

"Well, you got the potential. But I ain't got a hole for you to go down any further. So, I guess it's my word."

Looking back while racking the balls for the next round, Marty says, "I'm so glad you understand. I need to go all the way in this organization. Not get stuck in a hole. Now break. If you can."

Lining up for the break, Mickey strikes the balls, but nothing falls in the pockets. Marty takes over and sinks the next three before leaving another impossible shot.

"Seriously, dude. Can you at least try to leave me a shot?"

"Why in the hell would I do that? What is the point of giving you any advantage whatsoever?"

"Oh, I dunno. Compassion, for starters." Mickey attempts to shoot the cue out of the jam, but it falls flat.

Marty quickly yields not to the ball placement but, rather his, skill set. After all, a hustle is hustle when the other person thinks he has some sort of advantage or is better than the other person.

Mickey eventually wins this round, and never realizing the true ruse going on, he falls for the bait and challenges Marty to another round of pool, thinking maybe Marty just got lucky in the first game.

"Sure, pal. If that's what you want to do." Marty plays his poker face too well, enough for most players to believe him.

Meanwhile, Mickey is too confident in his own skills, albeit a little influenced by the alcohol he has recently ingested, and declares, "I'll double that bet to play ya."

Slowly raising his head, Marty complacently acknowledges the vain attempt that Mickey is employing in trying so hard to win this current match of pool between them.

After about five minutes and having cleared the table, Marty hits the cue ball to the eight ball in the side pocket, winning the game. "That's a cool hundred bucks you owe me."

Mickey takes his cue in hand and snaps it into two, throwing the pieces on the table. He inspects his right hand as though he might have gotten a splitter in the process. Seeing none, he still pats his hands on his pants.

Not backing down, Marty watches hesitantly before realizing that this guy is either stalling or is going to be uncooperative in paying back what he owes after losing so terribly. Granted, Marty flashed his pool skills maybe a little too quickly—he could have displayed them only after losing a round or two before miraculously starting to win with no explanation. Sometimes, it's hard to gauge these things and how to play them out.

He prefers to play how he normally plays, and that is to simply nail every pocket, every time. But it was an old adage that warned him of how to properly hustle and, more importantly, how to hustle to win copious amounts of cash. After all, what is the point of hustling pool if one cannot win a decent amount of cash and walk away with the other person, the hustled person, thinking that they lost only because they did not make the one important shot that they should have? Now that is the one true hustle, in essence. But not tonight—Marty just wanted to beat Mickey badly, for no other reason than just to be an ass.

Once he realizes the point of forking over the proper amount of cash to cover the wager, Mickey walks over to Marty to square up.

"So, Marty," he says as he throws a few twenties down on the table.

Cautiously, Marty gathers the twenties as though his life depends on it.

"How are your loan sharking skills?" Mickey continues.

"My what?"

"Exactly. You need to have a meeting with Forrester the day after tomorrow. Let me arrange it."

"If you say so."

"Oh, I know so. You got potential. I only hope you get aboard this train and ride it out to the end."

"What the hell are you going on about?"

"Never mind. Just be there at the meeting."

Marty tips his glass of whisky toward Mickey and says, "I salute you, my mentor."

"Don't you forget it." Mickey raises a glass and salutes back. "Don't forget those words, my protégé."

"How could I possibly?"

"You'd be surprised how many cocky bastards forget their roots or who brought them to this point."

"Well, shit, Mickey. I can't forget you," Marty declares.

"We'll see." Mickey raises his glass once more, wondering if Marty's words will stand true.

Forrester's loan-sharking class

"So. You're the guy everyone is talking about these days." Forrester, a throwback to the olden days of mobsters, sporting a classic fedora, studies Marty, who's sitting in the passenger seat.

"Marty's my name; gangster's my claim."

"Yeah, don't ever say that. I mean it. Ever."

"No. That wasn't my rap. Seriously." Marty attempts to regain face.

"Again. Never repeat it."

"OK. Fine. How's it going these days?" he says, switching topics.

"Better." Forrester takes another look at Marty before deciding on his next course of action. "Mickey wants me to school you on the fine art of loan sharking. Ain't that some shit. What am I, a professor or something?"

"Sure." Marty grins back, wondering if that was a joke and if he should be laughing at everything this guy says.

"Well, then. Let's go to work." Forrester shifts from park to drive. "We are going to pay a client a visit, and then we are going to the bar." Marty laughs at the word choice and then zips his mouth shut to continue to listen as Forrester rambles on during the drive until he parks the car up the street.

When they stop and get out, Forrester says, "So listen up. Watch and learn. He hasn't paid us back yet, not a dime—not any of the original money or the exorbitant interest. So. The first rule is, if we kill him, we get nothing. Keep the punter alive long enough to pay us. Does that make sense?" Forrester gives a questioning look as they walk down the street in a less-than-desirable part of town.

They confront the man, and Forrester performs the job like a mentor training a mentee. At one point, Forrester even stops screaming at the man to stress a point to Marty. Marty takes it all in, and Forrester eventually lets go of the man after collecting over two grand in cash and gold. They then walk down a couple of blocks and into a brewpub.

Once seated and having had their order taken, Marty thinks about asking if this is going to be on the test but withholds any smartass comments for the time being.

"Why would we even think about killing these people if they are supposed to pay us back the money? Wouldn't we be better off extorting some service from them instead?" Marty asks.

"Now that's the kind of progressive thinking we need in this business. Excellent question. And I have the perfect answer. Simply, we get nothing if they're dead, but it is a good bargaining chip to keep them alive. Alive does have various meanings to different people," Forrester replies in jest.

"So we must make them think we're gonna kill them."

"You got this, man. I ain't gonna teach you anything that you don't already know. Except torturing, but that's another lesson. Another day." He looks back to Marty, nodding his head in affirmation.

Meanwhile, Marty is still thinking about the repercussions of failing to abide by the time-tested loan-sharking rules and the consequences that could result. In his mind, the rules are black and white. Either you pay back the money you borrowed—plus some high-ass interest rate—or else you face some physical malady, such as a broken leg or broken arm or wrist, and you still have to pay back the money, with added interest.

In Marty's limited knowledge, before he had joined up with Mickey, the most unbelievable part was what the person who lost the bet was willing to trade when it came time to pay. Marty was sickened when some guys would literally offer their loved ones as payment in exchange for exonerating the debt owed. "Seriously, you'd sell out your girl because you can't handle your gambling problem?" Marty would sneer to these scum. Sometimes he'd even reluctantly offer one of his gambling tips if he thought it would help them, but it never did in the end. Then Marty assumes he would be stuck with some woman, crying and emotional, and he couldn't deal with that. Maybe it was easier just to break the guy's arm or shoot him in the thigh. Clean and easy. Reload and move on to the next client, after first taking any cash, jewelry, or anything of value from the guy, naturally.

As the food arrives, Forrester continues on. "You got to put the worst imaginable fear into these shitheads. I mean, come on, these bastards are willing to sacrifice their girlfriends or wives for their own personal problems? I mean, we may be bad guys, but I ain't no perv. Though I have to admit, this one guy's girl was so fine. But I wasn't gonna force myself on her, against her will. And she sure as shit wasn't gonna give in to pay her so-called man's debt with herself."

"What did you do?" Marty queries.

"I actually took the old girl out to dinner," Forrester answers. "Had a nice chat with her and, after a few rounds, asked her what the hell she was doing with this loser. And you know what the girl said?"

"Naw. What did she say?"

"You're gonna laugh, but she couldn't think of one reason why she was with said so-and-so asshat."

"No shit."

"Oh, wait. It gets better. The girl picks up her phone and calls the schmuck and dumps him right there. She then looks at me and tells me she is free now and is wondering if I have any current or future plans."

"Ha-ha. No way. What did you do?"

"Well, I'm gonna see here in about forty minutes." Forrester looks down at his watch to check the time.

"Bullshit."

"I kid you not. I told you this business is crazy. Now, don't you have routine business collections to do tomorrow?"

"Yeah. I do. I feel like an ass sometimes muscling old people, trying to extort money from them."

"Well, if it makes you feel any better, I used to feel that way until I found out some of those guys were millionaires and acted like I was robbing them blind. Then I'd see them drive off in BMWs to their McMansions in the suburbs. I tell ya, you can never trust people."

"That's nuts."

"Yeah. Well, don't take in every sob story. Though some might be telling the truth, most are just hustling you. You can count on it."

"Have you ever bargained with any of them?"

He turns to Marty. "Hell yeah. That's the whole point. I get free sandwiches from one place. Another gives me free gas. I call it the perks of the job."

"And the boss doesn't care?"

Forrester taps Marty on the shoulder. "The boss only cares if people pay, one way or other. As long as he gets his amount of money, he really doesn't care. Honest, I ain't bullshitting ya on that."

"Well, then. I need to get better acquainted with the neighborhood that I have to collect in, especially the delicatessens and bars. Maybe I'll refer to myself as the community rep."

"Now you're thinking. That's how you do it."

Marty flags the waiter down again. He tells the waiter that he will be paying the bill and to add another round on the tab. He then turns back to Forrester. "You know, I learned a lot. I'm kinda glad we had this meeting. Let me get the tab." The waiter brings the drinks and places them in front of the men.

Forrester nods his head in thanks. "I would never say no to that."

Raising his beer bottle and calling for a toast, Marty says, "Thanks, man, I appreciate your advice."

"Anytime, Marty. I always love a free beer and a free lunch."

"It was so worth it." He then laughs along with Forrester, his new friend and work colleague. "Don't you have had some place you need to get to?"

Forrester finishes the beer and says, "You're right. Gotta go. Later."

Marty watches his fellow gangster—or as he likes to say, coworker—depart the brewpub. He sits there a few more minutes before pulling out his phone to check his schedule for tomorrow. He studies the various businesses on the route, wondering which ones he can extort a perk from.

Shop talk

Marty wakes up in the morning and is full of enthusiasm. He has been looking forward to his meeting with Mr. Robinson, and he can hardly wait to go by the newsstand. He may let the first few collections go easy in his buildup to seeing the old guy and getting some information about the woman he saw in the store. He wonders if it was the old man's daughter or, more appropriately, his granddaughter. It doesn't matter how she is related; rather, it is about how Marty can use him to get to her.

Leaving the bedroom and heading to the kitchen to make the coffee is his first priority of the day. He loves his quaint and basic apartment because nobody bothers him—nobody messes with him in this nice part of town. To most people around here, he is just a guy who keeps to himself. A loner. Probably into video games or maybe an IT guy. He has met some of the other tenants and neighbors but keeps the conversation simple—hello, how you doing, the weather is great (or terrible), must be going, have a nice day (or evening). He even got the door for an elderly lady and held the elevator for a much younger woman who lived on another floor, but that's the extent of his display of social graces in this building.

The percolator stops making noise, signaling that his morning java is ready. How anyone could not enjoy the first taste of fresh coffee is beyond his scope of understanding. It not only tastes great, but it's warm and comforting, and he has a special kinship with this morning ritual. His daily life does not begin until he first holds the coffee cup, enjoying its warmth, and then takes a sip, eyes closed as he clears his mind.

"Ah," is the only sounds he utters until he opens his eyes to take the next sip from the mug.

After that, it's time to get ready for the day and read up on the daily news briefings. The boss tends to send, rather have some lackey send, updates and key items of interest. Sometimes, he even gives specific instructions in the emails, but they are always encoded. He can hear Mickey saying in his head, *You can never be too careful in this business. Someone is or will be watching you, at all times.*

Marty shudders as though a cold breeze has blown past him. Hearing such warnings reminds him: what he is doing is still illegal and against the law. While his vision of himself is just working a normal job—like in a cubicle— the police may see it differently.

Luckily for him, there are no other items worthy of note in the boss's email, other than noting "typical collects are up, but don't slack off," "nobody was killed in the last twenty-four hours," and whom they are under truce with and whom they are at war with. He closes out the email program and sets his phone back on the table. Now completely finished with his coffee, he ponders what to say to Mr. Robinson and runs a couple different scenarios in his head, trying to cover all the bases. Satisfied with most of the outcomes, he places the coffee mug next to the sink and heads to the back bedroom to finish getting ready for the day. Fifteen minutes later, he applies the final touches to his hair and adjusts his shirt in the mirror.

"Damn, Marty. You are looking way too good," he says to himself and checks the rounds in the gun before putting it back into the shoulder holster. He announces to himself that it is time to go to work and grabs his wallet and keys, heading to his front door. He locks it behind him and heads to the elevator. When the doors open, he sees it is unoccupied and steps in. The doors begin to close when a masculine shout from down the hall forces him to immediately place a hand in between them to stop them from closing. The doors then open back up, and an older man enters the elevator.

"Thanks for holding the door for me," the neighbor man announces, a bit short of breath.

"No worries."

They ride in utter silence until the noise of the doors opening, and Marty motions for the man to exit first. The man obliges and thanks Marty again, offering a token, "Have a nice day." Marty only smiles back, thinking, *He stole my line.*

He proceeds to walk out of the building and get into his car, ready to start the day of muscling small business owners for their periodic tribute payments. He reckons it is a fair exchange for the services rendered, with the boss's organization providing protection in return for the hefty amount they pay, which is based on an estimate of their gross sales. Their protection has led to many business owners feeling safe and having a resource to turn to if they are robbed at gunpoint, for instance. Most robbers don't dare to risk attempting to rob a place under a mob's protection zone. The pain of several broken bones and the lack of health insurance to fix said broken bones leave many criminals to go find a business to rob with much less risk.

Marty had heard the story of a guy who was apparently new to the area and wanted to show he was the new sheriff in town. He managed to hit two businesses that fell under Boss Mazoli's protection. The businesses were really ticked off and threatened to stop payments. Boss Mazoli was a fair man—a killer of many, true, but still just. He waived all payments until the perpetrator was caught. The boss then ordered everyone to track down this robber by any means necessary, and it came with a five-thousand-dollar bonus. It took a mere four hours and twenty-three minutes to find out who this guy was and an additional sixty-three minutes to track him down. No one wanted to know—and no one asked questions about—whatever happened to the guy or even if he was still alive. One thing was sure: all the money that the robber made off with was returned to the two businesses, along with a nice bottle of scotch, compliments of Boss Mazoli. Since that incident, there had not been any attempts on any of the businesses for many months. The boss continued extorting their money, but at least they were not being robbed.

After a few quick collections, Marty then strolls into Mr. Robinson's newsstand and convenience store, not realizing that from that moment forward, everything would change—for better or worse is debatable.

He maneuvers around the front of the store, making his way to the cash register. Mr. Robinson is looking down, stocking the cigarette display. Turning around, he then spies Marty staring back at him. A customer who arrived before Marty is between them, but the initial face-to-face meeting has begun.

Mr. Robinson takes the customer's goods and begins ringing them up.

He asks, "Is anything else you need?

"Yeah. Can I get two quick picks for the lotto? Can't win if you don't play," he says to whoever is listening.

"Ah yes. You are right about that."

"Has anyone ever won from this place?" the customer presses.

"Why, of course," the store proprietor responds.

Witnessing the conversation from the side, Marty chuckles inside, wondering if the old guy is just practicing a good sales tactic.

The customer receives the tickets and studies them. "You know, if I win, I will give you a cut of the pot."

"Then I hope you win the jackpot. Best of luck." Giving a smile as he adds the lotto tickets to the final price with the other goods, he then says, "That will be thirteen fifty-eight."

The customer hands over a twenty and receives his change, along with his tickets and the goods.

"Have a nice day—hope you win!" Mr. Robinson says.

"Yeah." The male walks out the door.

Marty then moves forward to counter and leans to one side. "Well. We meet again. Friend."

Mr. Robinson glares at Marty from behind the counter. "What brings you by today? Some smokes, or maybe a brewsky? I'm running a special on some of the twelve-packs." He points over Marty's right shoulder to the cooler.

Marty gives the cooler a momentary glance before quickly bringing his eyes forward to the old man. He thinks about the right moment to bargain for information and a chance to meet the stunning blonde woman who might be one of Mr. Robinson's family members or friends. Knowing he has to play this right, he chooses his words carefully.

"It's collection time, but you already know that. Or else you wouldn't be stalling like you are doing right now." Grinning, he picks up a small item from the counter near the register and says, "We can play this smooth, or we can play this out really bad. I assume you want this to go smooth. So. Let's change the rules this time around. Tell me how you would like this to go down."

The old man can't keep a poker face because he wasn't expecting these words from the collector. Rather, he is used to pleading that he has no money, and then they take what they can despite his attempts to hide some extra money here and there. Still, he gets the impression that this collector is different and maybe wants to bargain—but for what, he hasn't quite figured out. He decides to let this one play out and hope for the best.

"Suppose I don't have the money. Well, all of it. You know exactly what I mean, sonny. The amount you all steal from me every time."

"Yet we don't hear you voice your complaint when nobody robs your store or threatens you or your employees at gunpoint. Now, do you?"

Ouch. This guy has been practicing his retaliations or has been coached in how to respond to business owners' protests. Mr. Robinson thinks for a few seconds before responding.

"You talk about protection, but even the normal customers are afraid to come into my store. Thanks a lot for that. You know my sales have been declining every week," he says, trying a different strategy.

"Then prove it."

"What? How am I supposed to do that?"

"Open the register. Right now. Before you hide some of those big bills under the drawer or somewhere else." Marty acts unperturbed, like he knows what this guy is going to do.

The old guy starts to wonder if the mob has installed a hidden camera to record every move he makes and every attempt to hide his gross sales from the prying eyes of his protection enforcer. He hits a few buttons on the register, and it clinks open as Marty moves around the counter to inspect the contents inside.

Looking at the bills, he asks the old guy to lift the drawer. Unwillingly, he obliges, revealing a few more hundred-dollar bills lying there. Marty decides whether to take the bills or not.

Marty starts to reach from them, only to stop when he sees Mr. Robinson's pathetic expression. Stepping back, Marty decides to try something unorthodox, out of his normal routine. "Say—how about you close the drawer and I grab a couple of drinks for us? I want to talk to you. Or should I say, I'm willing to negotiate. Are you interested or what?"

Now the worried expression has turned to a quizzical one, but the old man decides to hear to what Marty has to say. "Sure. Grab us a couple of Cokes and bring them back here. Obviously, you got something to say. So say it."

With that, Marty heads to the cooler and reaches in to grab the old-fashioned glass bottles of Coke and hauls them back to the front of the store. Along the way, he grabs some potato chips as an added bonus. Mr. Robinson has the opener in hand and skillfully pops the tops off the two sodas. Marty grabs one and takes a big swig before he opens the potato chips and crunches down on a handful, and only then does he begin making his pitch.

After a belch that sends a potato chip flying out of his mouth, which he ignores, Marty says, "I like you, Mr. Robinson. I actually like this store. I especially like the blonde woman I saw you talking with behind the counter last week."

"Oh . . . You mean Amy?" Only then does he realize he spoke too soon, giving away her identity and a bargaining chip he had with this mobster. But he has the feeling that this Marty might be decent overall, so he is willing to gamble away with his granddaughter. "Why are you so interested in my favorite granddaughter? Wait a minute. Did she wrong you or something?" His tone suggests he is getting a little defensive.

Excited, Marty says, "Amy, is it? No. No. She didn't wrong me at all. Rather . . . I . . . I . . . am most eager to meet her. Er, I mean . . . I want you to introduce me to her." With this fumbling reply, he now realizes he just yielded his only bargaining chip to the newsstand owner.

Seizing this opportunity to his advantage, Mr. Robinson chuckles at this young stud on the other side of the counter keenly interested in his granddaughter, Amy. "Well. Well. You do have a soul, Marty. So you want to meet my granddaughter." He cracks a grin across his wrinkled old face.

"I'm willing to help you out if you are willing to help me."

Pushing the limit, as he now knows he has Marty in his pocket, the old man takes control of the situation. "What makes you think I will trade my lovely granddaughter for what you ask of me? What kind of person do you think I am? I told you, she is my favorite grandchild. Although she is certainly no child— she is a bright and independent woman."

Marty thinks before responding, "Because my intentions are honorable."

"Ha-ha. You got to be kidding, sonny."

Marty turns red in the face but maintains his composure. "Fine. Let's be honest with one another."

Mr. Robinson smiles, hoping he can bargain for a better deal than the one he currently has with the Mazoli gang. He's got nothing to lose, so he waits for Marty to dictate the terms.

Marty mulls it over. Still a little nervous, he says, "I ask only two things."

"Shoot. What are they? Reckon I might not be able to meet your demands. But go ahead anyhow."

"One. I want you to introduce me to your granddaughter, Amy. You aren't to tell her anything bad about me or who I work for or what I do for a living. I want you to simply put in a good word for me."

"It will be tough for me to lie to Amy, but I'll try." Although trying not to give it away to Marty, he feels the first request is pretty reasonable. He also hopes Amy will see right through him and tell him to kiss off politely. He now waits for the second request, thinking it must be much more. "Go ahead. What's the second demand?"

"I want to use your store as a safe house."

With a questioning expression on his face, Mr. Robinson says, "Describe in detail what you mean by safe house."

"Oh, it's quite easy. I want nobody else to know. I want access to the back anytime, twenty-four seven. I need to know I can hide out here for any amount of time. And at any time. I need a back room, nothing too big, with access from the alley behind the store. I'll be operating a numbers game from this store. Do you have any issues with that?"

"Hell, son, I thought you were gonna ask for something far worse. I suppose I can provide the safe house if that's what you want. There's a room in the back I don't use anyway. It should suffice for what you're talkin' about. You ain't gonna steal from me or rob me blind, are ya?"

"No. Nothing like that. I just need to know I can come here if I need to, well, you know, hide out if the circumstances dictate that I need to be hidden or out of sight. Catch what I'm saying?"

"Yeah. I reckon I can make a room for you in the back to hide out, if that's all that you want. But you'll have to explain this numbers game thing."

"Good. We have an understanding, then."

"Not so fast. As for Amy, well, you're on your own. I suppose I can introduce you two, but I ain't gonna force her to like you. Not that you're that bad of guy, given the circumstances."

Marty leans back to laugh out loud. "Agreed. Just give me the introduction. I can take it from there. But remember, you can't tell her anything about me other than I'm a good guy."

"Sure about that?" He slaps Marty on the shoulder. He actually is starting to like this fellow. "Now, what are you gonna do for me?"

Prepared from the moment he thought of and offered this deal, Marty responds, "Well, you still get your protection, but I will personally cover your protection money, until such time I don't. Until then, you will no longer have to pay a dime, at all. Nobody will harass you, either, from now on. Is that fair enough?"

"I suppose it is, and I should be grateful for your generosity. But there is still one issue that needs to be talked about."

Taken by surprise, Marty asks, "Oh, and what is that?"

"Well, I don't mean to be forward . . ."

"Yeah. Go on. Say what ya gotta say."

"You mentioned earlier about some numbers or gambling thing."

"Oh, you're talking about the numbers game."

Mr. Robinson swallows some air. "Yes, that. You want to run it from this store? Is that what you are telling me? Son, I don't know about such things."

"Yes. Ha. I get it. OK old man, your role is really easy. People come in and they'll drop off their bet and hand over the money. Just record the bet and the name. That's all. So what you really want to know is what your cut of the profits will be from this venture. Is that what you're asking me?"

"I reckon so if you put it that way. I am providing the store, and I'll have to start recording and taking the bets. Simple enough."

"Yeah. I guess you do. Well, how much you want? Ten percent? Twenty percent?"

"I don't want to be too greedy. I suppose you'll decide what is fair," he says, putting the onus back on Marty.

Without hesitation, Marty blurts out, "How does twenty-five percent sound? You think that's a fair deal?"

"I won't ask for more. Just tell me again what I gotta do."

"I can do that. Partner."

"Partner it is. I only hope Amy is as agreeable to whatever you say as I am!" he says in jest.

Marty chuckles at the joke. "Oh, don't worry. I will still run the numbers game with or without your granddaughter's decision to go out with me. But, you need to swear to me now: Our little business stays between us, understood?"

Mr. Robinson extends his hand out to meet Marty's. "A deal is a deal."

"Don't renege on your partner, ever." Marty grasps Mr. Robinson's hand tightly, squeezing too tight. "Now tell me some more about your lovely granddaughter, Amy."

"She will never go out with you."

"How much you want to wager?"

"Ah, the first bet I get to take. The odds are against you, my friend, and you'll lose."

"I always beat the odds. You should know that by now."
He puts an arm around his new partner in crime or, in this case,
partner in a new side venture.

"Fine. I will arrange for her to be here next week, Tuesday,
at around three in the afternoon. Will that work for you? I can
then introduce you as a financial and business consultant," Mr.
Robinson replies.

"Fine. See you next Tuesday, three o'clock sharp." Marty
turns to leave the store, sporting a wide grin on his face.

Mr. Robinson thinks about what he has just gotten himself
into by dealing with this guy and selling out his granddaughter.
But he knows she will see right through him and the sort of
business he is involved in. Well, as long as he gets his cut from
the numbers game, he can't complain too much, as the extra
money will be much appreciated. He turns to wipe down the
counter and rearrange the items next to the register, waiting
patiently for the next customer to arrive.

First impressions

Tuesday morning rolls around quickly for Amy. Her grandfather has been telling her all weekend about this guy he wants to introduce her to. Over the last few days, he has been saying over and over how wonderful he is and how he is going to enter a business partnership with him, although he doesn't give any more specifics. No matter how many times she asks, she can't get a straight answer or further information about this mystery man.

Mr. Robinson is standing at the register when she arrives at the newsstand on Tuesday. She gives her routine, "Good morning," and he eagerly returns his reply. He has a positive aura about him, and she thinks it means that this guy, Marty, who he is partnering up with should be all right. *Why else would Grandpa even talk to him or do business if he was bad?* She shrugs her shoulder and walks over behind the counter to talk to him.

"Do you need me to start the weekly inventory, or do you want me to watch the register?"

"Oh, I can take the register for a bit. Why don't you start the inventory in the cooler first and then, if you have time, do the canned goods. That would really help out your old grandpa!" He smiles back at her.

"You're not that old. Well, I haven't thought about putting you in a home yet. But if you keep pestering me about this Marty guy, I just might." Amy shoots back a menacing face.

Mr. Robinson is ready with a reply. "Amy, my dear, I don't you want to be lonely and working here all your life. Like I have. You're young. You should be out there." He points out the window. "Traveling and living life."

"No. I want to stay and run the store."

He nods his head. "Someday you'll get it. But enjoy life before you get stuck here every day of your life."

"Whatever." She knows he is right, but she refuses to listen to him, especially when she doesn't want to listen to him. Instead, she heads into the cooler, armed with her clipboard, to take inventory.

He watches her enter the cooler while ringing up a customer who came in for a pack of smokes. He is smiling inside, thinking that doing the inventory may help her cool off before meeting Marty in a few hours. Checking his watch, he realizes that it isn't even eleven o'clock yet. He wonders what else he can do to get her to relax and give Marty a chance. Maybe Marty will bring flowers or do something crazy to try to win her attention. He laughs about this, thinking of what he had to do to win the heart of his wife many years ago—and all the way up until she passed away a few years back. In his mind, he wishes Marty good luck.

His thoughts interrupted by the sound of the bell when the door opens, he steadies himself and greets the man and woman entering the store. "Good morning. Pleasant day, isn't it?"

Getting ready to meet

It is two in the afternoon, and Marty is fretting away in his apartment. He has pulled out a half-dozen shirts from the closet, trying to perfectly match the three different pairs of trousers lying on the bed. Not to mention the numerous ties that he will eventually have to narrow down to one that pairs with the shirt and pants. He wonders why he is putting in so much effort for someone he hasn't even met or talked to, rather, only seen in passing and heard briefly about from her grandfather. You would think he had finally found his soulmate—the woman of his dreams.

But Mr. Robinson's echoing words keep haunting him: *She'll never go out with you.* They remind Marty that he must dress even better than anyone would expect. He tells himself that he will never again try so hard to impress a woman. Maybe he should let her try to win him over instead. Assuming she finds him interesting. *And what woman doesn't,* the voice in Marty's head reminds him.

To himself, barely audible, he says, "Maybe I should just fight her, physically, before deciding to pursue her. Isn't that what they did in the olden days?" He laughs silently and then reaches for the perfect tie to match with the shirt and trousers he has finally selected.

Looking down at his watch and discovering it is a quarter to three, Marty hastily leaves his apartment and heads on down the street. Not wanting to deal with parking today, he flags a taxi because there isn't enough time to call for an Uber and jumps in. He realizes the taxi is more expensive, but his current expenditures are not a lot these days, so he can spend money frivolously without affecting his bottom line. He reminds himself that this may all change if Amy decides to go out with him. That would send his expenditures skyrocketing. But he doesn't want to get ahead of himself, worrying about having a potential girlfriend and how it will affect his savings and retirement accounts. *Can't take it with you, so might as well enjoy it and spend it,* he thinks. The taxi lurches forward.

Staring out the window, he suddenly jars himself back into reality. He's not sure how long he was out but realizes he is almost at his destination. He leans forward, and as they get close to his stop, he taps on the glass, signaling to the driver.

"Can you let me out up there?"

"Is past the corner OK, buddy?" the taxi driver shouts back in a local accent.

"No worries. That's fine."

The driver cuts across traffic in a show of his driving skills, despite the sounds of a few car horns blaring. He brakes hard and stops at the curb past the corner, reciting the total fare seconds later. Marty hands over a twenty and tells him to keep the change. The driver does not respond as enthusiastically as Marty would have thought, but he does say thanks. Marty barely hears it as he slams the rear passenger side door closed, never turning around to see the taxi rev off to his next fare.

He strolls down the familiar street, passing several businesses he had visited recently and collected the monthly protection money from. A couple of the business owners spy him coming up the street and acknowledge him, fearing that he may be intending to strong-arm them into giving more money. Smiling and waving to them results in confused return looks as Marty continues past them with a determined destination in mind. He wonders why they are looking at him in such a weird way, but he doesn't give it much thought as he slows down and enters the newsstand at precisely one minute before three.

The bell above his head rings twice, announcing his presence to all in the store. Glancing over to the left, he sees Mr. Robinson, who is standing in his routine position at the register but wearing a blank expression. Marty wonders if the old man is setting him up; maybe he doesn't have a chance in hell of hooking up with Amy.

Marty starts to panic inside, but the old man waves him over quietly as though he is about to reveal a plan of attack.

"Glad you finally showed up," Mr. Robinson says.

"What do you mean? I'm right on time," Marty says, defending himself.

The old man moves his right hand to hush Marty. "Yeah. Yeah. Not important. So. She's over there, down that aisle," he whispers, pointing to the third aisle over.

Marty looks to him, back to the aisle, and back to him again. It processes in his head as his eyes get big and he realizes what he must do. To spur him on, Mr. Robinson nudges him toward the intended direction.

He turns and heads down the aisle, where Amy is busy working, counting inventory, or doing some kind of business task for the store. He looks side to side, eyeing the cooler on one side and the chips and snacks on the other. His mind begins to wander, and he thinks that it makes perfect sense to pair the drinks and snacks in the same aisle, but then he reminds himself why he is in this aisle. He wipes the last bit of sweat from his forehead as he prepares to speak to this mystery woman he has been pursuing for the better of two weeks. He straightens up and coughs to clear his throat. It's now or never. After clearing his throat, he opens his mouth to deliver his well-rehearsed opening line but is interrupted by the woman holding the clipboard.

"Is there something you're looking for?" Amy asks in the standard owner-to-customer manner.

"I . . . no . . . I mean . . . yes." Caught completely off guard, he stutters and stumbles, trying to make a coherent sentence so that he sounds like he's normal and not a crazy or illiterate person.

Amy stops writing on the clipboard to look up, her eyes meeting his. Marty is transfixed by her gaze, but a part of his brain is screaming at him to listen to her as she is speaking.

He catches the last bit of what she was saying: "What did you say you were looking for?"

Attempting to project the image of a competent adult, Marty evaluates his words before constructing a sentence. "Yes. I'm looking for something to drink."

Her face drops slightly, but she always tries to help the customers, no matter how bizarre their requests might be. "Excellent," she says, adding a little humor in her tone. "You're in the right aisle. The cooler to your left is filled with many different choices. Soft drinks are that way, and the beer is the other way." She lowers her head back to the clipboard.

Appreciating that she has not given up on him by running away, Marty steps up the charm and tries a tactic to keep her engaged. "What would you recommend?"

Amy raises her head and starts to deconstruct his last question as Marty adds further information, hoping to avoid confusion. "I'm looking for beer."

Her expression is more relaxed than earlier. Marty feels he is making progress and listens intently to Amy's response.

"Personally, I prefer craft beer." She motions to a cooler to her right. "But . . . if you're economical in your purchases"—she points behind her toward the end—"those would be your options."

Marty takes a step toward her. "If I were trying to find a craft beer that you would like, which one should I pick?"

She laughs, realizing she is being hit on. She takes a second look and finds the guy in front of her to be kind of cute in a goofy way. She takes the bait and flirts along.

"I'm not sure. Unless you're a high roller, I seriously doubt you could afford my brand."

"Try me. I bet I could!" He grins toward her with a happy smile, comforting and warm.

"Oh? Do you want to bet? Well, then, shall we make a wager? Are you a gambling man, or am I wasting my time?"

"Let's hear it," Marty says with a smile.

"What are the chances I will go out with you? I have a percentage in my head. Do you have a number?" she asks, laying down the terms and even raising the stakes. He now knows he's committed and has to take her bet.

He mulls it over for a split second. "I do, but let's up the game, shall we? I will say, oh, let me see, I will say eighty-five percent—but only after I ask you one question that you have to answer." He's thrown his cards down, metaphorically speaking, and everything rides on how he delivers the question—that is, if she is willing to listen to it.

"Hmmmm. Eight-five percent. You must feel confident. Sure. I'll take the bet. But I must answer your question, correct?"

"Absolutely. Though I must make a side comment that I find it very brave of you to take such a risk." They smile at one another, both enjoying the flirtation.

"All right . . . uh . . . you know what? I don't even know your name. Perhaps we should introduce ourselves if we are to bet with one another. After all, this sounds pretty serious, and I'd hate to win and not even know who I've beaten." She smirks at him, waiting for a witty reply.

Marty extends a hand, formally, to the woman in front of him. He squeezes it tight when she places her hand in his. "Marty's my name. Mighty fine to meet you, finally."

She receives his hand, cautiously. "Amy." She then lets go of the handshake and raises an eyebrow. "What do you mean finally?" she says defensively.

Marty racks his brain for a snappy comeback that won't result in him being called out for being creepy or being a stalker. "Sorry. I meant I finally get to meet someone worthy of meeting and willing to take a risk every now and then." He waits to see if she buys it.

Nodding her head, Amy accepts the answer as reasonable. She then flips back to their previous conversation. "OK, buddy, here's your one shot at this. Ask your question. You better make it a good one." She glares at him defiantly.

He coughs once in his closed hand. "Do you want to go to dinner with me tomorrow night?"

Amy's eyes widen, and she shows signs of relief that the question is better than what she had assumed and prepared for in her mind. She is about to answer his question in the affirmative when another voice cuts her off, heard from afar.

"Of course she will," Mr. Robinson booms, giving the response Marty was hoping to hear from Amy and not him.

Amy smiles. "Well, there's your answer."

Marty jumps in. "I would like you to answer it too!"

"Yes. I would love to." She holds her hands out.

He grabs both her hands in a nervous way. "I assume it will be just the two of us for dinner?" He gestures behind him with his head, referring to the voice from the distance.

Never letting go of his hands, she bats her eyes and says, "Yes, silly. Just the two of us, Marty. And here's a hint. You need to buy that beer on the second shelf to the right."

Marty had almost forgotten what brought about the conversation in the first place but makes a mental note of what beer Amy prefers. He reaches in the cooler and grabs a six-pack to stock up his fridge.

Flower power

The next day, Marty goes over the timeline he created yesterday for the tasks to accomplish before the date. He checks his email to reconfirm the dinner reservation is set by opening up the email one more time. Check. He has laid out a different clothing ensemble, this time with a sports jacket. Check. He dug out some old cologne to try his luck. *Maybe she will like it, or maybe she will get nauseated after smelling it. OK, no strong cologne—maybe just some light, non-scented deodorant.* Check. The only thing left to do is pick up a nice bouquet of flowers— from CC's Florist, of course. He knows they're going to razz him once they find out he's got a date, but he secretly wants to hear Cindy's advice on what flowers to order. He's willing to lose a little face if he gets the right kind of flower bouquet and it makes Amy ecstatic.

Chad is in the back of the store, cutting the latest drug shipment and organizing the delivery schedule. Cindy is the front part of the store, maintaining the illusion of a legitimate florist. She continues to assemble preordered flower arrangements. They have built a decent business and a steady stream of clients, both normal customers looking for flowers and the drug customers.

Raising her head to acknowledge the person who just walked, she giggles upon recognizing that it is someone she knows rather well. "Hmmm. Let me guess this. I know why you're here!"

She finishes tying up a nice bouquet for a guy who wants to make up with his wife after an argument—or more like the guy wants to make out, and this will help set the mood. One more adjustment and then she looks it over, satisfied that the flowers should get the guy to second base, at least.

Cindy strolls around the counter and walks right up to Marty, giving him a big hug. Marty knows that Cindy's hugs are fierce and has prepared himself for the greeting ritual. She then plants a wet kiss on each of his cheeks. All he can do is receive them in kind and return the same gesture. Such is the way with Cindy; he heard she had lived in Europe for a fair amount of time.

"How are you doing, sweetie?" she asks with penetrating eyes.

Marty swallows a lump in his throat. "Fine."

"So let me get this right," she says, gleefully grinning back at him. "You're here on your day off."

"Yeah."

"And you don't smoke weed."

"Not for a long time." He does think about starting back up, but when you see the product day in and day out, it kind of loses its luster. He then feels a slight punch from the woman in front of him.

"Don't drift off yet—I ain't finished with you."

"Yes, ma'am," he says, eyes wide. "Please continue."

"That only leaves me to conclude you are buying flowers . . . for a girl." She erupts in laughter and then shouts out to the back, "Hey, honey, come on out here. You'll love this."

He starts to step back, but she already anticipates him fleeing and wraps one leg around his while grabbing his right arm.

"Oh no you don't—we ain't done with you yet!"

The curtain separates, and the bulky, strong, six-foot-plus man appears as though the show on stage has just started. He pushes the curtains back to the closed position and then surveys the room, always ensuring safety and protocol are adhered to at all times.

He then sees his wife in a rather untoward—but for the moment, necessary—leg and arm lock with another man. He has to admit, she does have him in an uncomfortable position. It is a good thing that he knows the man; otherwise, the situation might unfold a bit differently. Nevertheless, he still needs to have a little fun of his own.

"Just what the hell do you think you're doing with *my wife*?" Chad shouts.

"I . . . she grabbed me . . . nothing. Aw. Come on!"

Cindy counters, "He grabbed me—help me, honey."

Marty is most surprised by this reply from the one whose leg is blocking him, as their appearance would suggest she has grabbed him and has a tight hold on him.

Not bothered by the facts but only the insinuation, Chad grabs Marty and tries to put him in a headlock. Luckily, Marty takes the split second of being released by Cindy and jacks Chad in the abdomen, knocking him slightly off-balance. Marty regroups and steps back, ready to defend himself from the couple flanking him. Except the attack comes at him with open and outstretched arms, thus embracing him in a tight threesome clutch.

"What's this I hear? You come in here to buy flowers for a girl?" Chad asks as everyone finally ends the group hug.

"Yes. Yes." Still a few shades of red, he walks with them to the counter, standing on one side as the other two move to their side of the counter.

"What's her name?" Cindy asks the first question.

Marty looks at her quizzically. "What does it matter?"

"How else is my wife gonna design a special bouquet for your lady friend?" Chad chides.

"Huh?"

Leaning in, Chad squares up to Marty. "Tell her the name, and I guarantee your chances of scoring on the first date will double—of course, if you're willing to pay for the extra-special bouquet." Chad smiles and punches him in the arm.

At this point, Marty cannot tell if they are being nosy or actually trying to scam him. Still, he'd rather fork over the money to them—at the least, he still has to work with them most days of the week.

Surrendering to their will, he gives in. "Fine. Her name is Amy."

Gasps come from the two on the other side of the counter. Thinking that was a most peculiar reply, he decides to continue. He takes a deep breath.

"She works at the newsstand a couple of blocks over."

Chad slaps the side of his thick skull. "No . . . not Mr. Robinson's newsstand, by chance?"

He looks to Cindy and then to Chad; both have the baited expression of waiting in anticipation for the confirmation of what they suspect. At this point, he realizes he is all in and might as well confess the truth before they continue to pester him.

Reluctantly, Marty gives what they both have been waiting for: "Yes. That Amy."

A riotous cheer of affirmation fills the room. Chad and Cindy turn to one another, and both start blaring away on everything they know about the girl from sharing stories with the owner and frequently visiting the business. He waits it out until they finally turn back to him.

"Aww, she's such a nice girl," Cindy says. "Why does she want to go out with you?"

"What the fuck, people? You're crazy!"

"Aw, we're just messing with ya, Marty!" Cindy laughs.

"Yeah. Serious. I mean, Cindy here could whip up a really beautiful bouquet that will impress Amy. No doubt about it," Chad adds.

"Or I could add in, some, well, you know, a sprinkle of weed perhaps?" Cindy says, continuing her teasing.

Marty throws both hands outward. "*No. No.* No extra stuff. Please. Come on, people. I want to go out with her. Not get her stoned."

Chad asks curiously, "Are you sure about that?"

"Well, I . . . no. No. I don't want to do that. Wait a minute, are you thinking about trying to get her to be one of your regular customers?" Marty turns the tables and decides to go on the offense.

This throws Cindy off for a second. Chad remains mute on the point.

Then Cindy scolds, "I can't believe you would think such a thing. Sure, we are always looking to expand the business, but in this case we can't because she is already one of our best customers."

Back on the defense, Marty counters, "Bullshit."

"How do you know?"

"I . . . I don't. You win." He pauses, almost losing his cool because of their consistent teasing of him. "Cindy. Would you make a pretty bouquet for me, please?"

"Sure. Why didn't you say so in the first place?" Cindy turns around and begins to gather various flowers for the arrangement because she already has something in mind.

Worn down, Marty yields a simple, "Thank you."

"Oh, sorry. One more question. Did you say you want me to plant some extra stuff in the bouquet?" She is grinning, despite trying not to show any further excitement toward him.

"No extra stuff. But after dealing with you two, I may come back later tonight for some for myself."

Cindy hears Marty reply but shakes her head, ignoring him. "And you're positive she's not into it?"

"No. But why would I take the chance?"

"Oh. Because if this guy"—she points over to Chad, who is leaning against the counter—"or any guy gave me an ounce of weed, I would be most grateful and probably put out. Provided it was good weed!"

"OK, funny people. Just give me the flowers. How much do I owe you?"

"Oh. Your money's no good here, Marty." Chad steps to the register, ringing in a no sale with zeros flashed across the screen.

Cindy hands over the beautifully done bouquet, complete with a bow. Even Marty has to admire the details in the flower arrangement. "I'm impressed. Thank you both. I mean it too."

"Oh, trust us. The pleasure was all ours." Chad slaps him on the shoulder.

"Just tell us if the bouquet worked!" Cindy adds.

"Or not. No, wait. We don't want to know if it didn't, do we, honey?"

"Hush. You're making him all nervous now. Have fun on your date with Amy. I'm sure she will put out." Cindy continues to snicker. "Or not!"

Marty takes the flowers and waves goodbye, wondering why he even bothered coming here in the first place. He closes the door behind him and hears his phone ringing.

Don't answer the phone

His phone is ringing. Marty is carrying the beautiful bouquet of flowers and doesn't answer it. He figures it isn't that important and will check who called when he gets to his car in a few more feet. However, he hasn't even reached for the keys when the phone rings again. He puts the bouquet down on the hood of the car. He pulls out his phone and sees it is Mickey calling him.

"What's up?"

"What do you think?"

Marty opens the passenger door and carefully places the flowers on the seat. He goes around to the driver's side and gets in. "I'm starting to think this is not a social call."

"I would be lying if I said it was." Mickey pauses on the phone. Marty closes his eyes, fearing the worst. "I need ya, man. I need you tonight."

"Shit."

"Come again?"

"Nothing. What time and where?" Marty slams the dashboard in a fit of rage. He tries not to give away to the caller how pissed he is.

"For a second there, it sounded like I'm bothering you. I'm sorry—do you have other plans this evening?"

Only a date with a woman I've been trying to hook up with for some time now, Marty says to himself.

"Because if I'm inconveniencing you, then too fucking bad. I not asking you; I'm telling you! Are we clear, crystal fuckin' clear?" Mickey yells.

Marty pauses to sigh and put the phone down for a moment and then opens his eyes, putting the phone back to his ear. "Sorry, Mickey, I meant no disrespect. What can I do for you?"

"You can fucking apologize all you want later, but right now I need a second shooter. Tonight. Bruno is out with the flu, in case you're wondering. You say you can do it, now is the time to step up."

"Absolutely. I'm on my way and will be at your place within the hour."

"If you're not here in forty-five minutes, I will personally hunt you down and shoot you myself," Mickey says before ending the call.

Sitting in his car, Marty mulls over what he should do. Whatever it is, he'll have to do it quickly. Seconds later, he roars out of the spot and speeds off toward the newsstand. He has less than three blocks to come up with what to say, and he better make it count.

The door opens to the newsstand, and Mr. Robinson is surprised to see Marty practically running in and beelining straight to the counter. There is a customer finishing a transaction, so he must wait. Fidgeting, he pulls out his phone to check the time. Mr. Robinson bags up the purchases while keeping an eye on the crazy guy with flowers who is next in line.

"Thank you and have a great day," Mr. Robinson says.

Both men watch the customer leave.

"What are you doing here? You not supposed to pick up Amy for another three hours. Oh shit, you ain't bailing on her, are you? Don't lie to me, boy."

Laying the bouquet on the counter, Marty pleads his case to Amy's grandfather. He continues even when another customer enters the store, looks over to them for a second, and heads back toward the cooler and chips aisle.

Mr. Robinson watches the customer but turns his head back toward the raving man standing in front of him.

"Yes, I know, but something else came up, so please tell her something. It will sound better coming from you. Make it sound good, and don't forget to give her these," he says, pushing the flowers a little farther toward the other side of the counter. Marty is nervous and quite talkative.

"What the hell do you want me to say to her?"

"Hell. I don't know. Just come up with something." Marty throws down two fifty-dollar bills. "Just remember, don't tell her anything . . . else." He smirks. "I'll make it up to her somehow." He turns and rushes out of the store.

Mr. Robinson quickly picks up the fifties as the other customer brings her goods to be rung up.

"Hello, Amanda. How is your day going?" Mr. Robinson asks as he rings up her items.

Amanda, a community response detective, would normally give the typical response of "Fine" or "OK," but she feels the twinge of her policing skills coming to the surface. "Better than that guy's day, apparently." She turns, facing the doors, before looking back. "Say, do you know his name by any chance?"

Mr. Robinson feels that the detective is testing him. It is not the time to lie to Amanda—or any police officer, for that matter. Still, he has a partnership with Marty. *What is the worst that could happen if I mention his name to her?* he thinks.

Bagging up the last of the purchases, he tells her, "Oh, it's Marty. He's helping me out with some . . . er . . . investments. Financial planning stuff. That will be eight dollars and thirty-two cents, please."

"Oh. Yes, of course. One must always plan for retirement." She digs out a ten from her purse and hands it over. "Say, that's a nice bouquet of flowers you got there. Did he bring those in for you?" She laughs, trying to make a joke in the tense situation, sensing he is not being entirely truthful with her.

"Yes. I mean, no. He got those for Amy." He hands the change to her and maintains a blank facial expression.

"Well, that's mighty thoughtful of him. Marty. I'll have to remember him . . . if I need any financial planning as well." She exits the newsstand, forgetting to say goodbye, lost in thought about this Marty guy.

Pool shark

Marty speeds and makes it over to Mickey's place in just under twenty-nine minutes. Standing at the door, Mickey shakes his head impatiently as Marty approaches.

"What?"

"You have a chance to start making a name for yourself, and you were going to diss me for what? No, don't tell me, I already know. Let me guess, for a woman!"

"Cindy must have tipped you off."

"Well, yeah. But what else could it possibly be? Now get your ass inside—we gotta have a talk." Mickey is still holding the door, and Marty barrels on past him and inside the house.

They both walk down a hallway and enter the first room on the right. Inside, it looks like an old-time parlor room, except there is a billiards table, along with fully stocked bar off to the side. Marty almost makes a comment regarding Mickey's bachelor status but decides to remain quiet for the time being. Instead, he heads to the bar and, without hesitating, grabs the decanter, pouring whatever libation is inside.

"Next time, ask. That's some expensive scotch."

"Good. I don't like to drink the cheap stuff." Picking up the two glasses and handing one over to Mickey, Marty raises his own glass to smell the peaty fragrance.

"Cheers. Now rack them. I got time to whoop your ass on the table before we need to leave." Mickey directs him over toward the rack as he starts emptying out the pockets and rolling the billiard balls to the other end.

Enjoying his second sip, Marty savors the taste and then puts his glass down on the bar. He racks up the balls. "Are you going to tell me anything about the job we have to do tonight?"

Taking the cue and chalking it up, Mickey says, "Eventually. I'm breaking."

Eager to goad his opponent whenever the chance may arise, Marty says, "Good ahead. It won't matter. You and I both know I'm gonna win." He walks over and randomly selects a cue, not even bothering to test it for straightness or weight.

"We play first. Then we talk." With that, the room echoes with the sound of the crack of the rack and balls scattering about on the table. Marty sits back and takes another sip of his scotch, waiting until Mickey misses a shot.

Mickey misses after the third shot.

"Aw . . . shit!" he shouts, but Marty is already scanning the table, figuring out how to clear it. Taking a step up to the table, he carefully lines up his shot and then sinks the next four balls, only taking a break to head over to the table and sip on the scotch in his glass.

"What the hell you think you're doing?"

"Kicking your ass at pool, by the looks of it." Marty tips the glass in his direction before setting it back down on the counter. He grabs his cue and twirls it a bit and then sinks two more balls, although the second shot could have been judged a little sloppy.

"You're really gonna take that one?" Mickey shouts.

"Of course. It was legit." Marty crouches down in order to line up for another shot, moving on to strike the eight ball for the win.

"You cheatin' ass."

"Fine." Withdrawing his cue, Marty proclaims, "If you didn't like that last one, then the table's all yours." He steps back and waits for the reaction.

Not knowing what to do, Mickey contemplates his choices. Should he progress forward and take the callout, or should he just yield the table back to Marty and risk him running the rest of the table, winning in two more shots? He decides he wants to win rather than being moral. He lines up for a shot and misses by a few inches.

"Damnit," he mutters under his breath. "Fine. Go ahead and finish the game, you bastard."

Marty stands up and walks to the table. He glances back to Mickey with a smirk on his face and then proceeds to sink the next two balls. He throws the cue on the table as the eight falls in the called pocket. He turns back to Mickey with a straightforward expression. "If I was hustling you, I wouldn't have cleared the table so fast."

Mickey flips him the bird.

"Now can we sit down so you can tell me what I need to know? I'll even let you get the next round." Marty walks away from the pool table and heads over to a chair in the room. He's hoping Mickey is filling up their drinks.

Moments later, he is joined by the loser of the pool game, who slides a drink in his direction and sits in the chair next to him. Marty grabs the drink and slowly tastes it, realizing it's not the good stuff from the decanter. Oh well, a free drink is still a free drink. He continues to hold the glass, waiting for Mickey to tell him the plan of operation for the night.

"Do you ever shut up?" Mickey leans back in the chair and glances at Marty with menacing eyes, then stares back at the pool table.

Marty picks up the glass of cheap whisky and chugs it down, slamming the glass back down on the table. "You know. Even before you start telling me this and that about what I gotta do, I want to say . . ." He pauses, gathering his courage to tell his immediate supervisor off.

"Is there something you want to say to me?" Mickey glares back, knowing or betting on why Marty is so pissed off.

Marty's mind is feeling the effects of the alcohol as he raises a finger and points it in Mickey's general direction. "You. *You.*"

"What?"

"You fucked it up for me."

"How so?"

"I had the perfect date with this gorgeous woman. Tonight," Marty confesses.

"Oh. Sorry, man. Shit happens. I'll make it up to ya." Mickey puts his drink down, signaling to Marty to go get the next round.

"And how are you gonna do that?" Marty grabs the empty glasses and walks over to the bar. He is tempted to grab the decanter but decides to make an easy mixed drink.

"I got connections, you know."

"And what are these connections going to do?"

"Well, for starters, they can provide a dinner cruise down the river. You know, the one that's always booked weeks in advance? You think you and your girl would like that?"

He mulls it over. Yes, that sounds great—he's thinking Amy might actually forgive him if he offers something hard to get like the dinner cruise. Still, if he has any chance of a second date, well technically, a first date, then he needs to figure out damage control. Except he doesn't have the time to call Mr. Robinson at the moment. "OK. Sounds good. Let's get to that later. How about you telling me what we are going to do tonight?"

"Good. We can finally talk business. So. This is how it's gonna go down tonight. Listen up." Mickey then tells of the plan of what he wants them to do.

"No shit?"

"Just shut up for a second, will ya?"

"But wait. It's just that it sounds . . . sounds . . . what's the word?"

"Unusual?"

"More like weird, I'd say."

"Doesn't matter. Are you set? Can you be the backup?"

"Absolutely. What are we waiting for?"

Mickey stands up. "Let's get going, then. We got a BBQ party to crash." He then moves to the door, ready to leave. Marty finishes his current drink and rests the glass on the table, then follows him out.

Driving down the boulevard, Mickey shuts off the radio for a second to ask about the date that Marty allegedly had planned for tonight. He wants to hear it straight from the source before shooting him down and starting to preach about loyalty and duty first. Still, it is fun to hear about someone else's million-to-one chance being pushed aside by a higher priority, such as reducing the competition—specifically, in this case, killing a vital person in the rival gang's hierarchy. But Marty doesn't need to know all the details just yet.

"Man, this girl sounds like something special," Mickey says, offering a short-lived moment of sympathy. Trying not to burst out laughing, he adds, "Dude, I dunno how you could ever get a second chance with this broad. I mean, who ditches on the very first date? Only a class A asshole!"

"You're not helping," Marty mutters under his breath.

Mickey doesn't let up. He goes on and on about how he has never ditched a girl on a first or even second date. He describes how that is not his style and a trashy thing to do. "Naw, man, you're screwed. You might as well kiss this Amber goodbye."

"It's Amy. Amy."

Looking back at him, Mickey says, "It doesn't matter. She won't ever talk to you again. Ever. You're so screwed!"

"You're a real pal, you know that?"

Changing lanes to avoid being stuck behind a slow driver, Mickey maneuvers to the left and to the right numerous times before staying in the center lane for more than five seconds. The light up ahead changes to yellow, and Mickey decides to brake hard and not run the light, unlike the last three traffic lights. He puts the car in park temporarily and turns to Marty.

"OK. We got a second. Let's drop this Amy talk because, quite frankly, she will be dropping your ass anyway." After pausing for a moment to let it sink in, he continues to the important part of the conversation.

Sulking but deciding to actually get in the game, Marty abandons further talk of the date he almost had tonight. Instead, he nods his head and turns to Mickey before the light turns to green. "Fine. What are we doing anyway?"

"We need to shoot this guy, clear and simple."

"Where's it going down?"

"At his house. He's hosting a BBQ pool party."

"Well, it's the perfect day for it. So we are going to roast his ass?"

"That's one way to say it." Mickey shifts in the car seat. "Another way is to say it is a straight scare-and-shoot job."

"And what the hell is that?" Marty questions, as he's never heard the phrase.

Leaning back as the car propels forward, Mickey continues to stay focused on the road up ahead while deciding how to explain the mob-lingo phrase to his passenger.

"A scare-and-shoot job is really brilliant. You want to scare the other side and send a clear message that they are easily accessible and can be hit anytime, day or night. Also, it makes them be on guard in the future to anything after the fact."

"Why is this so effective?"

"Because it shows them they are vulnerable. They then go on the defense rather than the offense. They call in the forces and retreat back to guard the headquarters."

"So how does this benefit us?"

"Ah, I was getting to that." Mickey slams on the brakes, almost hitting the car ahead of him. He waits patiently for traffic to begin moving again. He then answers Marty's question.

The car moves forward. They coast along at almost 30 mph until he makes a sharp right turn into a subdivision. The similarity in the landscaping of the rows of houses of almost the same shape and size is obviously dictated the bylaws of the neighborhood's housing association.

"It helps us out because we can then start taking over and moving into their territory while they pull all their forces back."

"Oh. That makes sense."

"Good. I'm glad you understand because we are almost here. I need you to be backup while I do everything. Don't let me down."

"Just curious—what happened to the other guy who usually backs you up?" Marty checks his gun to ensure it is fully loaded and ready for action. He climbs out of the car and walks along with Mickey as they head toward the front door of a typical suburban house with numerous cars are already parked up and down the street. They've clearly arrived at the BBQ party.

"Don't worry about him. He's sick or something," Mickey says. Pointing to the right, Mickey motions to the fence with the door leading to the backyard. "You go that way and find the door to the house and position yourself there."

"Should I grab a burger for you from the grill too?"

"Grab me a hot dog, but only if they're charred. I hate undercooked hot dogs," Mickey replies.

Not sure how to take it, Marty moves toward the gate to the backyard and enters. He looks back, but Mickey has already entered the house, so he wanders around, acting like he belongs at this backyard party. He decides to head to a cooler and grab a cold one. Some stranger approaches him, and Marty starts to reach for the gun at his back, hidden under his shirt.

"Hey, buddy. Can you hand me a beer?" The stranger looks at him as though a cold beer is his only desire in life. Marty reaches in and hands him a beer, with some ice still attached to the can.

"Thanks," the stranger says before walking off. Marty can hear the sound of a beer can opening. He shrugs his shoulder and grabs a cold can of beer for himself. After closing the lid, his field of view now includes a dirty blonde in a tight shirt and shorts to match the hot temperature of the day. "Hey. Hey," she says, smiling at him. He has a hard time seeing her face because the sun is directly behind her.

"Where's the pool? It's so hot out here. I'd rather be swimming than drinking this," Marty says as he points to his beer, smooth talking the guest. If the Amy thing is going to fall through, maybe he should talk to several women at this party, he thinks. He quickly scans the crowd, seeking other potential women hanging around the pool.

The woman sizes him up, noting his choice of canned beer. "Well, honey. You didn't bring your swimming suit. Unless you're gonna . . ." She stops herself, letting out a cute giggle. Then her attention falls back on the cheap beer can he is still holding, and she sighs. She remains mute, waiting for him to reply to her with some cheesy pickup line or a witty response. Neglecting the opportunity, he instead finds a way to exit the conversation.

"Say, pretty thing, I gotta get me one of those burgers before I die of starvation. But I will be looking for you afterward for a swim in the pool."

"Sure. Whatever." The woman moves on as Marty heads in the opposite direction. He glances back and sees that his "friend" has found another man to try her luck. He puts the beer down as he makes his way to the position near the sliding glass doors to the house. He can already smell the scent of charred hot dogs and overcooked burgers permeating the air around him. He doesn't let that distract him as he reminds himself that his job is to be the backup shooter.

It's an odd coincidence that the other backup shooter is out with the flu, or some illness, despite it being a hot and lovely autumn day. How can one possibly get sick when the weather is great, bordering on freaking awesome? Marty pauses in his thoughts, wondering if "out sick with the flu" means shot up and lying in a hospital bed full of holes. He'd rather not ask Mickey about the exact interpretation of the phrase. In his own analysis, he decides the guy just wasn't able to make it this time. It doesn't matter if the guy is available in the future. What matters is that Mickey has trusted him enough to be the backup, so he should probably play the part.

However, the smell of the burgers grilling away is distracting him. *Wait a minute, is that cheddar cheese they're putting on those burgers, or it is Swiss cheese?* Either way, he wants to head to the grill before the shooting starts. As he makes his way closer to the table of food, he hears a commotion coming from inside the house. That only means one thing: he needs to be moving toward that direction. And one more thing: no burger for him.

Marty casually opens the French glass doors and closes them with a quick locking motion before moving forward into the house. It seems to be a nice house—clean, with an open design. But he is not house shopping. He is searching for the source of the commotion and loud voices. He hears another shout from an unfamiliar voice and decides to head in that direction. He passes through the kitchen, zeroing in on the source.

Stopping at an archway where he can hear voices, he cautiously enters to find a different sort of party happening in this room. Marty quickly counts six people, including Mickey, who is currently pointing a gun to a guy's head. The rest of the guests are circling around as though they're not sure what to do. Three of them react when he walks into the living room.

"Oh, it looks like the party has started without me!" Marty exclaims, causing temporary confusion among the occupants.

Mickey motions for him to continue the path he has started. "Howdy, stranger. Why don't you step forward." Marty gets that Mickey is playing the card of not knowing one another. Still, he feels for his gun to make sure it is there in the back of his pants and ready for action. A woman eyes him deviously as he continues into the living room.

"What the hell is going on in here?" he says, fully playing the part of someone who enters a room and sees a guy pointing a gun to another guy's head, people circling around, and a beautiful woman checking him out. "Is this the meth room or something?"

A few snickers and giggles emanate as he poses his comment, causing a distraction from the main point—which is being Mickey ready to blow out the brains of the guy from the competition. In the meantime, he might as well practice his comedy routine, even if he is the only one who laughs at the jokes.

"Boy oh boy, is this a tough room or what?"

Mickey continues to play along, recognizing the script they had practiced earlier, one of several scenarios for how this could go down. He begins to heckle the comedian who just entered the room.

"Hey. Funny guy." He points with the gun to Marty.

"What? You not liking my jokes or something? Whatcha gonna do about it? Shoot me too?" Marty continues to add to the distraction and now assumes the other people in the room have no idea what the hell is really going on.

"Yeah. I tell you what. If the next joke is not so funny, then I'm gonna shoot this guy. How's that for your confidence? Let's see how funny you really are."

Marty looks over to a few of the other people in the room for confirmation and support. He begins with the expected comments about how crazy this guy is and how he clearly has no sense of humor. He then elbows a random guy, asking which joke he should tell in the event this lunatic is going to gun all of them down. The guy, clearly in fear for his own life, is shaking and offers no support.

Marty decides the disguise has gone on long enough and signals silently to his partner that the scene in the room is about to change quite quickly. Marty then reaches behind and pulls out his gun. He then slowly points it around the room, getting a response of hushed awe from the other occupants. He continues to wave the gun to and fro and then settles on a target, pointing it at the guy who has had a gun pointed at him the whole time. Marty takes aim and shoots him point blank in the chest. The guy crumples to the ground, and the rest of the people in the room panic. One collapses, two others scream in fear, and the final occupant has added to his already-confused expression. All are in shock and too terrified to move between the two men holding guns.

Mickey stares at Marty in utter disgust. "You had to shoot him, didn't you? You just had to do it." He then takes aim, pointing the gun toward Marty, but then turns slightly and begins gunning down the rest of the people in the room. One bullet per person because that's all that's needed. Mickey kills three of them, mercifully, and Marty finishes the job by shooting the one who initially collapsed to the floor.

The guns that just committed homicide five times over are finally lowered. The two men still standing begin to plot their next move.

Mickey speaks up first. "Go outside to the pool and scare the people. You got enough rounds to take a few of them down, right?"

"Sure." Marty rechecks his clip and finds he has a few rounds to use before he even bothers switching to his backup clip. He looks down at the mass of bodies and sees that one of the women lying there dead looks similar to the woman in the bikini he had seen at the beer cooler earlier, but her hair is a different color. *Naw, just a coincidence,* he thinks, although it would be sad if he killed her because he needs a backup in case the Amy thing doesn't pan out in the next few days. "And what are you gonna do?" Marty asks.

Pulling out his phone, Mickey places a call and waits for the other end to pick up. When someone answers, he then requests for a cleaner to show up at the prescribed address. He gives the thumbs-up to Marty and waves for him to go outside. Marty turns around and makes his way back through the kitchen to the sliding door, only to be stopped by the woman whom he talked with earlier, who is attempting to enter the house. He immediately grabs her in an arm lock around her neck and shoots three rounds in the air to scare everyone off in the backyard. He then pointing the gun to her head and closes the door. Mickey appears beside them and begins to speak to the woman.

"Ah, I see you have met my colleague." Mickey slowly moves over to her. Despite being in a headlock with a gun pressed against her head, she is, surprisingly, not shaking in fear.

Marty presses the gun barrel a little harder but feels her attempting to squirm away and has to press his body tighter against her to get a better grip.

She relaxes slightly, realizing her struggle is futile, and gives in to being controlled, for the moment. "Hey, buddy, ease off a little bit. We're not on a date or something."

Marty ignores her, saying, "Now, is there any reason why we should let you live?"

The woman decides to take a risk and gamble her life for the knowledge she is holding. "Well. I'm assuming you killed off nearly everyone who knows where the money is stashed in this house," she says, shaking slightly.

"Wait a minute," Marty interrupts. "I just met you minutes ago at the cooler. I never got your name."

"Carrie. And what's yours?"

"Marty. Say, you do look amazing! Are you free later today?" He starts to lower the gun he has pressed against her temple.

Mickey coughs as he slaps Marty upside his head. He then pulls out his own gun and presses it to Carrie's stomach. "If you two don't mind, I would like to hear more on what you got to say."

"Oh. Sorry. Yes." Carrie now has another gun pointing at her but maintains her composure. She inches back as Marty withdraws his gun from her head and releases his arm hold. She now focuses her attention on the current gun pointing at her, Mickey's gun.

"As I was saying, since you slaughtered everyone else who knew where the money is hidden, I would like to make a deal. Because if you kill me, then you will never be able to open the safe where the money is kept."

"But we could just torture you until you cave," Mickey sternly replies and grabs her hair tight, getting a good grip.

"You know, your friend was a lot nicer. Plus, he held me a lot softer than you. He knows how to treat a lady. He was a real gent. I'd rather have him be the one holding me."

Mickey chuckles and lets go of Carrie. "Except he ditched a girl on a first date." Smiling, he says, "Hey, Marty. I got a new name for you. I'm going to start calling you Marty the Gent. The woman requests the honor of your grip."

Carrie decides to double down on her bet. "That's better. You know, I wouldn't mind joining your gang, mob, or whatever it is called these days." She smiles back and forth between the two. "Besides, I'm looking for new people to hang out with because all my other friends, well former ones, are currently dead at the moment."

"Lead us to the money and we'll let you live, and then you can plead your case to the boss man. Fair enough?" Mickey shakes her hand and expects her to lead them to the secret safe.

As she leads them down the hallway, Marty thinks to himself that they probably would not have discovered this secret stash—if there really is one—and so maybe this Carrie is worth keeping around. Of course, she could be bullshitting them.

Maybe she knows where a hidden gun is and thinks she'll be able to shoot one or both of them. Either way, Marty is on guard for anything from this woman and has to trust his instincts. He does get a good vibe from her, despite having put a gun to her head. *I hope she has no hard feelings about that. She should be happy she's still alive. Hell, she knows how to save herself from getting whacked, and in this business, that's a viable skill to possess*, Marty thinks.

Meeting the boss

Having agreed to the terms of the deal that is keeping her alive for the time being, Carrie continues down the hallway to the bathroom. Mickey and Marty follow her, carefully, and then Carrie stops and turns toward them.

"We have a deal, right?" She shows a spark of hesitancy, although she has no other choice than to trust these two mobsters. She reckons they will either take the money and whack her like the others, or they will take the money and then maybe turn her over to their boss. She reckons she's got a good chance to plead her case, or in this case, plead for her life. Mickey nods his head in affirmation.

She smiles at both of them and then hits one of the tiles in the shower to open the hidden compartment, revealing a secret stash. This is no small change either. Rather, Mickey withdraws stacks of cash, a bunch of small gold bars, and one large standard gold bar wrapped in cloth.

"Damn, woman. What are ya'll keeping in here?"

"Our retirement fund."

"Apparently. This will definitely go toward your favor with the boss. Whatever he decides is the final say. You're still taking your chances."

"I know. I know." Carrie seems torn between taking the money and running versus signing up to join a gang. However, one of the guys lying dead in the other room was the only one who could fence the standard gold bar. She still hasn't told these guys where the other safe is hidden, as that's her personal stash. She will have to be careful about coming back to retrieve it eventually.

"Either way, we are all celebrating tonight!" Mickey tosses the standard gold bar to Marty, who grunts as he catches it after almost letting it fall to the floor. Not that it would have broken if he didn't catch it. Still, he'd never held a standard gold bar.

"WTF, hombre?" Marty holds the gold bar but looks stunned to be holding it. He almost throws it back but takes a second to admire it, realizing he is holding actual gold. "Hey, take my photo." He whips out his camera and hands it over to Carrie while holding the gold bar. "How much is this thing worth?"

"About half a million, I guess." Carrie snaps the photo right when Marty's jaw drops, thus producing a silly photo.

"When you two are done taking photos, can we get outta here? You know, the cops will be here real soon." Mickey grabs the gold bar from Marty and the bag of loot. "Come on. And you're in charge of her," he reminds Marty.

Carrie shoots a big smile to Marty. "OK, big guy, I'm yours." She then wraps her arm around his. "Are you gonna put me in handcuffs?"

"No. Come on," he says, and they all exit the home.

All the other guests who were outside have fled the scene by now and the cleaners are finishing up in the living room. Marty keeps looking back to make sure there's no lone vigilante or somebody sneaking up on them. Marty's arm is still intertwined with Carrie's, although Mickey has given the standard gold bar to Carrie to hold so that Mickey can fire his gun if need be. There is no reason for Carrie to flee at the moment, but they both reckon they are still taking a big gamble—she could somehow get away, taking the gold bar with her. *But a bullet to her back or leg would slow her down just the same,* Marty thinks. *A target is a target.* He never really thought much about the difference between shooting a man or shooting a woman. Nevertheless, he can't recall the last time he shot a woman.

It's a good thing the leader has an exit plan. They approach the fence toward the back property line. Mickey unlatches the fence door, and a waiting van is sitting there. He thinks to himself that proper planning always ensures a high survival rate. Or at least it has up to this point. Mickey slides the side panel door open, tells Marty and the woman to enter quickly, and then climbs in himself and takes a quick check before closing the door. Mickey relieves Carrie of the standard gold bar. The driver of the van waits for the nod by Mickey and then turns around and drives off.

The white van with big, blue letters on the side reading, PETE'S PLUMBING, drives down the road. It stops momentarily, and all the passengers in the back look to one another. The sound of police sirens gets louder and louder as they zoom across the path of the white van. After the third squad car races by, the van turns left, departing the scene.

After driving for a fair bit of time, the van pulls over at a mechanic's garage. When the van stops, Mickey springs up and opens the side door. "OK, folks. The first taxi ride is complete. Marty, you know what to do?"

"No problemo, Mickey!"

Jumping out first, Marty then waits for Carrie to exit. She extends her hand, and he helps her out. He maneuvers his hand in a twisting motion when holding hers, just in case she tries something funny; this way, he can twist and break her wrist, if needed. Luckily, no force is necessary. Carrie takes his hand and walks slightly in front of him, understanding she is still not to be fully trusted.

They stop in front of a normal-looking black Mercedes. Mickey places the loot bag and standard gold bar in the back seat, throwing a blanket over them. He then climbs into the driver's seat. He gives Marty an impatient look, suggesting that he speed things up.

Receiving the death stare, Marty groans, taking one last breath before what needs to be done next. Carrie interprets this as meaning she is about to be killed, and a look of horror takes over her face. She does not scream but is one second away from doing so when Marty pops open the trunk.

"Sorry to have to do this."

"You bastards." She starts to raise a hand to him, but it is quickly snatched and then flipped up behind her back.

"What do you mean? I ain't gonna shoot you!"

Her muscles begin to relax a little. "Then what are you gonna do? And can you loosen the grip slightly, please."

"Oh, sorry." Loosening the grip, he then whirls her around so that she is facing him. Carrie's confused expression signals that she is waiting for him to explain what is going to happen. "Please get in the trunk."

Carrie glances at the trunk. It appears spacious and clean . . . still, she wonders why she must ride in the trunk and not in the more comfortable back of the car, no doubt with leather seats.

Marty's patience grows thin. "I'm asking nicely the first time. Next, I will place you gently in the trunk."

"Fine. Fine. I always wanted to ride in a Mercedes. This is not how I envisioned it, though." After climbing in and getting into as comfortable of a position as the space allows, she smiles at him as he closes the trunk.

After tapping twice to ensure the trunk is closed, Marty walks to the passenger side and gets in the car. "The goods are loaded and secure."

"Ha-ha. I thought she was gonna put up a struggle. I kinda wanted to see you manhandle her into the trunk." Mickey reaches to turn the ignition key and starts the engine, and the car moves forward, exiting the shop and heading to the boss's house.

They arrive at the boss's property, and Mickey rolls down the window to greet the armed guard standing between them and the perimeter fence. Once the guard recognizes Mickey, he motions them to wait a second and runs into the shack to open the electrified fence. They both wave to the guard and proceed down the long driveway heading to the house.

Mickey parks in the adjacent garage that houses a fleet of vehicles. As soon as they exit the car, they are greeted by the welcoming committee: two more guards. Mickey calls out to one of them, "Hey, give me a hand." One of the guards moves quickly, indicating who has the authority to offer his assistance.

"Oh, Marty. Retrieve our guest and bring her to the waiting room. I will send someone for both of you," Mickey instructs him as he grabs the loot and walks with the guard, who is carrying the standard gold bar, through a door and out of sight.

Having watched them leave, Marty moves to the back of the car and taps lightly on the trunk. He shouts a warning and has his gun ready, as one never knows with these things. He motions to the other guard to be ready to shoot if the situation should call for it. He taps on the trunk one more time, signaling to her.

"Hey. That really echoes in here." Carrie's voice is a little muffled, but Marty takes it that she is ready. He whispers to himself, "Let's do this." He hits the button to pop open the trunk, holding his gun to the side in the ready position.

The trunk flips up, and he sees Carrie lying there, her eyes adjusting to the bright light. She gets up and climbs out of the trunk, dusting herself off. She glares back at Marty, who has a defensive expression, and she also notices his gun at his side. He then places it back in its holster. She looks around before saying, "Hmmm. Nice place. Can we go now? I need to know if I gonna live or die today. If not, I got an appointment I will need to cancel."

Marty smirks and flips the keys to the remaining guard. Grasping Carrie's arm gently, he guides her to move toward the house. There, he finds the waiting room, as directed, and stops her. She starts to sit down, but he still holds her somewhat tightly.

"Carrie. I have to ask." Marty seems awkward and uncomfortable.

She is taken by surprise. "What is it, Marty?"

He raises his shoulders slightly before asking the question. "Do you have any weapons on you, hidden or otherwise? Anything that can be construed as a weapon?"

She smiles, relaxing, but replies with a little sass, "No . . . ha-ha. You can search me if you want to!"

Unperturbed but forceful, Marty says, "Apologies, but I'm gonna have to do it now."

"OK, then. But this means you now owe me a dinner." Carrie stands with her arms out and legs spread apart. Marty looks into her eyes and begins to pat her down, starting with the arms.

Boss Mazoli is outfitted in a classic polo shirt and khaki pants as he lounges around the house. He sits at his desk in his favorite red faux leather office chair. The chair may be ugly and fake, but strangely enough, it has saved his life on at least one occasion. There is a bullet hole on the back but no exit hole on the front, indicating, presumably, a bullet that never made it to him.

The creaks of the old fake chair sound one more time as the other occupant in the room, Mickey, having first grabbed two beers from the fridge, moves to sit across from him on an old and raggedy couch. *You would think that with all his money, the boss would buy some snazzy and comfortable furniture.* He smiles but quickly conceals his internal amusement and sits down, sliding one of the beers across the desk while keeping the other one.

Boss Mazoli reaches for the beer and takes a deep chug, nearly emptying half the bottle. He slams the bottle back on the desk; it rocks to and fro but remains in place. This seems to be the normal place for his beer, judging by the years of water rings imprinted on the desk. He leans forward to speak.

"You know, it was never about the money."

Sure. It never is. "Absolutely. Although they were holding out on us, it seems."

"No shit. That standard gold bar is at least half a million alone. I tell ya what. Give all the guys a ten-grand bonus."

"That will make them all happy, I'm sure. What about Marty?" Mickey inquires about his second shooter on this job.

"Yeah." The boss stands up and starts to pace the room. He stops to look at an item on a bookstand. "What does Marty know? What did you tell him?"

"Nothing. I assume he figures it was a normal whack job. He didn't even question us killing the five people from the Asian gang." Mickey reaches for his beer, drinking it slower than the boss.

"Interesting. Is Marty that loyal to you? You don't think he would try to take us out someday?"

"Nah. Not Marty. He was more pissed that he had to break a date with some broad he's been trying to hook up with."

"Maybe he should go see Nunzio's pimp guy. What's his name?" Mazoli is waving his hand as if motioning to be thrown a lifeline because he can't recall the brothel owner's name.

"You mean Goosey? Oh yeah. We should call Goosey anyway and tell him his business is about to pick up after we give out the bonuses."

The boss is still thinking about Marty's allegiance to him and Mickey. He has heard good things about how Marty has increased the revenues, and he certainly knows his odds in sports betting. In fact, he is supposed to be one of the best bookies around town, from the latest word on the streets. So the question is, Why hasn't he tried to make a lot of money with his gift? "Say, Mick, what does Marty want?"

Mickey pauses to reflect on the question. He feels he knows where the boss is going with this and doesn't want to say something that will plant suspicion about Marty. He feels Marty is a good guy, just not greedy; he certainly seems content with the simple things in life—living, drinking, beating him at pool, and killing partygoers. In all his interactions with Marty, he has never seen any form of power-grabbing attitude or seen him act like a tough guy with a chip on his shoulder. He just exudes influence in simple ways, and people take note of him. They remember him.

Mickey snaps out of his thoughts. "Say, what are we going to do about the woman? Now there's another strange one. She could have hidden, kept quiet, and taken the money for herself. But she must want in, to be a part of a *family*!" He adds a hand raise while saying *family* to emphasize the point.

"What are you saying?" Mazoli asks, sitting back down.

Mickey knows the boss is messing with him, or at least he hopes so. "She seems determined she wants to join us," he continues. "She currently doesn't belong to any other gang—Marty and me made sure of that." He reaches to the side to feel his gun. "And she has paid a handsome fee to join us."

"Yup. That was a huge score. Well, bonus, at any rate. Do a background check, and if she's clean, I suppose we can bring her on board. We can even partner her up with Marty—from what you say, they seem to get along." Mazoli flips a switch for the CCTV that shows the waiting room, where Marty and Carrie are talking and laughing with one another. He turns the CCTV off. "If she's lying, then we'll send her to Goosey's place."

"Works for me. What about this Asian crime gang? I mean, we took out five of them at the house. How soon do we expect a retaliation?"

Mazoli stands back up and places both hands on his desk. "You mean when do we expect a war with them? We don't know because you say Marty killed the turncoat before he was going to speak!" He pounds both hands down for added effect.

"Yeah. I take ownership of that. Sorry. I should have told him to shoot him but make sure he damn well survives."

"You need to trust Marty more if I'm going to. Now bring him in so he can be rewarded. I'm giving him a little extra. In the twenty-five-grand range."

"He does deserve it. When are you talking with the other boss about forming an alliance until this new mob is wiped out?" Mickey gets up and collects the empty beer bottles, putting them back at the bar.

"Meeting is this afternoon. I'll have a talk with you afterward. Now go get Marty and bring him in here. Then go have a talk with Carrie. See if there's anything else she wants to say."

"Later, Boss. Remember, Marty's one of the good guys. I vouch for him." He closes the door and heads down the hall to the waiting room, confident he went to bat for his friend.

Marty is ushered into Boss Mazoli's main office by one of the guards. The guard closes the door as Marty scans the room, remaining silent in a show of respect. He spies the boss staring at a golden, jewel-encrusted knife sitting on the mantel.

"Go fix us two drinks," the boss barks, fixated on the knife and never turning to face Marty.

Marty looks from left to right, sees the bar, and moves quickly toward it, where he pauses. He can't decide between the six to ten bottles of various liquors and almost asks what the boss would like. But he shuts his mouth in an instant, realizing it would be best to just pour them a couple of drinks. It's assumed any of the choices are good because this is the boss's private bar, so Marty ends up selecting a decent scotch from the collection. He fills the glasses and stands by the boss, waiting for him to acknowledge the offered drink, then hands the glass to him.

"Marty. You done good. People are saying good things about you. Cheers to being part of the family." The boss raises his glass in salute and praise. Marty matches and slams his glass against the other one. Luckily, it doesn't break or crack, and Marty takes a big gulp of the brown liquor.

"Go on, sit down." Mazoli directs him to the couch. He then sits down in his own red leather chair and, leaning to one side, stares at Marty. A smile breaks the serious face.

"You did good . . . back at the house. And brought in a substantial amount of money."

"Thanks, Boss."

"No. No. I should be thanking you." He pulls out an envelope from the top desk drawer and slides it across the desk. "Here. This is for you. A vote of appreciation."

Marty stares at the stuffed envelope, realizing it's larger than expected. He snatches up the envelope, and it feels heavy—he'd rather not know how much is in there. *At least they value my services.* He holds it with one hand for the rest of the conversation.

They talk back and forth on the events of the operation and then switch over to straightforward topics, including sports betting. Marty supplies some picks, personally, for the boss. The boss then finishes his drink. Marty thinks the meeting is done and stands up, the envelope in one hand and the empty glass in the other. He walks over to the bar to put the dirty glass on a tray and heads for the door. The boss stops him as he is about to leave.

"Oh, Marty. What's your opinion of Carrie?"

Marty doesn't hesitate in his answer. "She seems all right. I get a good feeling about her."

"Are you sure about that?" Mazoli goads Marty even further. "Would you vouch for her?"

"Yeah. I mean, I hardly know her, but I reckon so."

"That's pretty bold of you," the boss says, raising his eyebrows.

"I think she's a good bet. That's all." Marty excuses himself and leaves the boss's room, tapping the envelope to his forehead and eventually finding his way to leave the house. He steps outside and takes out his phone. After turning the ringer back on, he quickly dials a number—one that he has been wanting to try since he broke the date with her. But Amy's number just rings and rings and doesn't even go to voice mail. He hangs up, frustrated that he might have messed up his only chance.

One month later, Marty leaves Boss Mazoli's office. He feels discontented but thinks it better to keep it to himself. The reason is that his partner for the day is none other than Carrie, the newest member of their organization. She has been with them for barely over a month, but the boss completely trusts her— well, there's also the nearly million dollars she led Mickey and him to at the shooting job.

"Marty. Marty. You are walking way too fast. It's like you're like trying to ditch me or something. Wait. Is that it? Marty!" The petite, stringy-haired blonde hastens to catch up. She extends her arm to latch onto his, but he shrugs it off.

"You gotta be quicker than that, lassie."

"It's Carrie. I'm not a dog. Asshole," she shouts.

Marty stops in his tracks. He tries to explain that he was using some European vernacular and not actually referring to her as the dog from some old TV show. While he is standing there trying to defend himself, he notices she is listening to him with a wide grin on her face.

"What's so funny?" Marty demands.

"I finally got you to stop. Ha-ha! I knew what you meant, mate." She punches him childishly in the arm, then tags him. "And you're it."

After the punch, Carrie immediately takes off, running out of the boss's house and toward the car they will be using today. She opens the passenger door and climbs in before Marty even gets out of the house. The shade of red in his face begins to slowly match the color of the car next to the one he gets in.

"You know, we gotta have a—"

125

"No tag backs!" she says, cutting him off, smiling as she watches his frustration build.

Starting the engine and closing his eyes, he listens to the sound of the revs before opening his eyes again. He taps lightly on the gas pedal as he looks at his passenger. "Are you ready to do this?"

"Sure thing, sport. Let's go find this bastard."

The car pulls out, and they head down a long driveway toward the wrought-iron gate. It slowly opens on its own, thanks to the poor sucker who is guarding and working the gate, Marty presumes. They leave the grounds and turn left, heading into town, as the gate quickly closes behind them.

After a couple of miles of quietness in the car, Carrie reaches over and turns on the radio. She thumbs through a few stations until she hears a sappy love song and begins to sing along to it, turning up the volume. Marty races with his free hand to turn it down first, then turn it to a different station.

"Whatcha doing? I like that song!"

"Only the driver gets control of the radio. Period." He turns it to a Top 40 station playing a song by a rather annoying female popstar but leaves it on.

"Since when do you make the rules?" She flips it back to the love song.

Turning it back to the Top 40 station, Marty declares, "It's not just a rule; it's practically gospel. It's similar to the preset. You don't mess with a driver's presets, no matter what."

She leans forward and fiddles with the controls to find her station again. She then presses the button marked "1" and pushes it, holding it for three seconds. Satisfied, she declares that her station is now a preset channel.

"It doesn't work like that." He turns down the volume, figuring it's a battle he might win. He attempts to switch topics. "So you've been here a month now? I do find that amazing."

Carrie reaches over for the window release and cracks the window open slightly to let in the breeze. She almost sticks her hand out but figures the driver might be waiting to trap her hand in the window, and she doesn't want to give him the satisfaction. Instead, she tries a crack at her own strategy. "Oh, I almost forgot. Did you ever get a date with that girl? What's her name?"

"Amy." The car brakes harshly for a second.

"Yeah. Amy. Sweet Amy. Oh, I remember now. That was, ironically, the same day when you and Mickey shot up the place and killed all those people. My friends. Weren't you supposed to have your date with her by now?"

"Yes. It was that same day. What are you getting at? Is there a point to all these questions?"

"Oh. I was wondering why you were, coincidently, hitting on me at the party on the same day." She smiles back at him and then boldly changes the radio station.

Marty's voice cracks as he begins to defend himself. "No. No. No." He shakes a finger back at her. "No. And that's how rumors get started. I was not hitting on you at the party."

"I would have gone out with you. I thought you were cute, especially when you handed me the beer."

"Bullshit. You're lying your ass off."

"No. It's true. I knew a lot of guys there at the party, and you were special. Well. You were different. Not like the others." She tries in vain to refrain from laughing but can't hold back anymore. She reaches down to take her can of cola and raises it up to take a drink, but the car brakes suddenly and the backsplash comes forward like a wave across her face. "Aw, shit! Marty, you bastard."

"Sorry. A squirrel ran out in front of the car, and I didn't want to hit it. Sorry. I really am." This time, he sports a shit-eating grin and as he continues heading toward downtown.

Meanwhile, Carrie finds some napkins in the glove box and begins to wipe herself clean. As she pats her face and her blouse, Marty makes a comment about why those napkins are in there and for how long. She decides to ball one of the dirty napkins up and chuck it at him. She raises her arm and squares up, about to releases, but then she looks past Marty's head, out the window.

"Stop the car. That's him. That's the guy!" she shouts while pointing out the window.

He takes his eyes off the road for a second to turn his head toward the sidewalk on the left. He blinks as he suddenly realizes that it sure as hell looks like the guy.

"Well, damn, girl—good eye," Marty says, impressed with his partner's ability to spot guys randomly on the streets who owe the organization money. The car turns a corner, and then it races down a parallel street as they drive up three blocks before pulling into a parking spot.

Marty shuts off the engine. He leans over to Carrie, ready to tell her the plan on how to nab this guy. "Now remember, we don't want to bring out the guns and shoot him directly. Obviously, because it makes noise, and then we have to deal with witnesses and all that shit."

"Right. We don't want him dead, either, because we don't get our money back. With added interest."

"Yes. With interest," Marty confirms, and they both have a laugh.

"Listen up," Marty continues. "I need you to detain him long enough that I will partially pass you. Keep him distracted until I get there, and then we can take him out. Think you can do that?"

Carrie waves her hand. "Piece of cake."

Marty leans back confident she understands the plan. He starts the car and heads back to the street where they saw the guy. They drive past him again, turn at the next corner, and park in the first spot on the side street. "Good. He shouldn't have noticed the car. Now, he'll probably recognize me right away. But you, lassie, he doesn't know you, and you need to reel him on in!"

She slaps the driver on the thigh. "Just be there to back me up, partner." She steps out of the car, and Marty pulls away, quickly turning the corner. She's thinking, knowing the target should be walking up to her position momentarily. Meanwhile, Marty parks and slowly walks to the back of the car, popping open the trunk slightly, getting it in the ready position to open it fully for their guest. He hears raised voices and knows that's his sign to intervene.

He sees Carrie pleading with a very confused man. She grabs him with both hands as she is begging for help and assistance. The man, obviously hesitating, does not want to get involved, but Carrie is persistent, and her pleas only get louder and louder. She even brings out the tears and latches onto him tighter, slowly guiding him to the corner and turning him around. She then screams, "Oh my God, that's my husband now! Nooooo! Don't let him beat me anymore!"

The man has no idea what is happening, and he turns around to see Marty approaching. His brain can only process the scene so fast, and right now, it is searching for a past memory

129

regarding how he knows this guy. A split second later, he experiences instant pain as he is cold-cocked in the jaw. His brain slowly catches up and almost remembers the other man, but the pain receptors overpower his thoughts.

"You son of a bitch." The man is face to face with Marty and has little time to counterattack. He feels an intense throbbing in his right knee, which then gives out due to the force with which it was kicked, and he falls to the pavement. All this causes disorientation, and he feels himself being dragged across the ground and lifted up and over something metal before falling into a thinly carpeted compartment. A trunk, clearly. Hands are grabbing his personal items, such as wallet, pocket, keys, and both of his guns. The trunk is slammed shut, and he now he lies in total darkness before blacking out.

They both get back in the car. Marty, perked up, asks, "You think we should drop him off first or go grab some food?"

"Hmmm. I'm getting kinda hungry myself. And you knocked him out pretty good. That should give us, what, an extra ten or twenty minutes?" Carrie smiles back at Marty, trying to put the decision-making onus on him. After all, he would be the one to have to explain to the boss why the guy died in the trunk while they were having a pitcher of beer and a burger. She thinks about it and creates a backup plan just in case. Although she would have to steal a car and convince Marty to cause an auto accident, it seems workable. Carrie is beginning to translate her thoughts into vocal words, but he beats her to the punch.

"Nah. We better drop the goods off first. Then maybe go for a drink."

"You meant to say two or more drinks, right?" Carrie clarifies.

"Something like that. So . . . call it in—the sooner we drop this deadbeat off, the sooner you can buy me the first round."

"So it's like that now?"

"And why not? I did punch him out. All you had to do was flirt with the guy. Too easy."

"Well, I must be really great at it. I did stop the two of you from killing me," Carrie responds in kind. She secretly reminds herself that it was both pure luck and her quick wit that saved her hide and led to her being alive at this moment versus six feet under.

Marty recalls that day. He wonders why they decided to let her live and not shoot her like the others. *Oh, that's right—she hinted about the money stashed away. That's what stopped us from pulling the trigger.*

Also, he had sort of fancied her for a second when he briefly saw her before going into the house. Maybe he did have a thing for her, but now that he is partnered with her, he doesn't think of her in that regard. Besides, he is still pursuing Amy and trying to score a date with her.

He steps on the gas suddenly and turns a couple of corners in an attempt to reduce the travel time in dropping off the package in the trunk. "Did you call it in?" Marty asks. He then realizes she is on the phone and turns his attention back to the road up ahead.

Hanging up the phone and putting it back in her purse, she announces she has made the call and they are waiting for their arrival. She waits for Marty to nod his head in acknowledgment but then continues to stare at him afterward, perhaps for a second too long. She wonders if he ever thinks about her the way she thought about him, but that was only when they first met.

As they pull up to the guard shack, the guard cautiously peers into their car. He smiles once he recognizes the driver and passenger. They both greet him and declare they have a package to drop off. He flashes a big grin, knowing there's some dude in the trunk, and that all he needs to know. He waves them on through after opening the secured gate and watches the car go up the long driveway before turning back to his assigned post.

The car stops in the massive garage, and two guards quickly move into position near the trunk. Marty and Carrie jump out of the car and head toward the rear of the car.

Marty makes a fist and pounds on the trunk.

Thunk. Thunk.

"Wakie, wakie. Time to get up." Marty signals to the two guards, who have their guns drawn as he hits the trunk release. The trunk pops open and snaps upward. The guards aim toward the trunk more precisely.

The man in the trunk does not move. Everyone looks to Marty, waiting for instructions on what to do next. Marty moves closer to the trunk, with Carrie right behind him and off to his right. The guards position themselves, flanking Marty on each side.

Marty looks down in the trunk. The man is facedown. He pushes on the back of the man and jumps back. Startled, everyone does the same. Marty cautiously approaches the trunk again and looks for any sign of movement. He starts to push the man again but stops due to the shouting behind him.

"*Would you all stop fucking off and drag his ass outta there—now!*" The source of the shouting is moving closer to their position.

Marty turns back to the man and sees movement. Realizing he has to act now, he lurches forward and grabs the man with both arms. Carrie assists and grabs the man's belt and a leg as they both, like a well-rehearsed routine, extricate the man from the trunk and drop him on the garage floor. The man starts to shake and twitch. They both step back as Mickey pushes them aside and picks up the guy, pinning one of the man's arms behind his back, and walks to the entrance to the house.

The two guards race to catch up to Mickey, leaving Marty and Carrie to stand there with glum faces.

"Well. Our job's done. Let's go." He gets back behind the wheel, starting the engine in the process.

Carrie gets in the car. "I'm with you. Let's get outta here and get that drink."

"Or two!" The car exits the garage and speeds down the driveway.

Visit to the newsstand

Two days later, Marty wakes up feeling refreshed from a good night's sleep. He conducts his morning routine and sits at the table, enjoying the ever-tasty mug of joe. He switched to a new brand a few weeks ago, on Carrie's advice, and wonders why he didn't switch years ago. The aroma permeates his apartment, giving a pleasant smell he thoroughly enjoys. It sure beats whatever smell will be emanating from his apartment if the cleaning crew doesn't get over here this week. He jots down a note to make an appointment with said cleaning crew.

Upon glancing at his day planner, it suddenly occurs to him that he gets to pay a visit to his favorite patron business, the newsstand. Suddenly armed with more vigor, he hastens through the remaining tasks and leaves for work a half hour earlier than normal.

Parking in the neighborhood, especially at this time of day, can be tricky to pull off. It happens that a rockstar parking spot opens up—a car is leaving right upon his arrival. Amazing! He didn't even have to circle the block countless times like usual. *A first-time go!* he thinks, and now he feels like today is the day Amy will forgive him and actually want to talk to him. He can only hope.

Marty exits the car and hits the lock, arming the alarm. Although he is well known on these streets, he still reckons there may be some business owner who is pissed off enough to boldly attempt to steal his car. He can find the humor in that, as he would probably do the same, but his ultra-sensitive alarm will give him an extra two to three seconds to look for the bold bastard.

He brushes himself down and makes a few adjustments; he must look professional at all times. It is one of Boss Mazoli's golden rules and has been instilled into him since day one. He has never attempted to show up with a less-than-ideal appearance, and he has heard gangster tales of some dude, who is no longer employed—and likely no longer alive—who had shown up for work dressed poorly one time and was never seen again. Although such stories are humorous and designed to scare him, he nevertheless doesn't want to be the guy the next story is about.

He makes it to the pavement and begins the walk to the newsstand. He is still one storefront away when Mr. Robinson steps out from his newsstand and confronts him. This catches Marty off guard, but only for a split second.

"Why, Mr. Robinson. It is as though you were waiting for my arrival!" Marty says, attempting to be friendly.

Never one to be rude, at least not to Marty's face, Mr. Robinson replies, "Why, my boy, I look forward to every time you step into my store. Now, what can I do for you today?" He smiles, knowing he asked a loaded question.

Marty, who never loses his cool or loses face, says, "Why don't we go inside so that I can grab the latest newspaper. Maybe buy some lottery tickets—I feel lucky today."

Mr. Robinson allows Marty to enter the store first. He feels he must always show deference to this mobster, even if he also happens to be a silent partner in an illegal numbers game. Although at times he feels he has made a deal with the devil or at least one of his nicer minions, the extra income has allowed him to hire additional staff, thus reducing his work week to just under sixty hours. "Here's your newspaper." He hands him today's newspaper with an envelope stuffed between the

135

business and sports sections containing Marty's weekly cut from the numbers game.

Marty grabs the paper and folds it so that the envelope doesn't accidentally fall out and tucks the newspaper under his arm. He nods his head in a silent acknowledgment of the agreed-upon terms of their numbers venture, which they try to speak about as little as possible. That way, it stays only between the two of them, lessening the risk that anyone else will find out about it.

Marty had casually mentioned it to Mickey just to be on the safe side, and it was sanctioned by Boss Mazoli. Marty still has to pay tribute to the boss, but he also gives the odds for the boss, which is more valuable than the money Marty makes off his venture. The only stipulations are that the boss gets the more accurate odds, and Marty has to adjust the odds in his own game. Everyone is happy, everyone makes money, and above all, Mr. Robinson has no recourse to rat him out to the boss or the police for this illegal scheme.

"How's Amy?" Marty says, getting straight to the point.

"Oh, she's fine. She did ask about you a few days ago."

"Really?" He hears what he wants to hear after all this time. Perhaps she has finally forgiven him for standing her up on the first date.

Knowing he's gotten Marty to take the bait, Mr. Robinson continues to reel him in. "Yes, as a matter of fact, she was wondering if you were still stalking her every day." He lets out a snicker as he watches Marty's face turn a reddish hue.

"Not funny at all. Not cool, old man." He can't threaten Mr. Robinson because he is partnered with him in the numbers game. Plus, he's the only person Marty knows who has some influence on his granddaughter. He tries to ignore the latest ribbing from him and try a different tactic: pleading as man to man.

"So," Marty begins his speech, "what do you think I should do to get her to talk to me? She won't answer my calls, and she is never here when I come by. Did you fire her or something? What did she do? No, wait. Where is she, and how long will she stay mad at me? What should I do?"

"Would you stop acting like a knucklehead for a minute? First, no, I didn't fire her. She is on vacation, which apparently might be something you should consider yourself. And two, why don't you try buying her some flowers again? You know, women like that sort of thing—when the man has to apologize for screwing up." He slaps Marty upside the head lightly, but his point is made.

"See. I told you it was my lucky day. You gave me a great idea."

"Glad to help. Now don't you have other businesses to extort from?" Mr. Robinson says forcefully, smiling but basically asking him to leave.

Marty tips the folded newspaper with the envelope in it to his forehead and says, "Thanks, old man." He then leaves the newsstand.

Mr. Robinson watches him leave and wonders how long he is going keep pursuing his granddaughter. Stalking is a better word, but he is trying to be nice about it. The store door closes, and then Amy appears from the back of the store, telling her grandfather she has completed the cooler inventory and has placed the orders for the week.

Amy asks, "Have you been busy? I thought I heard you talking to someone, but I assumed there was only one customer out here."

"It's slowed down in the last hour. Had only one customer and, boy, was he a chatter."

Next time, say it with flowers

A visit to the florist shop is always unpredictable for Marty. He hesitates on the street in front of the store, debating whether to go in or not. Of course, they are going to razz him. They always have and always will—that will never change. They were most upset that he had to break the date with Amy. "The first date—who does that?" they asked. Apparently, he does, as he is reminded constantly by everyone. Now he trying to win a second date, although technically it would be the first date. Everyone is pulling for him to succeed. That is, everyone except, apparently, Amy.

He debates in his head and finally decides to just open the front door and walk straight in. A bell rings to announce the entry, and right away, Cindy laughs vociferously when she recognizes Marty entering the shop. "Marty, what are you doing here?" she queries as she grabs him for a big embrace.

With little time to prepare for the affectionate hug from Cindy, he resigns to her ways and takes it all in—in this case, being squeezed to the point of bones beginning to break.

Chad always seems to pop out from the back at the very moment Marty is in his wife's arms. Patiently, he waits until his wife lets go and then waits a few more seconds for Marty to start breathing again.

"What brings you by today? It's not a delivery day." Chad then wonders whether it is a delivery day and he just forgot. His deep thinking and blank facial expression are broken when Marty affirms that it is not a delivery day.

"No. No. The next delivery is in two days. This visit isn't work related." Marty regrets divulging that bit of information.

"Oh no. Are you gonna do it?" Cindy chimes in. "Did she finally submit to your constant apologies?"

"Or stalking. Do you need more flowers?" Chad adds.

"Uh . . . yes. Yes. I do. But I want them delivered to the newsstand this time."

"Uh huh . . . Marty's being super sly. Like a fox. I will have to get on it right away." Cindy turns around and starts looking about the shop for items to make a distinctive floral arrangement.

"I was hoping you would make it extra special!"

"What's that? You want to me to stick the herbal stuff in there?"

Marty puts up his hands. "*No*. That's not what I meant!"

Chad leans across the counter, trying to talk to Marty man to man. He barrages Marty with questions, more like those coming from a father than a friend. "What are you going to do? What's the big plan? Did she actually talk to you?"

"Well, I thought I'd have the flowers sent to the newsstand, for starters."

"Yeah. Is that all you got?"

"No. Hopefully Mr. Robinson will text a photo of the flowers to Amy. He said she was on vacation."

"Or trying to stay away from you! Ha-ha!" Chad slaps Marty across the arm with his lame teasing.

Marty waits until Chad's laughter dies down before proceeding. "Anyhow. The old man sends the photo of the flowers to her, and she caves in, arranging for a date. That's my plan."

"Huh. Then you are betting on the floral arrangement to seal the deal."

"It's that or I look pathetic every week I come in here."

Chad stands up straight. "Well. We can't have that happen." He calls out to Cindy, "Hey, hon, you really need to make it great so that this guy gets a date."

She yells back, "I'm doing the best I can. Maybe we should just go over there and talk to her directly. Would that help, Marty?"

Marty looks appalled at Cindy's response but is hoping she's only kidding.

Chad shakes his head up and down. "There ya go. Cindy is the best when it comes to these sorts of things. Now, I've been meaning to ask you. Have you noticed the new gang in town? They haven't ventured this far south, but they are the hot topic on the streets these days."

"Oh yeah. Them. I wouldn't be too concerned."

"Why is that?"

"I heard their numbers dropped significantly last month." Marty stares back at Chad square in the eyes, not wanting to mention that he and Mickey killed five members of the gang at a party.

"We got nothing to worry about, then. After all, we got your guys' protection."

"Yup."

"OK, then."

Marty and Chad continue to square off. Marty is wondering what Chad is implying. Is he just slightly concerned, or is he testing Marty on what he knows and what they are going to do about the new gang in town? Chad doesn't see any reaction from Marty, and it bothers him. Marty has to convince Chad that the Asian Crime Syndicate (ACS) is more of an annoyance rather than a threat. For now, at any rate—at least he hopes.

Pool-hall sharks

Marty shoots the cue without even trying and still manages to knock in a striped ball. He begins to square up for the next shot but hears a voice screaming back at him. He turns to the familiar voice.

"You're gonna take that slop shot?"

"Why not? It went in," he replies to Mickey.

"I guess, if you have no honor, then." Mickey leans back on his barstool and takes a pull from his glass of whisky.

"Wait a minute! You think I'm cheating you?"

"Just saying." Mickey continues to hold the glass but looks elsewhere.

Marty, frustrated, slams the cue down on the table. He doesn't realize Mickey is goading him to take the bait. "Fine. Double or nothing on the next shot."

Nonchalantly, Mickey replies, "It's your money. If you think you can do it." He is hoping the mind tricks throw off Marty's game because there is no other way to beat this guy.

Regaining his composure, Marty shakes it off and lines up the shot. He second guesses and realigns before shooting in the striped ball plus the next three balls. He then calls the pocket and sinks the eight ball with ease. Turning back toward Mickey, he taps the cue on his opponent's shoulder.

Mickey reaches for his pocket and throws several large-denomination bills down on the pool table before taking a seat at a nearby table. He shakes his head in disbelief but gracefully accepts the loss. Marty snatches the bills and pockets them and then rests the house cue back on the rack. He flags down the waitress and parks himself adjacent to the seat of his adversary at the recently claimed round table.

"You got lucky," Mickey sneers.

"Skill, my friend. Perhaps I can teach you . . . sometime." Marty laughs as he raises a shot glass that the waitress placed on the table seconds ago.

Mickey pauses but then reaches for his own shot glass. He takes it and shoots it straight down, not acknowledging the person across the table. Marty ignores the diss and slowly sips his drink. He mumbles something about being an ass under his breath but decides not to say it louder.

"All right. This is what I signed up for," Marty says, throwing his glass in the air toward Mickey across the table.

"What, did you think you were joining the army or something?"

"You know what I mean."

Mickey looks around the place before facing Marty again. "Well, then. Enlighten me, smart guy."

Marty thinks about what Mickey is trying to say to him, whether he is bullshitting him or actually challenging him. Marty laughs inside, knowing Mickey is not the brainiac he claims to be. Also, he is really lousy at pool—and gets worse the more he drinks—but as long as Marty wins money off him, why should he say anything?

"Yeah. I was just thinking . . ." Marty pauses to gather his thoughts, but he has to wait because Mickey cuts in, like he always does.

"Well, then. This should be good," Mickey says with a chuckle.

Having thought about it a second too long, Marty describes, in detail, what he thinks of the mob world thus far.

Mickey nods his head along the way for most of what he hears, but inside, he disagrees on some parts the storyteller is getting wrong.

"See? You thought it was something different." Mickey waves his hand around the room. "We're not that much different from that guy or that guy," he says, pointing to two different tables.

"What about that guy?" Marty points to a guy near the bathrooms.

"Oh, that guy? Well, he's just homeless. Bad example."

"I get what you're saying."

"Then you should be buying the next round and not bitching about the job I gave you. Speaking of which, I have another job for you. Important one."

"What?" Marty pipes up, putting his drink down. "I get to muscle some more people out of their retirement checks?"

"No. Now listen up," he says seriously.

"Fine. You got my attention."

"Good. You and me will be on guard duty."

"You're not selling me."

"Shut up, will ya? We are guarding two bosses for an important meeting."

A long silence ensues. "Does it come with a free meal?" Marty finally asks.

"No, unless you are a fast eater. Although that's a good idea. Maybe next time you should ask for an appetizer to be included. But you ain't being hired to eat. Only to shoot back, if needed."

"I hope the entrées are good, then."

"And I hope you can shoot in one hand and balance a fork in the other."

"We'll have to wait and see, won't we?"

"As long as you keep the bosses alive, it doesn't matter if you fill up on free garlic bread."

Mickey and Marty have a laugh as they slam their empty glass down on the table. The waitress comes over, and both fight to pay for the bar tab, with Marty rescinding first and not having to pay. Mickey pays the enormous bill, and they both stand up and walk out of the pool hall. He puts his hand on Marty's shoulder before they depart.

"I would advise you to stay sober for this job."

"I hope you follow your own advice," Marty says, slapping him on the back.

Coworker dinner date

Marty graciously gets the door for Carrie. She steps out of the car with her lavender, miniskirt. He does not look a second time but was probably caught gazing the first time around. She blushes but laughs inside, for one wears something like this for obvious reasons.

Throwing the keys to the valet, Marty remarks, "Make sure you wash it and clean the interior by the time I get it back."

The valet catches the keys and gets in the car. Although he hears similar requests countless times a day, he still cracks a grin, hoping the patron tips generously, lame joke aside.

"Yes, sir." The valet takes control of the keys and drives off maybe a little too fast for Marty's tastes. Meanwhile, Carrie is still attempting to balance on her three-inch heels as she throws an arm toward Marty for support and balance.

Wrapping her arm around his, she mockingly jokes, "All righty, then. The car is secured. Lead us in. I'm starving." Carrie hopes her joking distracts from the fact that she probably shouldn't be wearing shoes she can't walk normally in.

Marty feels the strain from the additional weight he is now supporting but doesn't think much of it. "Come on—they are showing us to a table," he says as Carrie happily follows alongside him.

Having been seated in a fine restaurant without a reservation is not a huge surprise to Marty. Over the last few months, he has started to make a name for himself, and the word is spreading around town. But Carrie, who is still new to the game, is flattered by the people showing her so much attention, even if they are just colleagues and friends.

"Marty," Carrie says, reaching for his hand. "Are you a co-owner of this place or what?"

He is not thinking past her spoken words. "Naw. They just happen to like me here, I suppose." He reaches for the freshly poured water glass to take a sip.

Carrie reclines in her seat and then reaches for the menu. "Should we order a bottle of wine or something?"

"Oh, babe. I got this. Let me pick it."

She smiles at him, feeling relieved. "OK, then. Impress me."

Still studying the wine list as the waitress appears, Marty takes a moment to lift his head and give his best wine choice. "We'll have this Italian red."

"Excellent choice, sir." The waitress scampers off to fulfill his order.

Marty takes a quick glance at the entrée menu before looking back at his dinner date. "Carrie, have you decided on anything? What sounds good to you?"

She is going back and forth between two choices, meat ravioli or fish with cream sauce. Knowing what Marty plans to order would help her decide. However, he is still debating between his own choices, and thus her decision-making process is all the more difficult. "I'm not sure—what are you thinking?" she asks.

"Oh, I was thinking the meat lasagna or the meat ravioli with vodka sauce," Marty states without looking up at her. Which is good, because Carrie is looking at Marty with a happy expression, but he doesn't see it or recognize it yet.

The waitress drops off some fresh bread and a plate of herbed olive oil to dip it in. She then asks if they are ready to order and if they have any questions. Without hesitation, Marty replies that they are ready. Carrie starts to feel the pressure of ordering.

"Oh, Marty. Go ahead. I can't decide," Carrie says. Deep down, she is waiting for him to order so that she can make her own decision—and she's interested in getting a taste of what he orders, provided it is something she's interested in.

"I have the meat ravioli with the vodka sauce," Marty states.

The waitress replies, "Excellent choice." She then turns toward Carrie, who is quickly rescanning the menu.

"I will have the pasta . . . No, wait . . . I will get the fish with the cream sauce."

"Fine. Is there anything else?" the waitress asks of the table.

"Nope. That will be all for now." Marty hands over the menu.

Carrie is still looking over her menu. She reluctantly hands it over as the waitress quickly snatches it and leaves to input the orders. Marty does not think anything of it. Carrie, however, is wondering if she ordered the right dish.

The wine arrives shortly. The steward opens the bottle, nearly spilling it all over, but he makes a quick recovery. Without missing a beat, he pours a sample into Marty's glass. Marty picks up the glass like a professional taster and sniffs the wine first, then swishes it around in the glass. He then lifts the glass to take a sip and puckers his lips as the liquid flows from his mouth and down his throat.

The wine steward waits patiently for the response.

"Ah yes. That's lovely." He gives a nod of affirmation.

The wine steward tops off Marty's glass and then fills Carrie's before placing the bottle in the middle of the table.

Both reach for their respective glasses and then lock eyes. There is an awkward moment, and Marty quickly says something by giving a toast. "To great friends and great company tonight." They both clink their glass together and then hastily retract them to savor the fine vino.

Carrie is the first to place her glass down. Granted, she has enjoyed the wine and this innocent dinner date. However, she knows they are only friends and work associates. Still, she wonders if Marty has ever thought of her as something different, something more. She gazes back at him from across the table, lost in her own thoughts.

Marty feels the gaze from the other side of the table. He searches for words to say, something to break the silence. He pauses for a second to look at Carrie, actually admiring her as a woman. As he studies her, he realizes she is fairly attractive, and the miniskirt she is wearing is an added bonus—she is dressed to kill. He would be lying to himself if he didn't appreciate the effort she put into looking great for this friendly dinner event, although he deviates for a second to think about the other woman, Amy, he has been lusting over. In his mind, he plays the awful comparison game of what he desires versus what is directly in front of him. Yet, he keeps reminding himself that Carrie is a work colleague and that he definitely should not date someone he works with. He should stick to his plan of trying to win Amy's heart. Yet, he is comfortable going out to dinner with Carrie and realizes that he truly enjoys her company. Marty reaches for his glass of wine and takes a big gulp.

"Hey. Slow down. You still gotta save some for your dinner." Carrie places her hand over Marty's hand in an attempt to halt him from emptying his glass.

Marty feels Carrie's hand and pauses before withdrawing his. Now embarrassed, he attempts to quickly suggest a new conversation topic.

"Mickey tells me you are picking up the job rather quickly."

"He is a good mentor."

"I agree with you on that."

Carrie looks at Marty. "Oh, I didn't realize he mentored you as well."

"Yeah. Although sometimes I feel I bring more to the table." Marty begins to explain the numbers game and the betting skills he has, in addition to being a master pool player whom Mickey is unable to beat.

Carrie raises a glass in his direction. "Maybe I should be asking you who to bet on from now on. It is March Madness coming up. I could use some extra money." They both share a laugh. Then she continues, "Oh, I am so inviting you over for the Kentucky Derby in May. Unless, of course, you are booked up!"

Leaning back in his chair, he casually replies, "Carrie, I turn off my phone a week or so before that race. If you could only imagine." He reaches for the bottle to refill the wine glasses, starting with hers. The waitress then brings out the entrée dishes, and they eat in silence.

She is the first to put her fork to rest. "Oh my gosh, I don't think I could take another bite," she says, although she has been tempted numerous times to have a taste of Marty's dinner choice.

Marty finishes up his own meal and looks at Carrie's plate a few times, mulling over how rude it would be to take a bite of her entrée. He makes the better decision not to, but he wonders if he should have asked anyway.

"What? We still got dessert to figure out. I'll make a deal with you. You choose it, and we'll split it. I just couldn't finish one off on my own." He smiles as he takes the last bite of his meal before surrendering his cutlery to the plate.

Carrie is hesitant to order a dessert, being so full already, but upon hearing his deal, she realizes she is only responsible for half of a dessert plate, and it makes her more inclined to go along with his proposal. She snatches up the dessert menu and bypasses the coffees and after-dinner drinks, instead perusing the sugary selections just as the waitress approaches. Without even asking for Marty's input or advice, she simply states to the waitress, "We would like the chocolate cake with the proper whipped cream."

Marty sees the happiness in her eyes upon voicing the dessert request and decides he should give her this one. Besides, her choice actually does sound quite appetizing, and he would probably have selected it himself. "Sure. Sounds like a winner. Make it so."

The waitress clears the dishes, and their dessert arrives minutes later. They both scarf it down in record time. Carrie takes every bite of the chocolate cake as if it were the last piece of cake on the planet.

They both make small talk, and then Marty reaches for his wallet to square up the bill. Carrie makes a polite attempt to offer to pay half, but Marty adamantly declares that this one is on him, and she backs off. Later, she thanks him with a peck on the cheek as they are putting on their coats and departing the restaurant. Marty takes her by the waist, more to guide her in the direction toward the exit than to show affection, and she comfortably yields to her fellow colleague. She feels his arm tense as they exit onto the street. Suddenly, she feels the full force of his arm pushing her down toward the pavement, and he shouts, "Get down!"

In a flash of a second, she hears the sounds of bullets flying through the air. Falling to the pavement, she doesn't have time to see who's making the attack on them but feels Marty move his arm from pushing her down to reaching behind his back, pulling out his gun. He then returns fire toward the source of the bullets. At that moment, she reaches into her purse, hoping to aid in the return fire. A bullet flies past her head and into the brickwork behind her.

"Get down! Get down!" Marty shouts to her.

Carrie hears him but finds her gun in her purse. She raises it and aims toward where she feels is the source of the bullets. Her colleague has just emptied his clip and is reaching for another clip. She smells burning flesh first, then realizes there is a hole is Marty's jacket, near his shoulder, and knows he has been hit.

"We gotta get outta here," Marty shouts while still crouching down to avoid possible bullets.

"What do you suggest?" Carrie says, not really knowing where the bullets aimed at them are coming from.

"Ditch the shoes. Follow me—and cover me." Marty stands up halfway and fires his gun in a more precise pattern, as if he is actually aiming specifically at known targets. The rounds returned to them are lessened as they move toward better cover.

Carrie has no clear idea of what is going on, compounded by the fact that she is quite full from dinner and dessert and has a slight buzz from the bottle of wine they polished off with the meal. She takes Marty's hand and follows him down the street and then into various alleyways. After about ten minutes, they eventually stop at a door in an alley.

She whispers, "What are you doing?"

Marty is punching in a code on a keypad as he replies, "Getting us off the streets and safe for the time being."

The door clicks after Marty enters the code. He pushes it open and takes Carrie's hand, pulling her into a dark space. He closes the door behind them and then guides her to an area about ten feet away from the door. It is only then that she sees a light come on as Marty pulls a chain to illuminate the room.

"Where are we?" Carrie's mind is racing, not able to fully take in the totality of what is happening and what just happened.

Meanwhile, Marty returns from the main part of the store with bottles of water and some paper towels. He hands her a paper towel, and she uses it to wipe her forehead. She notices he is doing the same.

"Damn. We got ambushed."

She finishes wiping her head and says, "Is that what you are calling that?" Throwing the balled-up paper towel toward him, she adds, "I thought you were just looking to get out of ending the date."

"Dinner. Not a date."

"Whatever."

They hear a noise, and both turn their heads to the door leading to the front of the store. Marty stands up and takes on a defensive posture, with his gun held low in his right hand. He inches forward as he momentarily pauses to look back at Carrie, putting a finger to his lips to tell her to be silent.

Cautiously moving toward the sound, Marty keeps his gun at his side. He pushes the door outward and sees a familiar face, and the tension in his body releases as he steps through, the door shutting behind him. He calls out to the figure standing in front of him, "Jesus. I almost shot your ass."

"I would have not liked that. Not to mention my granddaughter would never think much of you."

Hearing the response, Marty heads to the older man and gives him a friendly slap on his right shoulder. "And just how is your granddaughter these days? Are you still putting in a good word for me?" Marty uncocks the gun and places it on safety before returning it to the back of his pants.

Mr. Robinson acknowledges the gesture as he watches Marty disable the gun. Much to his relief, he feels better without a gun in the mix, and he grabs Marty as headlights shine through the store's front windows.

Both automatically duck for cover, but after realizing it was a false alarm, they each stand erect, facing one another.

"Hello, old friend," Marty says to his business partner.

Mr. Robinson taps Marty on the chest. "Who are you calling old? Speak for yourself, sonny."

Another car's headlights beam through the windows as it rushes down the street. Reacting accordingly, Marty ducks down again. Mr. Robinson takes note and does the same.

"I dare say, boy, you seem most jumpy this evening." He spits on the ground. "You ain't wanted or something?"

Shocked by the accusation, he replies, "No. What are you going on about?"

"Just saying."

"No. And I got a friend in the back." He points toward the stockroom. "We are just lying low for the time being."

Mr. Robinson shakes his head after Marty mentions a friend. "She's a work colleague," Marty says, clarifying his statement.

"Uh-huh." Mr. Robinson gives Marty a judgmental glance.

Not wanting to get into a full-blown discussion, Marty retreats to the stockroom to check on his friend. He calls out for Carrie, telling her the coast is clear and to come out. Marty hears movement as Carrie emerges from the darkness and walks closer to him and the light. She moves cautiously until she is standing side by side with Marty, wrapping an arm around him for moral support versus claiming him. Mr. Robinson watches it all and takes it in.

Marty attempts to diffuse any suspicions by making the introductions. "Here is my work partner and not my girlfriend, Carrie." The woman draped around Marty steps forward with an outstretched arm toward the old man.

Continuing onward despite the awkwardness, Marty announces, "And this is my business partner. He owns the store, and I have been pursuing his granddaughter for quite some time."

Carrie and Mr. Robinson contemptibly step closer to one another and forcefully shake hands. Each is studying the other as though they are ready to do battle at a moment's notice—against one another or perhaps teamed up against Marty. It's still unclear after the horrible introductions. They release hands and retreat back to their respective corners.

Realizing he made the situation worse, Marty says, "OK, then. Everyone knows one another." He glances at Carrie. "We need to hunker down for the time being. Grab what we need." Carrie listens and then departs to gather the items. Marty then turns back to Mr. Robinson, who is standing there, awaiting further instructions. Marty walks up to him, more as a friend than a business associate.

"Listen," Marty says, pleading his case. "As I said, she's a work colleague and not my girlfriend. There are people out there trying to kill us. We are going to hang out here for a bit. You OK with that, buddy?"

Taking it all in, Mr. Robinson throws an arm around Marty. "Why didn't you say so in the first place? You know, she's a real nice gal. Maybe you should pursue her instead . . . I dare say you probably have a better chance with her than with Amy."

"What? More than Amy?"

"I see what I see. Advice is free in this store. Everything else, I'm charging you for."

Marty shakes his head. "What is up with Amy anyway?"

"What do you mean?"

Getting upset and raising his voice, Marty exclaims, "I mean she never returns my calls, never replies, and is never here when I stop by."

"Women. What can you say?" He just shrugs his shoulders.

Marty stares in response to Mr. Robinson's latest reply before grabbing him and throwing him against the wall. "What are you saying, old man? I'm not good enough for your granddaughter? What is her deal?"

"I don't know how to tell you this." He knows it's something Marty doesn't want to hear.

"Tell me what?" Marty thrusts the old man tighter against the wall.

"She is just not into you. Sorry."

Marty pauses for a moment to take it in. "And why not?"

"Oh, I might have mentioned your employment in conversation."

"You sold me out?"

Mr. Robinson pushes back, giving himself some breathing room. "It was not my intention to do so. Sorry."

Marty releases him and puts up his hands. "Fine." He struts off, heading toward the stockroom and calling out, "I'm gonna check on Carrie."

Mr. Robinson watches Marty leave and begins to contemplate his life choices—in other words, he wonders if Marty is going to shoot him dead in the next ten minutes. *Well,* he thinks, *this is one of the few times I might deserve it.*

New beginnings

A few weeks later, Marty drives down the road and parks in the street parking area. He checks the sign and verifies he is still within the legal limits. He grabs the bouquet of roses sitting on the passenger seat and exits the vehicle. He nervously steps up to the brownstone building, which has several buzzers. He selects the appropriate one and waits for the callback.

"Hello? Identify yourself," a feminine voice says.

"It's Marty." He waits patiently, and the buzzer rings seconds later. Upon hearing the buzzing sound, he reaches for the door and opens it. He moves forward through the door, and it closes behind him. He races up the stairs, ignoring the elevator in lieu of getting to her floor quickly.

Upon exiting the stairwell at the door for her floor, he continues down the hall and arrives at her door at the same time as she begins to open it.

"Oh. Hello, stranger," Carrie remarks, opening the door with a seductive smile and leaning against it. She poses as the gatekeeper, as though waiting for him to say the right thing, like something sweet about her, before she lets him in. She waits patiently in silence.

After looking down momentarily while trying to catch his breath, Marty then looks up at her. Carrie is just standing there, waiting for a response of some sort. She fidgets for a second but then recovers. She waits for her guest to answer first and tries to goad him into saying something nice.

"Well, Marty? What do you have to say for yourself?"

He thrusts the bouquet of flowers toward her and, still out of breath, stammers, "I . . . I bought these for you."

"Why, I don't know what to say!" Carrie is surprised by the gesture—well, at least she acts completely overwhelmed by it.

Marty moves forward, bypassing her door-guarding block, and beelines toward the living room. Planting himself on the sofa, he looks back toward Carrie. She puts the flowers in a vase and then heads toward the fridge, grabbing two cans of beer.

She flings one to Marty as she opens the other, one-handed, without much effort. Marty catches the flying beer and also opens it one-handed, in one swift motion. He chugs half of it before stopping and looking at Carrie.

She has only begun to sip her beer.

"Are you not hanging out with me tonight?" Marty finishes his beer and crushes it on his head, then throws it aside. He knows he will have to clean it up momentarily but acted it out for the effect.

"You only dream of keeping up with me!" Carrie, too, slams her beer and flattens her can before tossing it aside, hoping Marty picks up her crushed can as well.

"Well. It seems I finally have some competition."

"Serves you right." She blows him a kiss.

"We'll see." This time, it's Marty's turn to retrieve the beers from the fridge. Returning from the kitchen, he then tosses a beer at her, keeping one for himself.

Carrie puts the beer down on the table and squares up to Marty as he puts his beer down on a different table. They meet halfway and embrace one another. They flinch at the same time as they begin to tussle back and forth, but it's the kind of game where both participants are winners. Marty eventually gains the upper hand and pins his girl to the floor.

"Oh. You finally got me. What are you gonna do?" Carrie mocks him while still struggling haphazardly.

"Why, I should . . ." Marty thrusts his force down on her.

"Oh, baby . . . give me your best! I surrender!" Carrie smiles back at him as if waiting for more, much more from him. She relaxes her body, giving in.

"Well, then. Let's play this out." Marty takes advantage of the situation and continues toward his objective, and Carrie is happy to oblige.

Next day

Marty wakes up in a strange bed.

Strange as in not his own but not totally bizarre, as he is quickly getting accustomed to it. It is as though he hasn't woken up in this bed before but will most probably wake up in it many more times in the foreseeable future.

A soft, warm, feminine body shifts position and then maneuvers toward him, attempting a spoon position against him. He can only oblige and shift his own position to be a better recipient of her moves. He feels the sudden increase in warmth and then starts to wonder about his own body temperature. She is now much hotter than he is, and his own temperature starts to increase as she snuggles closer. Maybe he should think about what he is going to do next, as it's becoming more clear to him—with him and Carrie, of course. He begins to take the lead in their early-morning romantic dance to and fro. Or in this case, up and down.

After the deed is done and both have taken showers, they switch to a more business-like mode as they prepare for the day's adventures—or work, depending on what needs to be accomplished.

Marty stands at the breakfast bar munching on an apple when Carrie comes out of the bedroom and walks past him, lightly slapping him on the ass. Marty jerks for a second and is ready to respond in kind, but instead, he leans over for a more benign response—a kiss. He decides he'll get back at her, in another way, later today.

"What's up, dear? You got anything exciting going on at work today?" he asks nonchalantly, knowing perfectly well that her schedule is similar to his. Namely, because they are assigned to the same team.

Rolling her eyes, she opens the fridge to grab the OJ. "Really. That joke is starting to get old. Like you, honey." She laughs out loud in her very identifiable laugh, almost spilling the juice all over the counter.

"I only say it because it makes you laugh. I rest my case."

"Keep telling yourself that. As long as you find it funny," she replies.

"See?" He points to the counter and the juice glass. "You almost lost it! I should quit my day job and go into standup comedy."

"The only thing we're gonna lose is our asses if we don't get a move on. Mickey wants to see us both in thirty minutes. Did you forget about that?"

"Waiting on you, dear, as always," Marty says, the *as always* part being a soft whisper. He flashes a cheesy smile back to her.

Carrie may or may not have heard his whole reply, but she assumes it was some smartass comment. Maybe not at the moment, but she assumes there has been one and there will be another one. She lets whatever she may have missed go for the time being because, for the most part, she does have Marty wound around her finger, and it would be a shame to fight over something petty. But then the making-up part might be all the better. She grabs her purse and moves closer to him. "*Vamos.* Let's go, partner."

He looks back at her intently with soft eyes that show he is happy to be with her. She hopes so, thinking of the effort she puts forth to make him happy. But she benefits all the same, so it is worth it for both of them.

Taking her arm, they walk out of her apartment. She stops to double-check the lock on the door, and they stroll down the hall as one happy couple.

Mickey's meeting

A couple of weeks later, Mickey, who is standing outside the back door, throws down a cigarette butt and stamps it out. "Oh, shit." He remembers the boss's policy about littering—specifically, the shitloads of cigarette butts dotted around the property he tasked a bunch of guys last week with cleaning up. He quickly picks up the butt and chucks it farther in the bushes. "Hell. I'll make Joe, Mike, or somebody go clean it up later!"

A car approaches, and Mickey looks up, assuming it's who he is waiting on. He watches as the car pulls into a spot and two people, a man and a woman, get out, whispering to one another as they recognize him standing there.

"Well, well. I hope this meeting didn't inconvenience your schedule today. Did the two of you have plans for a nice stroll through the park?" He gives the eye to Marty, but it is Carrie who strikes first. Namely, with a punch to the shoulder.

"You're a funny guy, you know that?" Carrie says. Why, if I wasn't romantically and sexually involved with Marty at this minute, I would have considered you."

Marty blushes. Mickey stands there, his mind blank and without a witty response. Carrie beats him to the punch before he has time to come up with one.

"No. No. I would still be with Marty," she says, giving him a once-over and brushing him aside.

Mickey cracks a half grin, more like a smirk. Marty strolls on by, not looking to either side but chin raised slightly as he passes him. He turns around as they both pass him, heading toward the house.

"All right. You two wiseasses get a move on. We got some serious work to do." He closes the back door and pushes Marty slightly forward, heading toward the boss's office.

Upon entering the room, the first two people take their respective places near the sofa, where all invitees stand, as is customary. Mickey enters the room last and closes the door, taking a seat on the sofa. Boss Mazoli is sitting in his chair, reading some papers. He finally acknowledges everyone, in his own time, naturally, not theirs.

In unison, Marty and Carrie both recite, "Good afternoon, Boss."

Boss Mazoli is never one for formalities or ritual, but he is schooled in the old ways of showing the utmost respect. It brings him joy when his underlings show him proper respect. Even Mickey stands up to give him respect.

"OK, Mickey. The show is yours." Boss Mazoli turns toward Mickey first and then stares directly at the other people in the room. "Please, you two, sit down." Both race to grab a seat as Mickey stands up and paces near the boss's desk.

Mickey is about to speak, but the boss cuts him off. "Carrie, will you fetch us all some drinks?" Normally, Carrie would think that was an old-school or sexist remark, but in actuality, she is the lowest-ranking person in the room. She resigns herself to making the drinks, reflecting that there was an earlier time when she stood in this room, seconds away from being dead. It was the good graces of the boss and her showing them where the money was stashed that had kept her alive. And she can't honestly complain about how her life has changed. She has steady employment with great pay and benefits. She is now with a great guy, Marty. She smiles as she pours the drinks and turns around to serve them to the men of the room. She takes her seat next to Marty as he pats her on the knee, more as a signal of appreciation and comradery than affection.

Savoring the taste of good scotch, Marty reflects on whether any of the whisky bottles in his own cabinet would measure up to the level of this beautiful and expensive selection. There may be one or two that rival it, but he can always count on Carrie to grab the most expensive bottle at the boss's bar and pour it for everyone.

Boss Mazoli impatiently taps his fingers on the table, waiting for the show to get moving. He signals Mickey to get started. Mickey takes his cue and begins his dialogue.

"So. Let me start off by reminding everyone how Marty and Carrie were ambushed a few weeks back."

"Yeah—" Marty starts to speak but then goes silent after a gentle nudge in the ribs from Carrie.

Mickey hears this but ignores it. "Yes. You two were ambushed and, luckily, fled to a safe house. And we later found out the attackers were associates from the Asian Crime Syndicate."

"Yes," Boss Mazoli chimes in. "They have been trying to move in on my territory! The nerve of some people. We have some businesses that are actually refusing to pay their tribute because they feel we can't protect them anymore. You know, in the old days, we would just set fire to those businesses. Teach them all a lesson. They are being rebellious, and it will soon spread to the paying businesses. We may have to shoot some before it starts getting out of hand, right, Mickey?"

Carrie and Marty look at one another and nod their heads, having heard similar complaints from some of the customers on their routes.

Mickey takes another sip before continuing, ignoring his boss' last comment. "I'm hearing word on the streets that some businesses who are refusing to pay us are now paying someone else, presumably the ACS. Even our other businesses are starting to suffer as well," Mickey says, beginning his briefing on the decrease in revenues from these other businesses.

Marty reflects privately in his own mind for a second, recalling a slight drop in bets and revenues reported by Mr. Robinson over the last two weeks. He figured it was a coincidence or a couple of off weeks. Now, after listening to what Mickey is saying, he wonders if the ACS is causing the decline in his side business.

"Boss Mazoli has decided to be proactive and do something about it," Mickey announces as Marty snaps out of his daydream reflection. He is jarred and gives a startle response, but Carrie quickly places a hand on him in an attempt to help him regain his composure. Once he is all right, he squeezes her hand to reassure her. She slowly withdraws her hand and continues to listen, with much interest, to the big pitch from Mickey.

"What are you saying, Mickey?" Carrie asks.

Giving her the eye, he says, "I am just coming to that. So listen up."

They both readjust themselves on the sofa. Carrie is feeling the vibe of something really important about to come forward. Maybe she will have a bigger role this time around. After all, she was invited into the room with Marty, Mickey, and the boss. They must want her for something big or significant—not just fetching drinks. She leans back in anticipation.

Marty, too, senses something big. But being the more cautious of the two, he believes that Mickey is not quite telling the whole truth. Something along the lines of someone in this room is going to die. Or maybe all of them are going to die. In this line of work, "kill or be killed" is often stated. He ponders on whether they are taking the ACS too seriously or not seriously enough. He only knows how to stay alive and how to make the odds in his favor. However, with Carrie recently added to the mix, he may have to readjust his odds.

From Mickey's tone, the odds do not seem to be in their favor. He may have to place a bet with Mr. Robinson that the chance of him walking away is slim. Of course, if he is right, then it doesn't matter—he will be dead. If he is wrong, it would be one of the few times he's been wrong, but he would be alive. But then his reputation and odds-making skills would be harmed. Better for him to be right and dead, even if that's a shitty way of looking at it.

"Boss Mazoli believes it is time to form alliances for the greater good," Mickey boldly proclaims to the room. "If the ACS is moving in on everyone's territory, then we must be proactive and stop them before it's too late."

"Who are we teaming up with?" Marty demands.

The boss speaks up. "Nunzio's gang."

"How are we gonna do that?" Carrie asks.

"Very carefully," Mickey chides. "We are setting up a meeting, ironically, at the favorite, neutral restaurant of both of the bosses. They are old friends, in case you didn't know," he says to Carrie. "They go back many, many years."

"Nunzio will be onboard, I'm willing to bet," The boss says. He stares at Marty for a second. "We have had this happen before, decades ago, when the Irish gangs were encroaching on our territory." He then looks at Mickey as he sips the last of his scotch, wondering if Mickey still has any deeply buried animosity. He continues to watch Mickey, but he doesn't seem to display any hostility, so the boss doesn't dwell on it.

"What do you want of us?" Marty asks carefully.

The boss nods to Mickey, indicating for him to continue. Taking it as a cue to reveal the plan, he turns toward Marty and Carrie. "You two." He points to each of them. "You two are the guardians."

"Or targets," Carrie remarks, placing her empty glass on the table in front of her. She leans back, thinking a bit before asking, "What are the odds that the ACS is going to be there?"

"As long as they don't catch wind of this meeting?" Mickey responds.

Switching topics, Carrie quickly thinks up of a different question. "What do we have to do, then?"

Mickey stands up, giving renewed spirit to his presentation. "Good point. Here's the plan."

Marty, despite remaining quiet, sits up to listen to his friend give the details of the plan. Carrie starts to reach for her empty glass and then decides to make a play for Marty's half-empty glass. She leans in at the same time he reaches for the glass and grabs it, without actually raising it to take a sip. He never looks over, but she suspects he is laughing on the inside.

"I want Carrie on the front door and Marty at the table with us," he says, issuing the orders as the boss nods in affirmation.

The boss then adds, looking at Marty, "You will be watching my back as well as Nunzio's. Yes, his man Bruce will be there, but you are there to protect me and Nunzio, not to eat a free dinner." Marty nods, but Carrie snickers at the last comment.

"I don't know what you're laughing about. You will be targeted first before they get to us. Perhaps you might want to have a hard think on that," Mickey says to Carrie. "And might I remind you, the ACS is growing in numbers. They could be anyone or anywhere."

"What? You mean like the waitstaff or bartenders?"

"Exactly," Boss Mazoli adds in. "Hence why we picked this place for the meeting. Besides, it is one of my favorite places to eat. The stuffed ravioli is perfect, just like my nana used to make."

"Then we are all in agreement," Mickey says, finishing up his dialogue. "Everyone knows what's at stake here. We need to team up with Nunzio's people if we are going to thwart this ACS gang and take them down. At the very least, we need to be seen in large numbers to stop their advancement into our territory."

"Here, here." Boss Mazoli raises his glass, and everyone else follows suit. Carrie raises her empty glass, going through the motions. Marty's glass is nearly empty, not as empty as his girlfriend's, but he manages to take a sip as the toast is completed. He finishes off what little he has and then collects the other glass from Carrie before walking over to the bar. Mickey grabs him on the way and whispers in a barely audible voice, "I'll need to have a word with you before this goes down."

"Sure. You want to play pool tonight?"

Mickey steps back, calculating how much money it will cost him. "Fine. Whatever. Eight thirty tonight."

"That'll work. It's your money," Marty says, goading him. "You know, you could just pay me now and save yourself the embarrassment." He grins from ear to ear toward Mickey.

"Be serious for once, buddy. Because I actually am." Mickey uses a different tone that causes Marty to rethink his last comment.

Carrie's comments

As they walk out of the room and down the hall, Carrie is practically sprinting, heading to the back door and eventually outside. Once she exits the building, she turns around, stops, and screams, much to Marty's chagrin.

"Shh. Wait until we are off the property."

Carrie is having none of it. Rather, she is most vocal about what she just heard in the meeting. "Holy shit. We are teaming up with another mob to take down another gang. Possibly even stronger? Damn."

"Well, now that you put it that way," Marty responds to her summation of the meeting. He didn't really have time to think too much about what would actually transpire from what Mickey was saying. Now that he has a second to ponder, the picture is becoming a lot clearer and more in line with how Carrie described it.

"Shit is about to get real," Carrie says, confirming Marty's thoughts.

"No shit," Marty agrees.

"Well, then. We need to throw down tonight. You know. Go out. Get fucked up. Enjoy each other's company." Carrie doesn't add *before one of us or both of us die* but instead puts her arm around his neck and massages it, causing a strange sensation to run across his skin. He slinks away for a moment after experiencing the willies.

"You know I hate that." He pushes her back.

"Your body is telling me something different!" Carrie attempts to put her hand back on his neck, playfully this time. He doesn't jerk it away and actually starts to relax his neck and shoulder muscles. He closes his eyes until he hears the sounds of others, men's voices, off in the distance.

"Fine. I like it a little." He grins back at her.

"I know." She pulls her hand back as they walk toward the car. Marty gets in the driver's seat, starting the engine and turning on the radio to find a classic rock station, as he needs to hear something that rocks at the moment.

Grabbing his hand on the radio knob, she pushes it once, forcing the radio to go silent. She turns to stare at him as if waiting for a reply. "You never answered me. Where are you taking me out tonight? I'm adding a caveat. No dive bars or ones with cinder blocks this time."

Slinking back in the seat, he replies, "Aw, babe. You know we have the best time in those hole-in-the-wall joints. But I hate to break it to ya." He pauses, trying to soften the news.

"What? Tell me!" Carrie says loudly.

Hesitantly, Marty tells her he has a meeting with Mickey tonight, first, before they can have their little party this evening. He tries to explain that it is important because Mickey sounded serious. None of this translates to Carrie, who has already formed her own opinion of said meeting.

"You expect me to believe that shit? Oh, you and Mickey are to have this all-important meeting? Where at? I suppose it will be at the Irish pub on Fourteenth Street? Am I right?"

Marty thinks in his head that there is an Irish pub on Fifteenth Street, but it is not important to clarify this point to her. She clearly is livid and in pissed-off mode. Maybe she knows about another place, but he isn't going to bring it up at this point in the conversation.

"Listen. I'm going to the meeting with Mickey. I suppose I'll have a couple of drinks and all that. I'll listen to what he's gotta tell me. After that, I'll leave ASAP, and then you and me can meet up later on to continue to party until dawn. Is that fair enough?"

Carrie ponders the words spoken by her partner, her current man. She decides to agree to his offer—but with a caveat. "You better be ready for anything goes tonight. You know what I mean. Afterward? You hearing me?"

"Of course, babe. You know it. I hear ya!"

"You better."

Marty only hopes this meeting with Mickey is all about business and not about drinking—although he has no problem with either. He just has to remember to be somewhat coherent by the time Carrie calls for him. Then it will be another issue he has to deal with.

Mickey's meeting

Marty is watching patiently as one dart after another hits the board. He smiles cheerfully and takes another sip from his local craft beer. He studies his opponent, Mickey, as he withdraws the darts and tallies up the score. A low number at that, but Marty cheers on his adversary with some token phrases like *good job, way to go*, and the classic *you'll do better next time.*

He then steps up to the line and throws at the dartboard, nailing a triple twenty and a triple nineteen, hitting only the single seventeen and missing the triple seventeen by a mere hair.

"You're an asshole."

"Or you could say, 'Nice throw, Marty.'" He casually walks up to the board to withdraw the darts and jot his score down on the chalkboard.

Mickey stands at the line. He takes a second to comprehend the act of throwing a dart at the dartboard versus aiming one at the back of Marty's head. After his last three turns, though, he doubts whether he could even hit Marty's arm.

"Oh. Nice throw, asshole."

"That's better. Thanks." Marty returns to the table to sip his craft beer while laughing tremendously on the inside. He wonders when this guy is ever going to realize that he can't beat him at most leisure games.

"Well. Maybe pinball," Marty says out loud before realizing he is talking rather than thinking.

"What's that?"

"Uh . . . you're doing . . . great. Go for the triple twenty."

"Yeah, right." Mickey throws the third dart and hits the "1." Marty realizes that his comment was more like goading his competitor rather than offering support. He takes another pull from the beer and calculates what he needs to win this game in three throws. He then steps up to take his turn. After Marty's third throw wins the game, Mickey resigns, saying that he has had enough, and they both walk over to a table to listen to the house band.

"Whatcha want?" Mickey gruffly asks.

"I can't remember. Were we playing a dollar a point?"

"Piss off. Order your two shots, and we'll call it even."

Marty decides not to bait him anymore and celebrate his victory in private. "If you insist. And some popcorn too."

The waitress comes by and smiles at both of them. Maybe she fancies one or even both of them. But she also knows men tip her better if she smiles—especially ones who order the expensive stuff versus a round of PBR in a can. She touches the arm of the younger one as she leaves, hastening to get this tab going because she figures the two guys look like some serious drinkers who are willing to part with their money.

Receiving his drink with a much-too-friendly grin, Marty leans back to throw down the shot first and then nurses the second drink. "Thanks for the drink. Now tell me why you ordered me here."

Mickey eyes the bar tab being quickly consumed by his mate on the other side of the table. He takes his own drink in hand and splashes it around the glass before announcing, "This isn't gonna end well."

"Tell me about it. Me working under you and whooping your ass in pool and darts and God knows what else."

"Cut the crap. For a moment." Mickey then shifts his eyes, and Marty knows this is for real. He decides to change his position and lean forward.

"OK. What do I need to know, then?" He moves the empty glasses out of the way and readjusts the items on the tabletop. Satisfied with the new arrangement, he then shifts his eyes back to a patient, yet somber Mickey.

"I think we are going to get ambushed. Clean and simple. And there's not a damn thing we can do about it because these . . ." He trails off, pausing in his monologue to formulate what he wants to say. "Because these guys have to have their traditions and certain ways of doing things." He grabs for his glass and slams it down.

"I sense you're not liking the idea of this dinner meeting?"

"Look at the clever one." Looking about for the waitress, he shouts, "Honestly? A dinner meeting out in the open? We might as well advertise in the newspaper what we are doing."

"Uh . . . nobody buys a newspaper anymore."

Mickey makes a fist and slams it down hard on the table. The waitress comes running by, apologizing for not getting there sooner. Marty waves her apology off, telling her the action was not due to her inattentiveness.

"Just another round, dear," Marty says, quickly taking over to calm the tense situation and make the waitress feel less stressed. She stares at him for a long second before smiling and then scampering off to fetch the drink order.

Marty watches the waitress leave the area. He turns back to Mickey and asks, "So what can we do about it?"

"Absolutely nothing."

"Serious?"

"Pack an extra gun. Buy a bulletproof vest. Pray. Because you will be needing it, my friend. Oh, I will tell you this. One of us isn't walking out of that restaurant. You can figure out the odds for you and me." He pauses momentarily, finishing the last bit of liquor in his glass.

Reaching for Marty's arm and pulling it closely, he says, "Let me tell you this bit of info. Between me and you, it's important, especially if I'm one of the people who gets whacked at the dinner meeting."

"What the hell are you going on about?" Still confused, Marty leans forward to listen to the words from the sage. Or in this case, Mickey.

"There will be this guy, Bruce," Mickey begins. He's a good guy, although there's a lot of talk about him and his past. Something no one has ever figured out or investigated thoroughly. Mostly gossip talk, I guess, but one never knows. Be that as it may, it doesn't matter. I would trust him with my life, and he will be the one guarding Nunzio. You are assigned as the backup shooter for him. You cool with that? Remember, I say Bruce is all right."

The waitress arrives. Maybe she heard some of the conversation, or maybe she didn't. She could have heard some of it but decided not to react to it. After all, she has heard much worse and much scarier words spoken in her many years of slinging drinks to all types of clients. If she had heard, she would be rooting for the younger one to be the one walking of it alive.

Mickey grabs for her arm. The waitress tenses up but is used to men, mostly drunk men, employing this tactic to get her attention. She shrugs his arm off, wishing the other, less creepy, one was touching her. Instead, she shifts her eyes back toward the older one, obviously the one in charge and most likely the one who will be paying the bill tonight. "What do you need?"

"Cash us out, will ya?" he says plainly. She had assumed his demeanor and tone would be much worse.

"Sure thing, sweetie. You want me to split it?" The other one reaches for his wallet but is too slow; the older one simply throws a credit card down on the table without even bothering to ask how much the bill is. She reluctantly grabs the credit card, wishing the other one had time to throw his card, too, as then she could see his name. "No problem. I'll be right back." She takes a quick glance toward the other one and winks. He sees it but doesn't think too much of the gesture.

"Well, thanks, buddy," Marty says. "Though my night is only just beginning."

"How's that?" Mickey is inquisitive as he finishes the remaining drink until the glass is bone dry.

"I'm supposed to meet Carrie afterward."

"Hmm . . . Well, then. Don't let me hold you up. Enjoy it, man, while you're still alive." Mickey gives these haunting words before Marty leaves the bar, waving to the waitress as he departs.

Safe-house precheck

Not thinking anymore about leaving Mickey to pay the bar tab, Marty looks down at his watch, noting the time. He should call Carrie and tell her he is on his way, but first, he must do something else. He hails a cab, gets in, and heads over to a familiar neighborhood. He jumps out of the cab and enters a store to pay a visit to the old man, a.k.a. his business partner, Mr. Robinson.

Walking in like he owns the place, Marty glances about, eyeing the merchandise and displays, more particularly, casing the place for how many customers are in the newsstand. He notes two other patrons and then casually shops as though he is looking for a specific item but not finding the item in question. After witnessing the two other customers finally leaving the store, Marty decides to confront his business partner.

"Well, well. Hello, old partner." He grabs a piece of candy from a counter display to chew on, not making an attempt to pay for it.

"Yeah. Greetings to you, Mr. Marty," he replies in a monotone.

Marty believes he hears a hint of sarcasm in Mr. Robinson's voice, as he has never addressed him like that before. Maybe something has changed in their relationship, and Marty is about to figure it out, although that would be a surprise because Marty is still counting on this steady stream of income coming in, plus the use of the safe house in emergencies. To lose either of them—or worse, both—would definitely change the dynamics of their relationship and their future business dealings.

Proceeding with caution, Marty leans on the counter toward Mr. Robinson and decides to question him about his granddaughter.

"How is Amy? She obviously doesn't ever want to speak to me. Does she even ask about me?"

Mr. Robinson sheepishly stares over Marty's shoulder before replying back in a noncommittal tone, "Oh, my boy, she is just not happy with your . . . ah . . . how do we say . . . career choice. Ah, and your business dealings."

Ignoring the first statement, Marty instead emphasizes the second part. "You mean the one you and I have, right here? Operating out of this store? What does she have to say about her grandpa partnering with me?"

Eyebrows raised, Marty ponders his last comment before realizing that Amy is now standing behind him. He slowly turns around to face the woman, once of his desire, now standing in the flesh approximately ten feet from him. Not missing a beat or losing his cool, he simply acknowledges her presence.

"Amy. Good evening. Nice to finally see you again," he says, sounding uninterested.

The slender, fair-skinned woman approaches Marty with a defensive posture and stops in front of him, as if ready to fight.

"Well, well. If it isn't the original Mr. Gangster himself. To what do we owe the honor of your visit?"

"Maybe you should ask your grandpa. No, wait—this is business just between us menfolk. Or business partners, I might add." Marty finds himself getting more and more livid toward this woman—who once garnered his desire but now more so his scorn.

For a moment, Marty even starts to wonder why he was ever attracted to her. Maybe it was just a physical thing because the limited vocabulary he has heard from her thus far would suggest he might have grossly misjudged her. He is much relieved that he has hooked up with Carrie—she is way more of a woman than he has ever wanted, and they share a commonality in employment, which helps. He even begins to second-guess what attracted Amy to him in the first place, and now he doesn't have to find an excuse to visit this store anymore. Still, he has business dealings with her grandfather, both of which are illegal, but neither is with her nor requires her judgment.

Sizing her up, he decides he has time for some additional smartass commentary. "I guess you never liked the flowers I sent or my numerous phone messages to ask you out." He throws all his cards on the table, relieving himself of any feelings he might have had for her.

Amy feels insulted by the accusation of her being an awful person after all this time. She now feels she has to be on the defense, first for her honor and, second, to somehow terminate the business dealings her grandfather has unfortunately been swindled into. Sure, she may have had found this guy interesting and cute, but that was only for a moment by the beer cooler. She has come to realize that with most men, give it a little time, and they always show their true colors. Marty certainly failed this test. But in her mind, he's still a dangerous person and can make her life and her grandfather's life more difficult. She must be tactful in dealing with this mobster.

She stands her ground before walking around Marty. "So. You think because you bring money to our family-run business that gives you the right to all things, including me?" she says, lashing out.

"Well, no. But I was actually interested in you and wanted to go out with you on a date. Is that so wrong? I actually liked you once." Marty shifts the blame back to her. Mr. Robinson is silently laughing as he listens to the argument between these two—it sounds more like they have been married for years. But he is resolved to stand back and let them have at it.

Amy is taken aback that he was truly interested in her but continues to maintain her position, despite possibly erring in her judgment. Yet, her grandfather had blatantly confided in her that Marty is a mobster and should never be trusted, nor should she ever think of going out on a date with him—or any of his associates, for that matter. She has always believed in her grandfather, despite realizing he is profiting, quite nicely, from the illegal numbers game that both he and Marty have set up and currently operate out of the store.

"You may have my grandfather in your schemes, but you will never have me," Amy shouts back at him in a fit of desperation. Mr. Robinson sinks a wee bit lower in his stance behind the counter.

Marty takes a step forward and stops, a breath away from Amy. She shakes a little from the nervousness of what he might do but maintains a firm position of defiance. Starting to raise a hand to her head, he stops and then withdraws it. "I was so into you," he says softly. "But you know what? I don't need you. I don't care about you anymore." He then turns toward Mr. Robinson and speaks directly to him.

"I assume we still have our arrangement, and I will hold you to honoring our agreement. Pray that I do not find cause to terminate it." Marty then points in the direction of Amy and finishes with, "Or anyone who wants to change the arrangement because I will then have to personally deal with them."

Having kept silent the whole time, Mr. Robinson decides to speak up and says, "I understand you."

Marty moves past Amy, practically pushing her aside. He then walks up to Mr. Robinson and starts to reach into his coat pocket but resigns himself to simply placing his right hand on his shoulder, smiling.

Mr. Robinson shudders at Marty's touch at first and then takes it as a sign of continual business dealings with Marty. It is Marty's numbers game that is fetching a fair amount of money for him, although illegal, and he is not quite in a position to have it end so soon. Even if his granddaughter disagrees or is not interested in Marty anymore, it doesn't matter to him.

"So, Mr. Robinson," Marty says. "Are you with me or not?"

Amy almost says something, wishing to get the last word in, but thinks the better of it because she is now bargaining with her grandfather's life—she doesn't want to be the reason for his untimely death. She keeps any further comments to herself.

Mr. Robinson stares blankly at his granddaughter before giving the expected response. "Of course, nothing has changed between me and you. Do you think otherwise?" He closes his eyes, trying to avoid the heat of the disapproval from his favorite granddaughter. *You can't please everyone unless they are paying the bills.* Mr. Robinson figures it is easier to make amends with family than a guy who has killed many people before and won't hesitate to add two more to his résumé. He decides it's better to side with Marty this time but wonders if this is the last time he will. More importantly, how can he get himself and his family out of this arrangement for good?

Carrie lines up the cue ball and breathes at a rhythmic pace. On her next exhale, she releases the cue, which strikes the cue ball and in turn hits the eight ball and falls into the corner pocket. She scoops up her winnings and then glances around the room for any more punters to hustle their hard-earned money from. Nobody comes forward. She returns to the front end of the table and racks the balls. She starts the process of methodically placing each ball in its respective position, alternating a stripe and a solid. When almost complete in her task, she hears a familiar voice calling out to her. Concealing her smile, she never looks up but accepts the challenge of this newcomer.

"I got a hundred bucks that says I can beat you two out of three. Are you gonna accept, or are you just another pretty face in this place?" The all-too-familiar voice rings out, trying to goad her into taking the bet.

"Sure," she passively calls out to the newcomer, without even raising an eye. "Put your money down on the table. I will gladly take anyone's money. Without prejudice, of course."

"I'll only throw money down when you actually beat me at pool," the newcomer says.

"Then let the games begin."

"So let it be said." The newcomer acquiesces the break to her, and the game begins.

Carrie studies her shot and shoots toward the one ball, like so many times before, but with the particular angle she has always found to be successful. She starts the game and strikes the rack, with the pool balls flying every which way before settling down, with one ball falling into a pocket. *Good luck,* she hopes. Surprised by that fact, she lines up the second shot and sinks a striped ball. *Good, I have the advantage.* She shoots and nails another striped ball before barely missing on the next shot. *Oh shit, here's where it starts.* She calmly sits down and reaches for her drink as she watches her opponent step up to the table and begin his turn.

"You're stripes, right?" He smiles as he lines up his cue and begins the slaughter of clearing the next four solid balls before missing, slightly, on a tight cut from the last shot.

Oh, maybe I have a chance to beat this guy. Carrie steps up and surveys the table. Granted, she is down two balls, but it is her turn, and she is a decent pool player. At least she thinks she is, and now is the time to prove it. Maybe she could actually beat this guy after all. She looks back and forth and settles on lining up her strategy and finally nails the next shot. Unfortunately, she banks it too much to the right, causing her next shot to be off, and she barely misses the pocket. *Damnit. He's gonna run the table now.* She sits back down in resignation to watch her opposition take his turn.

Her opponent takes less than a second to figure out what to aim for and what to shoot at. He lines up his shot and sinks the first ball with ease. He then takes a second shot, and that ball falls in as though it was programmed to do so. One after another, solid balls fall into the pockets, clearing the table for the solid ball player. He steps up and calls the eight ball to the side pocket but misses by inches.

She tells herself, *OK, Carrie, this is your last chance.* It takes a second for him to acknowledge his miss on the last shot and relinquish control of the table. He eventually sits back down to watch his opposition play out her one last ploy. Standing upright with her cue in hand, Carrie claims the table and takes her last step toward it. Surveying the predicament, she thinks it through and plays it as though it was a desperate situation and she was playing for her life. She does manage to sink one ball, but with her eventual miss on the next shot, she actually helps the newcomer, Marty, in lining up the last shot. He does what he has to do, and that is to call the sinking of the eight ball.

"Eight ball, corner pocket." Pointing with the cue to the corner pocket off to the right, he taps it twice for good measure and then takes his winning shot, sinking the last of the balls he is required to hit.

The eight ball falls into the correct pocket, and the game is over.

The next game proceeds at a much faster pace. Carrie only has two turns to clear her balls before Marty clears the table of his striped balls, again. This time, he doesn't miss the first shot on the eight ball. Marty chalks up his quick two-game victory as the loser, Carrie, confronts him and murmurs softly into his left ear. "Marty, I owe you from our wager and will gladly pay it off . . . later tonight. But for now, how about us taking this private party over to a more secluded table somewhere over there?" She points to a less secluded area of the bar.

Marty shuffles out the area, replying back, "Sure." He walks over to a quieter part of the bar and claims an unoccupied table that will fit the bill.

Date night: part 2

Carrie sits down on the same side of Marty as opposed to sitting across from him. She thinks it is much more intimate to be seated next to the person versus looking over at them. Also, Marty happened to grab the correct side to see the band play, and she wanted to watch the band as well. Although the band won't be starting for another hour, she at least gets to watch the overhead TV airing some sports game.

"Well played, Marty. You know, schooling me back at the pool table. I never realized how good you really are. You can at least buy me a drink or two to help bolster my damaged ego."

"Mickey would agree with you—I whoop his ass in pool too." Marty laughs over his small victory and continual dominance over anyone and everyone at the table with his pool-playing skills. He finally catches the waitress's attention and orders some cocktails for both of them. The waitress departs to fulfill the drink request. He realizes he has a few moments of quiet time with his woman and brings up the topic that has been bothering him.

"You know. I feel like an ass," Marty declares and pauses for dramatic effect, but he instead receives a snarky observation.

"No worries. I could have told you that from day one. But I'm still with you, I guess. I have no other pressing engagements at the moment." Carrie puts her arm around Marty.

"No, I'm serious." He thrusts back and to the side. Carrie decides to pull back her arm before it gets caught in a painful way.

"I got it. You're an ass. You're not telling me anything new."

Marty looks back to her with hardened eyes. This is his tell that suggests she should listen up, as it's serious stuff. "Would you let me just say this for once, please?"

"Sure thing, babe." She wraps her arm around him once again in a show of support.

"Good." The waitress places the drinks on the table in front of them. They declare their cheers to one another and take the first sip. Marty explains the events earlier in the evening with regard to him, Mr. Robinson, and Amy. Carrie feels the pain of jealousy until he gets to the part where he tells Amy off, much to her relief. The story ends with him making a menacing threat before walking out of the store.

"Seriously? Why are you still doing business with them? Any of those bastards? You know, they would sell you out at any chance they get," she declares as she throws back the drink in her hand.

"Oh, it's simple. I need that safe house. You never know these days. And the numbers game still brings in a fair amount of income on the side. I don't have to hustle at pool to pay for these drinks." Marty winks at her as he, at the same time, flags the waitress to have another round delivered to the table.

"So you don't feel anything for her anymore? Positive?"

"Nope. Not a damn thing. And why would I?" He pauses to finish his drink and pushes the empty glass toward the end of the table as he slides his free hand around her waist. "I already have a great girl. That's all I need. She would be pissed otherwise."

Carrie immediately leans over to kiss him passionately, with the added buzz effect from the latest strong cocktail. She has been so happy ever since that fateful day when her life changed for the better. She reflects back to when he entered her life. She kisses Marty to the point of almost suffocating him. He recoils, more for a gasp of air, and they both retreat to their respective positions.

Marty reclines against the seat back. He takes a deep breath, as Carrie sucked away most of his oxygen in their last make-out session. He sees the waitress coming forward with the next round of drinks and decides to slow things down for the moment. The waitress places the drinks on the table, and he raises his glass to match Carrie's. They look deeply into each other's eyes.

"I gotta ask you a question. Completely off topic. Maybe you should take a drink first."

"You can ask me anything." She giggles, although she is thrown off by the suggestion to take a drink first. He must be messing with her.

"Are you sure? Are you sure you're up for it?" Marty goads her even more.

Carrie ponders this, wondering if he actually has something serious to ask her or if he is just messing with her. She decides to take a chance and will try to answer accordingly, although if he keeps ordering these generously poured drinks, she may not be in the right frame of mind to answer correctly should the "question" arise. She nods to him.

Marty picks up the signal to proceed. "You know, I always wondered . . ." After trailing off, he blurts out, "What was one of your worst dates?"

Surprised, she spits out her drink, spraying down the table. "With you?"

He shakes his head.

She then picks up on how to answer the weird question. "Oh. You mean, what was one of my worst experiences overall?

Got it, babe. Well, let me tell ya!" She moves forward and back, revealing a slight buzz.

"I so want to hear this one." He moves closer to her, readying himself for an entertaining story.

Carrie takes an additional pull from her glass, hoping more alcohol might help her tell the story. She steadies herself against the table as she begins her tale.

"So. You may have not liked my former self," she says, beginning with a declaration of guilt.

Marty interrupts. "How so?"

She pushes him. "Would you let me tell the story?"

"OK. Fine. The floor is all yours."

Carrie regroups. "You may not have like me a few months back. I was an absolute mess and a complete train wreck." She sees Marty ready to interject but waves him off.

"Choo-choo," Marty says, making juvenile sounds.

"I didn't know what life was to offer me," she continues. "I didn't know of this criminal underworld. I am only starting to realize the potential of what I can do. What we can do."

Marty beams but remains silent. He figures she is telling, with honesty, more of her life because of the several drinks they both have consumed recently. At this point, he feels he is starting to hear some of Carrie true feelings and experiences.

Waiting for some additional commentary but receiving none, she presses on. "Fine. You wanted to hear about some horrific experience I had with some guy prior to meeting you? Well, here you go."

Both of them reach for a glass and take a sip, adding to their drunkenness. Marty then strives to attune his listening ears as the other one coughs to clear her throat.

"So I was encouraged by someone I am no longer friends with to have a meeting with this random dude," Carrie recites. "Some guy that was a friend of a friend, and they said he was all right, I guess. They also said he was employed and had a car. I suppose my standards were quite low if employment and the capability for independent transportation around town were my top priorities. Anyway, it was a different time in my life, a time I'd rather forget and not reflect on. Ever."

Carrie pauses. "I mean . . . Come on. You saw me at that party. Did I look like someone who had their act together?"

"Well . . . I . . . don't know," Marty hesitantly responds, thinking of that day and only remembering what she was wearing versus her personality. He opts to remain silent as a better defense.

"Good answer," she remarks before getting back to the story. "I was a complete mess. I admit it. But here's the funny part. I was hooked up with this guy. You know . . . the friend of a friend. We meet up in this run-of-the-mill place. At the time, it was all I knew, so it was top class for me."

Marty snickers but then stops, waiting for her to continue with her story.

"I meet him there, and I knew right away he was Mr. Wrong. I dunno. Call it a gut feeling, but I figured I would give this guy a chance to prove me wrong. He didn't, and he even exceeded my expectations."

"No way. What did he do?" Marty asks. Then he adds, "Or what didn't he do?"

"No. You were right on the first question. What did he do? Well. I'll tell ya what he did. For starters, he picked the wrong place for a first date. The second, he ordered the wrong things for a first date. I mean, come on—how could one royally fuck that up?"

"Oh, come on. It's a first date. What could he have ordered that was so wrong?"

Carrie chuckles. "You won't believe this. Try a chili dog and chicken wings."

"That doesn't sound too bad," Marty throws back at her.

"Seriously? Have you ever watched someone not slop themselves when eating a chili dog, loaded with everything?"

"Well . . . I . . . ."

Carrie interrupts, waving a finger outward. "No, wait. The chili dog was only the beginning. I watched this bastard devour a ten chicken wings. Now, have you ever watched a date, a first date, one that is being screened for potential as a lifelong partner, devour ten chicken wings right in front of you? Before your very own eyes?"

"Can't say I have. Though you said he devoured—I mean, he ate—ten of them," Marty responds.

"Whatever the final count, it doesn't matter. You're missing the real treat, I'm tellin' ya. I mean, it's bad enough to pick the wing up with your fingers, but that's the easy part. Then he started to rip apart and suck the gristle, flesh, veins, and whatever else from the bone. I mean, seriously, to watch your date tear apart a wing with his teeth makes you wonder if this is the person you want to spend the rest of your natural-born days with. Not to mention kiss at some point in the evening." Carrie takes a deep inhale after finishing her monologue and wipes her mouth for good measure. She shudders even thinking about it.

Marty is in a quandary over his next choice in words. He definitely has made the vow never to order chicken wings, ever, or at least in the presence of Carrie, but at the same time, now he's hungry and wants to order something off the menu. "I know it's really bad timing, but I'm wondering if you are hungry for anything particular on the menu?" He points to it.

Carrie takes a quick glance and replies, without hesitation, "Nachos."

"That's funny—isn't that the same kind of food, the kind you slop all over yourself?"

"It is in the top three but after chicken wings and a chili dog. I can handle it much better now."

Marty smiles deep inside and says, "You're perfect. I love you, Carrie. I mean it. I love you, dear."

Not expecting that kind of response nor prepared for it, she never gives away her poker face. "I love you too. I think you are the first guy to really understand me."

"Then we should be going out for some New York–style pizza."

Not missing a beat, Carrie remarks, "I would have settled for Neapolitan-style pizza, but close enough."

Marty realizes the woman of his desire is right next to him, and without hesitation, he leans across the table to kiss her, as he has finally found his one and true happiness. She is the one. He's thinking that after the protection job tomorrow—if they survive—he's going to take her on an extended holiday. Maybe to the Caribbean or Mexico—somewhere other than here.

Next morning wake-up

Marty wakes up in the morning, this time without a drinking glass in his hand. He shifts in the bed, trying not to wake the woman next to him. He wishes it was a memory foam mattress so that he could easily slide out, undetected. With this mattress, however, the slightest movement will awake the partner. He still tries, nevertheless, and makes it out of the bed and onto the floor, walking quietly to the bathroom for a nature call.

Returning to the bed, he forgets that his body temperature is cooler by a few degrees as he carefully moves back into bed, only to awake the person he is sharing said bed with. A terrible and failed attempt and all for nothing.

"Brrr . . . What? Did you go outside or something?" She utters in her half-sleep state before rolling over and returning to sleepland, snorting blissfully at a high pitch. Marty wraps around her in the spoon position in an effort to fall back asleep. It grossly fails, as Carrie is roused and stays awake. Meanwhile, Marty falls back to sleep. Carrie gets up and heads to the living room to catch up on her reading.

A few hours later, Marty wakes up from his slumber. He heads out of the bedroom and into the living room, beelining toward Carrie to kiss her lightly on the back of her neck. She pulls back, feeling an emotional response and goose bumps running up and down her body. "That's lovely. Good morning, dear."

Marty scans the kitchen and says without really thinking, "Did you make a pot of coffee?"

"Seriously? Is that the first thing you're thinking about?" Carrie plays with a piece of her hair in an attempt to tease him.

Never seeing the innuendo or picking up on the hint, Marty heads over to the kitchen to make his own coffee. He wonders why Carrie is staring at him in weird sort of way but ignores it as he brews the coffee for his morning fix.

Having satisfied the caffeine craving, he starts to see things more clearly and begins to realize the sexual innuendoes Carrie has been signaling to him over the last ten minutes since he got up. Clearly, she's been expressing her intentions, but he hadn't picked up on the blatant signals. He is learning very quickly, though, as Carrie calls from the bedroom, "Hey, Marty, can you come back to the bedroom for a minute?"

Marty doesn't fully understand the extent of his part, but he hears the call and answers it in haste, returning to the bedroom to satisfy Carrie's wants and immediate needs.

Moments later, Marty finishes up and retreats to the bathroom to clean up and breathe deeply, realizing the need for a moment to catch his breath.

Carrie calls from the bedroom, "Are you coming back, dear, to finish what you started?"

Marty swallows his pride, pumping his chest before returning to the room to complete the task. "Sure, sweetie. I'll be there in a second." He takes one last glance in the mirror and then returns to finish off the conquest he started earlier.

Lunchtime.

Marty rises to the occasion a second time today and heads to the bathroom to take a shower. Granted, Carrie is already in the shower and starting the process, but with his entrance, it only slows it down. When both are finally clean and satisfied, they exit and towel themselves dry.

Marty hangs up the towel and proceeds to the bedroom to finish getting dressed, whereas Carrie is still applying lotion. Once lotioned up, she then heads to the bedroom to get dressed.

Marty pulls a shirt over his head. Carrie's process is a bit more challenging, as she dresses herself in layers. After finishing the last form-fitting layer, she turns to Marty for final approval. "What do you think—does this top look all right?"

"Damn straight it does." Marty nods his head in approval. He thinks to himself that today is going to be a hell of a day. Or, should he say what is left of the day as it is alright half gone.

Mickey is walking fast down the hallway, with Marty next to him and slightly a footstep behind. He's still talking about the upcoming meeting, but Marty is more concentrated on keeping up the pace, not trying to focus on hearing the details of the upcoming meeting. And then his mind begins to wander to last night and this morning with Carrie. Ah, Carrie . . .

He is slapped in the left arm by the tough guy next to him. "Have you listened to anything I just said?" Mickey asks. Mickey then pins Marty against a wall next to a table, with an expensive vase nearly falling over in the process, and Marty begins to reach for his gun. Mickey anticipates that action and blocks his hand.

"What?" Marty asks.

Mickey raises his other hand as if ready to slap him. He lets go of Marty's hand that was reaching for the pistol grip as Marty slowly backs his hand off the gun. Trying to plead with him, Mickey says, "Dude. This is important. This meeting is important. I need your head in the game."

Hesitantly, he replies, "You got it."

"Good. And you need to work on your reflexes. Maybe join a gym. You're getting soft on me. Maybe your girl can help you out."

Marty flips him off as they turn the corner and open a door, heading into Boss Mazoli's private office.

There is another man in the office conversing with Boss Mazoli. Judging by the laughter, they both seem well acquainted with one another. Marty also notices that each of them has a drink, which also suggests this meeting is not so serious. Or perhaps it is. You never can tell with these things. Marty steps back and waits for the proper introductions to be made, eventually, after all the laughter and banter stop.

Minutes go by, and Marty continues to stand in the back of the room, waiting patiently and respectfully. Mickey had already raced toward the bar, poured himself a drink, and joined in the conversation. Now, all three of the men are talking loudly and talking over one another about whatever. It really makes no sense to Marty. Finally, Marty has reached a point of not giving a rat's ass anymore and cautiously strolls over to the bar. He eyes several bottles and grabs a medium-priced liquor and pours himself a drink. He replaces the bottle and grabs his drink as the once-loud conversation goes dead silent. Closing his eyes and then opening them, knowing what his fate might be, he turns around to face all three staring back at him.

Mickey is the first to speak. "Nice of you to finally join the party." Then the room erupts in laughter from all except Marty because he is raising his glass to quench his thirst.

"Marty, my boy, grab that bottle and get your ass over here," Boss Mazoli shouts out to him.

After grabbing the bottle and topping up his glass, he drops the bottle off on the boss's desk and finds a seat. He was going to just lean on the desk but figures the boss would not take to kindly that. He simply sits down next to another guy, a guy named Bruce.

Bruce studies the new guy up and down and then diverts his attention back to the conversation. For what Marty has pieced together, Bruce is the all-around second-in-command guy for Boss Nunzio's gang. Marty has heard Mickey speaks volumes on this guy, everything from running the show to taking care of the problems—he is the mob's mobster. A guy with a lot of experience in the ways of the mob and solving problems. But a mystery guy too. Of course, in this line of work, everyone has their own skeletons and demons. Why, even Marty runs an illegal numbers games out of his safe house, so he probably shouldn't judge this guy too much. You never know what a guy like Bruce can be like as a friend versus a foe.

"Marty's my name." He extends a hand in friendship.

Bruce slaps the extended hand back. "Yup. I heard about you. Marty, you say? Well, I finally get to meet the man in person."

That threw him off completely. Here he thought he was a nobody in this world, and now one of the top guys in a competing mob is happy to meet him. Maybe Mickey has been talking him up way too much. Or maybe this guy, Bruce, wants some bets for next weekend's matches. Somebody always wants something. Oh well—at least he seems friendly enough.

Boss Mazoli speaks up.

"All right. All right. Shut the hell up." When Boss Mazoli speaks, everyone within earshot listens. "We have a problem, and it needs to be sorted," he continues. "Now, not some point later on down the road."

There is a murmur among those in the room. Marty hears the competing sides of the debate. Notwithstanding, Marty takes a crack of speaking out to this crowd. "Fine. Everyone. I admit . . . me and Carrie hooked up."

Bruce lets out a chuckle.

"No. No, Marty. We really don't need to know any more details," Mickey says with a sigh.

Marty is unabashed about his confession.

"Fine, Marty. Thanks for sharing—or not," Mickey continues. "But that is not the most pressing matter. What we really need to know is more about the ACS. Have you got anything worth mentioning to the rest of the group? Well, do you?"

Marty goes over and over his specific assignment in his mind. He will be guarding Boss Mazoli as a backup to Mickey's primary role, and he is to guard Boss Nunzio, being a backup to Bruce's primary coverage. Easy enough: he's the backup guy on both accounts. Sounds like an easy gig, and he may even get a chance to sneak in a free appetizer.

"I still think I got shafted," Carrie replies while checking her gun in the passenger seat of the car. "Even more than you."

"How so? You got an assignment tonight. This is an important meeting, and I'm sure old Boss Mazoli will look upon you with favor," Marty says, offering his condolences in the nicest of ways.

"Yeah. Yeah. You get the men's table and will be wined and dined, whereas I get stuck outside and across the street. Out in the dark and cold." Click. Click. She looks down and rechecks the gun.

"Oh. I dunno. It won't be all fun and games for me." He tries really hard not to crack a smile or let her see him wielding a grin.

"Laugh it up, buddy boy. See how much you will be laughing tonight after this guard job. Oh, Marty. I feel a headache coming on tonight." She feigns putting her hand up to her forehead. "And you know the golden rule. If I don't get any, that means you don't get any." She snickers.

Marty slows down the car as he sees a drugstore coming up on the corner. He pulls into the parking lot. "OK. Go inside. I will be waiting right here." He switches the engine off and leans back, waiting.

Bemused and confused, she asks, "Why did we stop here? What the hell are you doing? What the hell is going on?" Carrie stares are him, continuing to barrage him with questions and querying eyes.

He lets out a chuckle. "You said you felt a headache coming on tonight. I didn't want to interrupt our quality time tonight after this job! So go inside and buy some aspirin. You know, so you don't have a headache . . . tonight." He maintains his shit-eating grin, trying really hard not to burst out laughing.

"Well. Well. Look who's the clever guy. I should be—"

"That's Mr. Clever Guy," he interrupts. "And while you're in there, can you get me a Red Bull? Thanks, sweetie." He pulls out his phone and checks the sports scores.

Carrie turns a shade of red but then thinks for a second and gets a laugh out of it as well. She gives her boyfriend and his quick wit some credit. Sometimes she doesn't get it right away, but she hands it to him for calling her bluff. Of course, because they are in a serious relationship, if she holds out, then that also means she isn't getting any either. She thinks about this as she enters the store and heads over to the cooler to get a Red Bull for her man. She then crosses the store and picks up a bottle of aspirin, just to maintain the running joke.

She gets back in the car and hands him the can of Red Bull. He thanks her and notices another item still in the bag. He makes inquiries about said item, but she simply tells him not to worry about it and that he will like it in the end. Satisfied with the response, he starts the engine and drives off to the restaurant.

Marty stops and parks across the street from Guigi's Italiano restaurant. Marty thought about taking Carrie, and at one time Amy, to this place for dinner, figuring if the mob bosses want to eat here, then it must be good food, although he has always felt this place was a little odd because it doesn't affiliate with any particular mob or gang. It has, surprisingly, stayed impartial and has been unofficially untouchable for decades. Thus, it is often used, as opposed to a church, for important meetings as a neutral ground—with the benefit of getting a decent Italian dinner. The restaurant's specialty is a homemade ragù sauce over gnocchi—it is to die for.

Marty sees the restaurant sign as he looks out the car window. He glances toward the car clock and realizes he has about ten minutes before he has to show up for the assignment inside.

"Whatcha thinking about, dear?" Carrie asks as she stares out the front window.

"Oh. Nothing. I dunno. I just have a weird feeling all of a sudden."

"What do you mean?"

"Just a weird feeling. Hey. It's nothing—probably gas or something." He looks back over to her and waves his hand as if it's not a big deal.

She grabs his hand. "Hey," she says in a more serious tone. "Talk to me. Are you all right? Honey?" She looks at him, worried.

"Hey. It's nothing. I'm all right." He takes her hand and squeezes it tightly. "I'm more worried about you being out here all alone and hungry while I'm feasting away inside with the menfolk!" He tries to divert her attention.

"Oh, rub it in." She doesn't think much more of his mental state and instead starts to get into her mobster work mode.

He leans over to kiss her on the cheek. She says, "I think you can do better."

"I think so too." Marty scoots a little closer and begins to passionately smooch his girl—in the car and in broad daylight. Several people walk past and notice the couple making out in the car.

"*Marty!*" Carrie pauses to catch her breath. "Where did that come from, and why are you stopping?" She giggles and attempts to recompose herself.

"Just wait until tonight, then. That was just a preview."

"Well, then, I hope this dinner meeting goes quickly." She gets out of the car and walks around to the driver's side at the same time Marty gets out of the car and stands there, waiting for her to walk around. She walks up to him and stops.

"I'll be thinking about you throughout the whole dinner." She smiles at him. "I love you, Marty. Honestly."

Marty takes her head into his hands. "I love you, too, Carrie. We need to talk about a vacation and other things after all this."

"Where are you thinking? Wait—what other things?"

"Anywhere. But the Caribbean, for starters."

"With the crazy, fruity cocktails and all that?"

"Sure. Anything you want." He kisses her, moderately, one more time.

"Then sign me up. I'm with you always until the end. And we'll discuss the other things as well."

"I hope so." He lets her hand go and walks across the street. His mind is elsewhere for the time being, and he is almost hit by a passing car. He stops short in time and turns around, seeing that Carrie is watching him closely. He waves back to her, and she waves as well, but it's more of a cautionary one.

He reaches the other side and grabs for the restaurant doors, taking one last look behind him and noticing that Carrie is already in her guard mode, watching the street up and down. He feels an utmost sense of safety in his mind that she has his back. He then turns around and walks into the restaurant, ready to do what he has been paid to do.

Dinnertime

Marty walks through the front doors of the old-school Italian restaurant. The smell of garlic permeates the place. He sees the hostess station and a cute woman, presumably the hostess, and makes a stop there first. He does a quick scan of the joint and spies a man waving oddly in his direction, so he assumes it must be for him. He doesn't immediately recognize the man but decides to head to that table.

"Good evening, sir. How many in your party?" The cute hostess smiles back at him, waiting for him to answer her simple question.

"Oh. Sorry, dear." His attention had been diverted to the person waving to him, but he quickly recovers and answers, "I believe I'm with the party over there." He points to the table over her shoulder.

The hostess tightens up when she learns that he is with the important party this evening. "Oh. You're with that party. Excellent. If you'll follow me please." She is quivering a little as she quickly departs her station. She doesn't know what to do, so she simply takes his arm, guiding him to the designated table.

Deep inside, she is nervous but trying to hide it, knowing that these people are very important and even dangerous—they've probably killed people in the past. Trying not to let that fact cloud her judgment or her job, she simply plays along as though she is showing a wealthy customer to his table and party. In fact, she thinks he's kind of cute and that maybe she should have chatted him up. Returning to her station, she waits patiently for the next guest, hoping he or she is normal and not some mobster.

Marty watches the hostess depart and then waits for the stranger—now recognizable as someone he knows, Bruce—to stand up and give him a saltatory greeting accompanied by a friendly hug before sitting down.

"Marty, Marty! I feel you and I are going to see a lot of one another. I hope you can hold your own on the pool table." He smiles jokingly while holding a brown-colored drink in his hand. It could be scotch or it could be bourbon—hard to tell. But Marty can definitely smell the potent alcohol.

Marty waits good-naturedly for the waitstaff to come by and take his drink order. He figures he can get in one or two drinks before he has to be on guard and, more importantly, maintain somewhat of a semblance level of sobriety. He sees the waitress heading in his direction and signals to her. Bruce, without hesitation, orders another round.

In due course, the bosses arrive. The only way Marty knows this is the case is because he is having a conversation about sports with Bruce when Bruce receives a text and immediately reacts, leaping out of the chair and beelining for the front doors. Moments later, Bruce is escorting Boss Nunzio, and he makes the proper introduction to Marty.

Nunzio says to Marty, "I have been hearing great things about you. When are you coming to work for me?"

"I would love to work for you, sir, but Boss Mazoli has a great dental plan," Marty responds with tact.

Nunzio gives him a tap on the cheek. "Come on by sometime. We need to have a chat about your future." He adds, "And not just your teeth," giving Marty a light slap on his cheek.

"Thank you, sir." Marty smiles and then sees Bruce giving him the evil eye. He wonders if this Bruce guy is jealous of him or what. He starts to say something to Bruce, not planning to be overly direct, but there is commotion behind him. He turns around to see Boss Mazoli arriving, accompanied by Mickey. To his surprise, it looks as though Mickey actually shaved for the occasion—Mickey never shaves for anything or anyone, yet he maintains this look of never more than two days' growth. No beard, yet rarely clean-shaven, baby smooth. Marty could never figure it out because it seemed to be much more trouble to maintain versus just letting it go.

Boss Mazoli maneuvers over to greet his fellow mobster boss, Nunzio. They both square off to one another and then greet and hug each other like they are old-school chums.

"Mazoli. It's been too long," Nunzio announces.

"Nunzio. Where has the time gone?" Mazoli greets before they sit down, on opposite sides of the table, of course. Bruce takes up his position next to Nunzio, whereas Mickey sits next to Mazoli, unfortunately positioned with their backs to the door. Marty is, luckily, at the head of the table and has the best view and vantage point of anyone in the group.

Mazoli declares, "Before any business is to be discussed, I think we should order."

Nunzio replies, "For once, I agree with you." Everyone at the table laughs in unison, and as though in synchronicity, everyone immediately lowers their eyes to study the menu, finalizing their dinner choices.

"Well, I'm ordering the pasta in vodka sauce. It would be a crime not too," Nunzio declares. His words are met with a murmur of agreement. Meanwhile, Mazoli is ordering the special, the gnocchi in ragù sauce, and once again, everyone murmurs their affirmation.

The waitress assigned to this table, who is even more nervous than the hostess, gingerly approaches the table full of mobsters and mob bosses. She cannot tell who is the most senior or most powerful and so simply begins by asking the one who looks the oldest, "Sir, can I take your order?"

Mazoli recites his order and is followed by Nunzio and then the rest of the table. Marty places his order and then feels a little guilty, only for a second, because his girlfriend is outside watching the place. But he thinks she surely would have gotten Subway or ordered from some sandwich place by now. He laughs internally as the young, panicky waitress heads off to quickly put in the food orders for this table of important people.

Only then does the feeling that something strange is about to happen return to Marty as he, without hesitation, scans the restaurant, trying to piece it all together in mere seconds. He then thinks he hears a sound that would be odd to hear at this moment—what sounds like gunshots in the near distance. *That's strange,* he thinks, but that's not the only thing going on at that very moment.

Nunzio never sees it. Bruce never sees it. Mazoli never sees it. Mickey never sees it, but somehow Marty sees it, and it is this split second that will decide who lives and who dies this evening.

A man comes by carrying a tray with something on it that is covered by a white napkin. Marty thinks it is most peculiar because he is expecting the next round of drinks to be delivered, not some nearly empty tray. *Unless* ... The man is acting unusual, like he's lost or he is unsure what he should be doing as a waiter or even as the server of water or bread. Instead of serving something, the strange man immediately begins to flip the tray, revealing his hidden agenda. At that moment, Marty catches the oddity and immediately reacts to it.

He reaches out to his right and grabs Nunzio, pulling him down to the ground, causing Nunzio to miss the first bullet that zips past his head. Bruce had ducked down for cover at the same time, realizing what was about to happen, and then draws his gun, firing blindly in all directions.

Unfortunately, Mickey and Mazoli have their backs to the waiter/assassin, and a fateful round squarely plants itself into Boss Mazoli's skull just as Marty is pushing Nunzio down. Mickey slowly turns, feebly attempting to protect his own boss. Mazoli never saw it coming, literally, whereas Marty, being positioned at the head of the table, sees it all unfold. After yanking Nunzio to the floor, he pulls out his gun, aiming straightway toward the pseudo-waiter's head, with one purpose: to take him down before he takes anyone else down.

Too late. The shooter moves purposely from right to left. As Mickey turns, starting to pull out his gun, he is taken out in similar fashion to his boss next to him, although Mickey takes two bullets before the third, which unfortunately strikes him in the neck, finally brings him down. At that moment, Marty fires two shots at the waiter; one hits him in the chest, and the second hits a mere two millimeters away from where the first shot landed. Finally, the waiter ceasing shooting and collapses to the ground, dead.

The crowd in the restaurant erupts in a frenzy, with screams and shouting creating panic and chaos. Some patrons are standing up, confused, and others are running toward the doors. Those who are packing themselves produce their guns and have an eager stance, ready to start shooting someone, anyone. Marty flips his gun downward and then peers over to Nunzio.

Bruce is helping Nunzio back to his feet and brushing him off. Nunzio pushes Bruce aside as he slowly maneuvers over to Marty, who is slightly shaken but otherwise in a high-adrenaline state of alertness.

Bruce motions from behind Nunzio for Marty to holster his gun quickly. Marty sees the hand-gestured message and holsters his gun as he watches Bruce, who has his gun, for the purpose of guarding Nunzio, still trained on Marty's forehead.

Nunzio surveys the carnage and then stumbles forward, jarring the table in the process. "Marty, my boy. I owe you. Come work for me. I am sure I could use a person of your talents."

Marty sees his best friend and his mob boss face down on the table in front of him, dead. "I guess I have no boss anymore," he blurts out, trying to desensitize the situation, but it sounds awkward at best.

Turning to his right, Nunzio speaks in haste. "Let's have that chat sometime in the near future. Now get out of here. Leave—we'll be in contact." Bruce is helping Nunzio along as they both head toward the back of the restaurant and eventually out of sight.

Nunzio's gesture was offered with a smile, but at that moment, Marty realizes his worst nightmare could be coming true. He turns around and pushes past the few people who are lingering around the front entrance to the restaurant. He breaks free of the crowd and races across the street as the sounds of the police sirens come closer and closer. He sees the car but does not see any movement inside. In a fit of anguish with the realization of what he is to find, he bellows, "*No!*"

He dodges one last car zooming past him and reaches the car, which is parked on a side street. He peers in and sees her body, lifeless and still. He opens the car door, realizing his ultimate horror has come true. The body of Carrie, his girlfriend and lover, is lying there, dead and cold. He reaches for her to hold her one last time, half hoping for some kind of response. All their life plans and dreams are now killed off as well, like his girlfriend lying dead before him. At that instant, he wishes the bullet lodged in her head had been aimed for him and not her.

"Carrie. My love. Why did it have to be you? Why?" Marty weeps, holding the body of his dead girlfriend, one of the many who have died this evening, including his best friend and his boss. But it is her death that hits him the hardest.

"Carrie. Carrie." Marty's tear falls onto the cold corpse of girlfriend as the police approach the murder scene. "Goodbye, my love, until another time." Marty gently lays Carrie's lifeless body back in the seat and closes the door. He then turns around and makes haste down an alley and out of sight as the police begin to arrive on the scene of the carnage.

Fight or flight

Marty sprints, racing down the alleyway and never looking back. He runs and runs until he realizes he needs to stop but only after looking about to see where in the neighborhood he is currently at.

He sees something familiar and heads toward that direction, still hearing the police sirens off in the distance. He hasn't even had time to process it all. First, someone had started shooting; he thinks he remembers shots being fired that sounded like they came from outside. Then, he saw the waiter acting confused and strange, and without hesitation, Marty had pushed Nunzio down and out of the way. He hopes Nunzio isn't too pissed off at him for manhandling him, but it was the only thing he could think to do. Then again, Nunzio did offer him a job. Imagine that. Right after witnessing Marty's last boss get blown away.

Concentrate, man. Persistence is the key. Must make it through the night. Survive first to fight another day.

But he now comes to terms and realizes certain facts. His good friend, Mickey, is dead. His boss, Mazoli, is dead. His girlfriend, Carrie. Ah, Carrie . . . yes, she is dead.

Marty screams in horrified angst.

He wipes away the tears, and then his survival instincts kick back in. He concentrates for a second and comprehends that he is in some alleyway and can still hear police sirens in the distance. He understands what he must do. He needs to get off the streets and find somewhere safe, now. Thinking for second, he plans out his strategy. He surveys his location, trying to come up with the best plan for surviving the night—he can mourn tomorrow. It suddenly occurs to him that he is a couple of blocks away from his safe house in Mr. Robinson's newsstand. Making his way there in haste, he now has only the safe house on his mind. It is the only way he will be able to survive this evening.

Exiting from the alleyway, Marty approaches a cross street. He peers out to see a deserted street, void of any movement for the time being. After looking up and down the street, along with a check behind him one more time for good measure, he sprints across the street and makes it to the other side undetected. Relieved, he hastens his pace to reach the back door of Mr. Robinson's store.

Assuming he has the correct door—it is dark, and most of the doors look the same to him—he finds the cover for the keypad. He lifts it up and punches in the secret code; the door lock clicks once, and he quickly pushes the door open, entering the premises and closing the door behind him just as fast. He saw the beginnings of car headlights when he pushed the steel door shut.

Phew. That was close.

He leans back on the heavy back door as he waits for a second to give his eyes a moment to readjust to the darkness. He hears the car in the alley zoom on by, and he then counts a few more seconds before moving away from the door and into the back part of the store.

Ha-ha. I'm just waiting for old man Robinson to come around the corner with a sawed-off shotgun and blow my ass away, he thinks as he moves around the store cautiously.

He feels around in the dark for the light switches and flips one of them on. Light is produced but only for the back room. Good. He sees the boxes that should be hiding the secret room. He heads in that direction and moves the boxes to reveal a door with a lock on it. Only one more code to enter, and it's a simple entry, as one only needs to push the right combo on this push-lock. The door unlocks and opens, and he automatically reaches for a switch inside and to the left on the wall.

Marty then flips the switch on the wall outside the door to turn off the light to the back room. He closes the door behind him as he stares at the provisions laid out in front of him. There is a cot for his sleeping needs. Check. There is a mini-fridge, and he opens it to make sure it's stocked. Check. There is a sofa to sit or crash out on. Check.

Tired from the stress of the night's events, he flings himself out on the sofa rather than unfolding the cot. It feels a bit like the good old days of his collegiate years, and memories of frat house activities start entering his mind. Ah ... to be twenty-something now. Maybe he should be wearing a toga and chugging a beer. Well, he is surrounded by beer in the front of the store.

He sits up on the sofa after a few minutes, staring at the cot. Marty stands up and unfolds the cot, planning to lie down and rest. Although it takes a special way to maneuver on the cot for maximum comfort, he thinks he has it figured out.

Lying on the cot, wrapped in a blanket, he is suddenly hit by the realization that things did not pan out the way they should have. Granted, he is still alive, so at least that part is as planned. However, he doesn't want to trust anyone, and he is even paranoid about someone snitching out his place in the safe house. But these things to worry about are for another time. He closes his eyes and quickly falls asleep, as though it was part of tonight's plan all along.

The next morning

Although it only seems like a mere hour or two since he has fallen asleep, Marty hears some rattling around in the back of the store, near his secret room. He sits up, unsure of what to do, as he is not fully awake and is desperately in need of some coffee. Marty decides the best thing to do is to wait it out, remembering there are only two people who know about the existence of this secret room. And one of them is Marty. He then hears the sound of an unknown person working the lock. Marty stands up and steadies himself to the side of the doorframe, ready for almost anything.

That anything includes the barrel of .22 rifle entering the room first. Marty quickly reacts, grabbing the barrel and aiming it downward. He then pulls on it, and the perpetrator is revealed. Naturally, it is Mr. Robinson.

"What the hell are you doing?" Marty whispers as loudly he can, almost letting go of the rifle barrel but hesitating, waiting for the response.

Mr. Robinson is looking guiltier than sin but removes his finger from the trigger.

"I heard the news last night. But remember, sonny, this is my store," he barks in a show of defiance. "I'm just checking it's you in here."

Although he's surprised by the tone the old man used—it's the first time Mr. Robinson has spoken to him that way—Marty brushes it off, moving forward with plan B. He knows he'll need to find another safe house, as this one is now compromised, and he no longer feels it is safe. He decides not to mention to the old man that he will never use this one again. No need to tell him anything more than he has to or really wants to at this point. He no longer trusts anyone.

In an attempt to control the conversation and glean as much information about what went down last night as possible, he asks, "What did you hear about last night?"

Mr. Robinson pulls out a folded paper and tosses it over to Marty. "Here. Read for yourself. I don't even want to know if you were involved. But I will pray for your soul. Sonny."

Marty grabs the paper. Before reading it, he replies, "What do you think? Seriously?"

He waves his hand downward. "No, I told you that I don't want to hear anything about last night or your involvement. Nothing, you hear?"

"Well. It appears you assume I was involved," he says sarcastically as he moves to sit on the sofa. Mr. Robinson leaves quietly, closing the door behind him.

Marty unfolds the newspaper and reads the headline:

Mob boss and others killed, Possible mob war ensuing

He quickly scans the article, and it doesn't even mention Carrie's name. It only notes, "A woman was killed last night in front of the restaurant. Police are investigating and have not identified the victim. No further leads."

He throws the paper done in a fit of angst, lowering his head and using the palms of his hands to cover his eyes. There is a knock on the door.

"What?" he shouts.

Carefully, Mr. Robinson opens the door and hands him a donut and a cup of coffee. Marty reluctantly takes the offering. The old man starts to say something but is fumbling to find the right words.

"You know, now's not a good time," Marty says. He drinks the coffee, nevertheless.

"Yeah. Well. I gotta open the store shortly."

"Fine. I'll be out of here shortly." He takes a bite of the donut. Ah, it is quite fresh, like it was just baked.

"I . . . just wanted to say I'm sorry. You know. About her. About Carrie. She was a nice girl. I . . ." He then turns around and quickly exits.

Marty stares outward, first watching the old man leave and then watching the door close in front of him. He takes his last bite and chugs the rest of the coffee. "Well, I guess it's time to go and find a new employer." He gets up, leaves the room, and simply walks out the back door, never looking behind to see if the back door closed.

Amy waits a few seconds and then paces about in the back stockroom. She silently walks toward the secret room and rechecks to make sure Marty is no longer in there. She then moves to the back door that leads to the alleyway and rechecks it, ensuring it is locked tight. She turns back around to see her grandfather standing there, still with the rifle at his side.

"You know, he can't be coming around here anymore."

"Yeah. Yeah."

"And you have to stop that numbers game running illegally through this store. I don't care how much extra money it brings in. It's not worth it anymore." Her voice is getting louder and louder the more pissed off she is getting. The old man knows she is right about a lot of things, and he is reluctantly ready to admit it.

"Anything else?" he says glumly.

"Yes." She points to the lock on the back door. "We need to change the combination."

"He wouldn't be too pleased to find himself locked out of his safe house. He'll come after us, you know. He'll come after you, and I can't let that happen." He raises the rifle in a defiant stance.

"I'm working on that. I am going to meet with this police detective next week. Her name's Detective Amanda Goodfry, and she said she wants to help us."

"It's still a risky game you're playing with these guys. You heard what happened last night at Guigi's restaurant?" Mr. Robinson says.

Amy moves to the right, in front of him, and places her right foot on a box. She pulls her pants leg up slightly to reveal an ankle holster packing a small revolver. "It may be small, but sometimes a gal only needs one shot!"

"That's my granddaughter. I'm so proud of you. Now get your ass back to stocking the shelves and doing the inventory. This store ain't gonna run itself." Both head out to the front of the store and unlock the front doors, ready for the first customer of the day.

Marty leaves through the back door of Mr. Robinson's store, absolutely livid. He thinks about going back in there and just shooting the old man point-blank for being such an ass before deciding the better of it. Not to mention that he needs to collect one more week of the numbers game before he terminates it, as the rent is due on his apartment.

He struts down the alley, still peering over a shoulder now and then, watching for a cop or somebody with a gun to come forward and charge at him. Or fire a round or two in his direction. He knows the police probably have his photo plastered across every cop's desk in the morning briefing and now wonders if he'll be seeing his mug on the local 6 o'clock news.

"Ha," he says out loud to no one in particular. "I hope they at least got my good side." Moving quickly down the alley and coming out at a cross street, he immediately spots something near the next intersection—exactly what he was hoping for. Some poor schmuck trying to beat the system by parking on the street versus parking in a secured lot. Stealing a car from a lot with paid parking means you have to produce a ticket to avoid having to pay the full daily rate. The benefit of stealing a car parked randomly on the street is the part about it being free and not having to pay anything. He's known guys who've tried stealing a car parked in a lot and paying a whole day's rate, only to realize later that those specific parking lots have CCTV cameras recording everything and everyone.

A car parked on the street, especially an abandoned-looking street like this one, virtually calls to him, begging him to steal it. Marty is more than happy to oblige, whispering to himself as he pops open the lock and jumps in as though he owns it. In less than fifty seconds, forty-seven to be exact, Marty takes the now free transportation and drives toward his home.

"This is actually a nice car. Maybe I should keep it for a couple of days," he declares out loud before turning on the radio. He always sticks to just playing the radio in a stolen car. He remembers that once, with a car he stole last year, he thought it would be funny to play the current CD the owner had left in the stereo. The volume was turned all the way up, and it nearly scared the shit out of him, not to mention deafening him for a period of time, as it was some Euro techno beat that came blaring out of the speakers. He will never make that mistake again.

Aw, man, these presets are all off, he thinks as he quickly finds some classic rock stations and an alternative radio station in case the others have to go to commercial. Spinning the dial, he finally stops on one in particular. *Ah, finally, something good to cruise to,* he thinks as he drives off to his side of town, upping the volume on the stereo.

He drives to within a half mile of his apartment complex and stops in a large supermarket parking lot. He finds a spot midway down an aisle and pulls in. He thanks the car for the free transportation and casually wipes down the steering wheel. It doesn't matter too much, as there are often many fingerprints, and the police rarely ever obtain one, let alone his. The owner is usually happy about getting the car back in one piece rather than having the police find it at the bottom of a lake or its charred remains after it has been set on fire.

Marty begins to step out of the car and does his normal routine just in case there are any CCTV cameras that might pick him up or get a clear shot of him. First, he steps out but leans over. Next, he fakes a sneeze, and third, he turns away from the main entrance to the building. In that way, he reckons, the most somebody will ever see from the camera's perspective is a man covering most of his face before turning and walking away. He has done it every time he has ditched a stolen car and has never been arrested for grand theft auto, so why chance fate? It has worked for him successfully thus far.

This time, during his fake sneeze, a stranger walking by says, "Bless you," and he just gives a head nod in acknowledgment before trying to sneeze again. *Phew, that was close,* he thinks, as he was facing the store and the main camera might actually capture a good image of him, for once. He then cuts through the parking lot and heads to a sidewalk leading down to the main busy street. He moves up a couple of blocks, then turns to the right and heads up three blocks before turning left this time. He then walks down three-fourths of the block until he finds the door he is searching for along row after row of similar-looking buildings. He steps up the three steps and rests, raising a hand to punch in the key code to the open the first door. He walks in, then pulls out the card that will allow him to access the buttons on the elevator.

At first, he thought all these push-button codes and keycards were a waste of time. Nowadays, it is incorporated into his daily routine, and he feels it adds a bit of deterrence to anyone trying to break into his apartment complex. He's been here over two years and has never heard of anyone getting robbed or broken into. *Maybe the security does pay off,* he thinks as the elevator doors open and he whips the keycard against the reader, thus allowing him to activate the button for his floor. The doors close quickly, possibly part of the preventive security system.

As the elevator goes up, he remembers he has an appointment with Boss Nunzio next week. His actions directly contributed to Nunzio's survival of the shootout last night. Nunzio should be most pleased with his performance as a guard and security backup and will most likely honor the job offer with the organization. However, Marty feels he has let down Mazoli, but life goes on, and the living ones must endure now and mourn the dead later.

Marty feels the elevator stop on his floor, and the doors fly open, giving him barely enough time to exit the elevator. He walks down the hallway, still lost in thought over his former boss and the meeting next week to work for a new gang or organization. He walks down the quiet hallway, stops at his apartment door, and enters his home, slamming the door quickly behind, with the door automatically locking. He plans on not leaving his place for the next seven days and takes a quick inventory of food and supplies, also assessing what he might get as takeout or have delivered. Closing the refrigerator door, he resigns himself to beginning his search for the delivery menus in his junk drawer in the kitchen.

One week later

Marty had decided to leave the apartment one day to check his snail mail so as not to warrant any suspicion. He did not want a do-gooder to call to have a person check on him and having one's mail start piling up in the box is certainly a way to raise a warning flag. Last night he actually went out, way out of the area, and used a share-ride app to get to the other side of town just for a change of venue.

However, this morning, he had to steal a car to get back to his side of town. He ditched it not far from his apartment, deciding to walk the rest of the way. He even remembered to collect the mail en route.

Now, he feels relatively safe as he gets close to his building. Perhaps that's why he doesn't think much of the guy walking toward him, who passes him and then turns around, brandishing a knife toward his back.

He has little time to react other than to turn around, reaching for the said knife with one hand and pulling out a gun with the other. Although he moves rather fast, he turns around to see a gun pointing at his head as well as the knife inches away from his chest.

Marty takes a gasp of air. "Oh. Good morning, Bruce. You must be here to escort me today?"

The brazen, slightly older, hard-as-nails guy replies, "Yes, Marty. Today's the day. I thought of waiting in your apartment early this morning, but you are most late getting home from last night. I'd probably rather not know what you've been up to." Bruce smiles as he puts the gun away and folds back the knife before making it disappear as well.

"Well, it was a long night. I was on the other side of town, clubbing and celebrating my unemployment. You know, the one time I finally leave the apartment, and now you give me slack. I did have to acquire public transport getting back over here."

Bruce has to chuckle. "Clubbing? That, I'd rather not know about. So where did you ditch the stolen car?"

"Supermarket parking lot, of course. My usual go-to place. You'd be surprised how many stolen cars are in that lot!" Marty unlocks the front door and walks in, with Bruce following directly behind him and slamming the door after they enter.

Marty excuses himself to change clothes and clean himself up, leaving the living room and heading straight to the bedroom. Bruce takes a quick look around the main living areas, surveying Marty's modest living style and guessing how much money he spends on furniture and such. He even takes a peek into the liquor cabinet. Although it is about time for a morning pick-me-up, he is more interested in this guy's level of spending on liquor and other extras. Clearly, Bruce judges, Marty's not a bottom-shelf guy, as there's a fair number of bottles that are over forty dollars and even some decent bottles of scotch. *Hmm, maybe this Marty guy with fit right in.* Bruce definitely will make a point to stop by Marty's place more often for a friendly visit or a raid on his liquor stash.

Marty returns, cleaner, and he heads into the kitchen. "Do you want some coffee? Or a shot of something?" He asks, watching Bruce study the liquor collection and thinking he should offer his guest everything and anything just to be polite.

"Nah. Tempting. But coffee's fine. Black. With sugar." Bruce continues his survey, taking mental notes of the layout of the place. He had the idea of breaking in and scaring the shit of out Marty in the future, and he is making his nefarious plans in the back of his mind.

Turning back toward the kitchen, Bruce asks Marty, "So are you ready to have this meeting with Nunzio? He certainly wants to meet with the guy who saved his life."

"Reckon so, as I am currently unemployed at the moment. I suppose you'd rather wait until we're in the meeting with the boss to discuss . . . you know, what happened last week."

Nodding his head to Marty, he lets out a sigh. "Yes. Afraid so. Oh, I am sorry about all of them, your boss and your buddy and especially the woman. What was her name again? It slips my mind."

"Carrie. Yes. Thank you," Marty sternly replies, thinking in his head that was probably the worst offer of condolences he has ever heard. *Seriously? Does this guy have no compassion?* His face begins to tighten the more he thinks about Carrie, Mickey, and Mazoli. They were like family to him. And Carrie, yes, Carrie, she was something a little more. Now he has to man up and play the tough guy again, trying not to lose face. He hands the coffee over to Bruce, whose face is expressionless.

Each drinks his own coffee, and no conversation is spoken between them. Both look back at one another, waiting for the other to say something, but both stand mute—or possibly stubborn. In the end, Bruce puts his coffee mug down on the counter and slips it over to Marty, signaling that he has finished and they should go. They depart Marty's place and head downstairs, then walk to the spot where Bruce parked his own car, about a block away to. Getting in on the passenger side, Marty wonders if the car is Bruce's or if it was recently acquired, a.k.a. stolen. The car then zooms, off heading to Boss Nunzio's estate.

The estate is even more impressive than he imagined. They drive up a long driveway and eventually circle back around to the backside of the house. *House* is a very loose term to use to describe the impressive mansion estate before him. All Marty can think is that Nunzio's illegal operations have a lot more working capital than his former boss's did. He smiles, reckoning he's moved up to the big leagues now.

The car finally parks in the garage, a very large garage housing numerous cars—some expensive and, surprisingly, some cheap beaters. Marty laughs at the old Delta 88 with the whitewall tires before signaling to Bruce.

"Is this your other car, Bruce?" Marty points to the one car in particular.

"No. But it will be yours if you don't stop fucking around."

"No. Seriously. Who is driving that piece of shit?"

Without hesitation, the two of them move through the garage, and Bruce remarks, "Oh, you be surprised how many times we use that one. Besides, it's a lot of fun to just going cruisin' around town, and the sound system in that one is surprisingly awesome."

Marty is left with a blank expression, but upon thinking about it some more, he decides it would be kind of fun to drive a big old car like that. Maybe even jam some 60s surf music in the tape deck. Assuming it has a tape deck—it could be an eight-track. Bruce grabs his shoulder, and Marty is lost in thought as he is pushed toward the back door to the house. There, an armed guard stands sentry.

"Our first line of defense." Bruce turns to Marty. "Say hello to Joey."

Marty smiles and says hello to the sentry guy. The guy only nods his head in reply to Marty but acknowledges Bruce more respectfully. The two then enter the house and walk down a hallway.

At the end of the long hallway is a large oak door. The hand-carved door is beautiful and ornate. Marty is transfixed by the door and bumps into the guard standing next to it.

"You know, Bruce. If I had a dollar for every schmuck that bumps into me while they are staring at the door for the first time, I would be rich." Jim or Jimmy, the guard, states sarcastically.

Bruce snorts. "But you are rich."

"Apparently not rich enough." Jimmy opts not to say anything more on his wealth or how much he is paid, choosing his words carefully for fear of it getting back to the boss. Instead, he gives Marty a once-over and asks Bruce, "Who's the cherry?"

Marty gives a crazy look to Jimmy that almost scares him a bit. Marty lurches forward and gets into Jimmy's face, then withdraws and outstretches a friendly hand.

Jimmy cautiously puts out his own hand and shakes the new guy's hand while keeping his other hand on his sidearm, readying himself for anything.

"See here, Jimmy," Bruce interjects. "Marty is a little crazy, but he also saved Nunzio's life in the shootout."

"No way!" Pointing to Marty, he marvels, "This guy? No way. Bullshit."

"The very one and the same. Now cut him some slack before I cut you myself." Bruce brandishes a shiny knife toward Jimmy's throat. Not touching but close enough to give the guy a hurried shave. He then retracts the blade and puts the knife back into his pocket. Turning to Marty, he says, "Now, Jimmy has strict orders to kill first and shoot second if anyone tries to enter the boss's office when not called upon to enter. Also"—he points to cameras mounted in two of the corners of the ceiling—"the boss is always watching."

"The boss is telling me that he is ready to see you both," Jimmy interjects, "but he wants to talk to Bruce alone first." He turns his head and motions to the door, and that's when Marty can see the earpiece in the guard's right ear.

Bruce opens the heavy oak door and closes it immediately. Jimmy points to a chair, nonverbally telling Marty to sit. Marty takes the hint and sits down, waiting patiently to be called into the office.

A few minutes of silence pass until the guard leans over, whispering to Marty, "Say, I heard you're really good on sports betting."

"I'm decent." He has a silent chuckle in his head.

The guard was expecting a more confident reply but continues anyway. "So. You think you can supply me with some picks for this weekend? Maybe for a couple of games?"

"I dunno. What's in it for me? Do I get a percentage of your winnings?"

"Why, you greedy bastard," the guard says, raising his voice at first and then quickly lowering it, realizing he is supposed to be working, guarding the door and such.

"Come again? Do you have something to trade, then?"

"Well, no."

"Then twenty percent is a good number to start off with."

"Piss off."

Marty stands up and adjusts himself, brushing any lint off. He turns to the guard, smiling with a smug look. "Let me get this straight. You otherwise suck at sports betting, yet I'm rather gifted at it. You've even heard of my, let's just say, gift for producing winners. Yet, you still balk at the mere notion of me asking for a measly twenty percent when you could be winning eighty percent on sure winners. Well, my friend, money is money. It's kinda arbitrary how much you take home at the end of the day when you started with nothing. I'm not following your logic." He then turns to face the large mirror and checks himself one more time. In reality, he is waiting patiently and letting it sink in with the guard.

The guard starts to say something, but he then puts up his right hand to his right ear and looks at one of the cameras, shaking his head up and down. He turns to Marty. "The boss will see you now."

At the same moment, Bruce opens the door and waves Marty in. Being a little nervous, Marty steadies himself and coughs once to clear the lump in his throat. He then raises a thumb and finger in the gesture of a gun and points it at the guard, acting as if he is firing it, and tells the guard to think about his offer. He then steps into the office with Bruce, the door slamming shut behind them.

Meeting the new boss

The first thing Marty sees upon entering the office is Boss Nunzio standing behind his desk and holding a drink. The second thing he sees is the rather large mahogany desk that separates the distance between Marty and Nunzio. The third thing he sees is Nunzio putting the drink down and moving quickly around the large desk with his large arms outstretched, ready to give Marty a big bear hug.

"Marty! Marty!" The boss then squeezes Marty so tight that he can't even gasp for a breath.

Eventually, Nunzio releases some of the force seconds before Marty would have passed out from asphyxiation. He is still in shock from having the life-force choked out of him, but the boss is overly jubilant.

"You saved my life, dammit!" Smiling, he gives him a friendly smack on the cheek, still grinning from ear to ear. He shouts out to Bruce, "Get this man a glass of the finest scotch." He beams at Marty one more time and then retreats back behind his desk as the drink from Bruce arrives in Marty's hand. Everyone is motioned to raise their glasses for a toast in Marty's honor and then to sit down. Marty takes a sip from the extra-large pour, and he savors it even more upon taking the second sip as he sits down.

Everyone is all smiles, and Marty takes a moment as the alcohol begins to course through his veins and reach his brain. Distracted for a second, he studies the layout of the office, with its oversize windows and French doors leading out to a beautiful, well-manicured lawn with a small patio to the side. Returning to looking around the office, he takes note of where the bar is located, the various items on the bookcases, and even the massive eight-foot pool table off to his right. He thinks to himself that if he worked from home, this is how he would imagine his office to be laid out. He takes another sip and then puts the glass down so as not to drink too fast. The boss does the same thing.

Nunzio leans back to stare at the other two men in the room. He is still reeling from the joyous meeting in which he got to embrace the man who saved him from being shot and killed. But that moment is over now, and it is time to get down to business. He sits upright, scoots his chair in, and puts his hands together on the desk.

"Gentlemen. We have several pressing issues going forward after the attack from last week. But"—he pauses momentarily, deep in thought—"we must first do something necessary." He turns toward Marty. "We must offer employment and membership in our family to Marty."

Marty turns red but is proud, deep inside, to be part of a family again, even if it is a mob family.

Bruce commands Marty to stand up as the boss walks around the desk to where Bruce and Marty are now standing. Bruce steps back to retrieve the sword from the mantel and hands it to Nunzio.

Nunzio smiles at Marty. "As I swear a solemn allegiance to uphold the family name to my father and to his father before him." He then faces Marty directly. "I now ask of you, Marty. Do you swear allegiance to the Nunzio mob family to your death?"

"Uh . . . yes." Marty knows those words just bound him to this family until he dies or Nunzio dies. This is the way of the mob, traditional and demanding of unwavering loyalty.

"Very well." Nunzio taps the family sword on Marty's head twice. "Welcome to the Nunzio family." Bruce takes the sword and puts it away, then returns and gives Marty a punch on the arm, laughing. "Welcome, brother."

Nunzio steps back to the desk and withdraws a large, overstuffed envelope and throws it down on the table in front of Marty. "Here. This is for you."

Staring at the envelope, Marty steps forward and scoops it up, trying to tuck it into his suit pocket discreetly, but it is too large. He decides to place it on the table next to the rocks glass that is being refilled by Bruce. Marty wants to say something in regard to the bartending service Bruce is providing, but Bruce beats him to the punch.

"Listen. Don't get used to this. Today is your day. After that, you can get your own damn drinks." They all share a laugh.

"OK. Quiet down." Nunzio hushes the room, and they quickly fall silent, waiting patiently for the boss to speak.

Bruce and Marty take their seats after the boss sits down behind his large desk.

Nunzio takes a deep breath first and then says, "Now, the ACS took out two good men." Marty stares intently at the boss, practically giving him the evil eye, as it is written all over his face. Nunzio corrects himself, quickly adding, "And a good woman. We must exact revenge of the highest order, but now is not the time to strike." He pounds a fist on the table. Marty nearly jumps out of his seat.

Bruce and Marty try to maintain a poker face and keep their opinions to themselves for the time being.

Nunzio continues, "Therefore, we must regroup, and we must start to make alliances with our other brethren. There will be no knee-jerk reactions at this time. We must be smart, and we must be better, in order to defeat this common enemy that plagues our beloved territory. Ahem."

"Yes, yes," the two men in the audience agree, although they have no choice in the matter.

"In addition, you two will be leaving town for an extended vacation. Well, not exactly a vacation, but I have some business that needs attending to, and it involves both of you leaving town immediately. In other words, take a break from this town. Let these headlines about the murders die down in the media. The police are probably looking for both of you right now, anyway, for questioning. Let the police investigation get bogged down, and then, when the time is right in the foreseeable future, we can exact revenge for Mazoli and the others."

Marty goes from utter joy to utter disappointment with these words. He wants to hurt those who killed his boss, his friend, and his lover. He wants to do it right now, and instead he has been given a pass to leave town on some small-time assignment with Bruce. Well, maybe it is important to Nunzio, but Marty doesn't care about that at the moment. He was hoping they would be killing ACS gangsters this afternoon and be home by seven to have dinner. Instead, he has to flee town and go on a road trip. He resigns himself to unenthusiastically agreeing with the boss for the time being—Nunzio is now the new boss, the new employer. Still, he secretly vows to himself that he will take the chance to get his revenge, especially for Carrie, should the opportunity present itself in the near future. He makes a mental note that he has to visit one more place before he and Bruce hit the road.

"Yes. This all sounds great. I will do what you ask. Thank you, Boss." Marty smiles forcefully at Nunzio and stands up to his extended hand, shaking it. Turning to Bruce, he thanks him for fetching the drinks, telling him he did an excellent job, although the ice started to melt too fast.

"Don't push it, buddy. We're hitting the road and leaving this afternoon."

"Right, but I got a few things I gotta do."

Bruce looks down at his watch. "Fine. I will meet you at your place in three hours. Is that enough time for you?"

"Sure. Please don't show up in the Delta 88!"

"Wouldn't you just love that . . . Now scram. I gotta talk to the boss some more. Go see Joey to arrange transportation for you. I'll let him know."

Marty grabs his envelope and slams the drink down, but then he picks up the glass and returns it to the bar, quickly departing the office.

Say goodbye with flowers

Stopping the car, Marty spots a prime parking spot near to the store. He parks, figuring he's not going to get much closer, and turns off the engine but does not get out just yet. Taking a deep breath, he debates in his head whether to tell them his girlfriend, the one they were so fond of, died last week in the shootout. Of course, they are both tied to the mob in one way or another and have probably heard the news by now, along with the news of Mickey and Mazoli's untimely deaths. Still, they may be effective in running a drug distribution system, but they are the most caring people he has ever met, and they need to know, to hear it from him. He still wonders if they smoke some of the product they distribute all around town.

Eventually manning up, he steps out of the car and struts toward the store, thinking he will figure it out by the time he walks through the door. He arrives at the florist shop in less than three minutes.

"Good afternoon," Chad says. He is currently working on a beautiful rose floral arrangement and has his back turned to the door. "I'll be with you in a second, as I'm just finishing this up. Feel free to browse and tell me if you see anything you like."

Marty attempts to disguise his voice and says in a deep tone, "Sure thing, pal."

Not two seconds later, Cindy comes running out from the back and practically tackles Marty with a strong embrace. One second behind her comes the second round of hugs, with Chad wrapping his strong arms around both of them.

"Marty! *Marty*! What are you doing, trying to hide from us?" Cindy blurts.

"I ... I ... dunno." He strains to refill his lungs after having the life-force nearly sucked out of him, just like with Nunzio.

Chad lobs question after question at him. "Yeah, buddy. What have you been doing? How's that girl of yours? What's her name?"

"Carrie," Cindy says, completing his thought.

"Yes, yes—Carrie. She is such a sweet lass. When are we ever gonna meet her?" Cindy sends him a second glance, but Chad doesn't take notice of it or understand what he said to warrant such a look.

"She is," Marty replies gravely.

"So," Cindy says, keeping the conversation going," did she like the extra-special arrangement we made for her the last time you requested one? We both put our heart and soul into building that for her."

Chad laughs, turning toward her. "I almost forgot—she almost got an ounce of weed packaged in with the arrangement. Now that would have been funny. For us and not you, obviously!" Marty thinks he could use some of that stuff right about now.

Cindy leans toward him with a worried look, sensing something is wrong with Marty. He seems distracted or just not quite right. She takes his arm, asking, "Did Carrie not like the flowers, dear?"

Marty shakes his head. "No, no. It's not that." He feels his eyes dampening but maintains his composure and says, "There was an incident last week . . . You may have heard about."

Chad and Cindy look to one another with blank expressions. Chad responds, "No, we avoid watching the news, and we don't bother with social media. Hell, boy, we don't even have a TV. We mostly listen to the radio at work—you know, happy songs."

"Well, I'll tell you, then. There was a shooting last week at Guigi's restaurant."

Chad instinctively wraps his arm around his wife. Cindy tenses up but listens earnestly to Marty next words, although, in her mind, she is already preparing for the worst.

"I don't know any other way to tell you both, so I will just say it. Hell, you will hear about it soon enough anyway. I'm surprised you haven't already." Marty is nervous and just jibber-jabbering away. Cindy and Chad look confused and wish he would just say what he wants to say.

Marty tries a second attempt, more blunt. "A rival gang attacked us at Guigi's Italiano restaurant."

"Oh, that place. They have a real tasty ragù sauce. I remember the last time—" Chad is cut off as Cindy shushes him to be silent. Chad whispers he is sorry in very soft tones.

"Please, Marty. Tell us exactly what happened." Cindy pushes to the point of anguish because she wants to know, whether she will like hearing the rest or not, and wants to hear it from him. Meanwhile, Chad is still thinking of the Italian ragù sauce and the last time they ate there, wondering if he should take his wife out to dinner next week. He stops daydreaming once he hears Marty's voice.

"The two bosses, Mazoli and Nunzio, were having a dinner meeting to discuss . . . current issues." Marty decides not to mention the full scoop on the meeting. "They had just received their predinner drinks, and then the shooter, disguised as a waiter, approached the table and started shooting them. Point-blank. In cold blood. I mean, everyone thought, including me, I suppose, that it was a just a normal server or another waiter coming by to drop off cutlery or more bread. I don't know. I was guarding Nunzio, and I had a clear view of the waiter, well, shooter, and I took him down as fast as I could, saving Nunzio. But apparently, not fast enough." Marty pauses, choked up. "Not before he took out Mazoli and Mickey. They both had their backs turned to the shooter and never saw it coming."

"What about Carrie?"

"Yeah. Carrie." Marty loses it.

Cindy rushes to his side and holds him, wrapping an arm around him for moral support. At first, he brushes her off, but she doesn't relent, and he just accepts her next to him.

"Marty. Oh, Marty," Cindy whispers. Chad stands in from of him, not knowing what to do.

Marty regains the courage to continue. "Well, she was outside on guard duty. She never saw it coming—she never got a shot off. I am surprised. I would have assumed she would have . . . But ironically, it was probably hearing the shot in the distance—the one that most likely killed her—seconds before the server, or whatever, the guy with the gun, appeared that allowed me to be more reactive." Marty pauses, letting out a deep breath, only to have Cindy embrace him tightly again. "I wish I could have . . . maybe just . . ." Marty turns away as tears start to appear, and he hides his face from the two of them.

"Marty, dear. It wasn't your fault."

Marty looks at them, shame on his face. He takes both of their hands and tells them, "Carrie absolutely loved the arrangement I gave her weeks ago. It made her so happy, and she couldn't stop talking about the flowers. So thank you, both of you, thank you so much. She and I really did appreciate it."

Cindy begins to cry at this point. Chad attempts to comfort his wife while she bellows out, "Oh, Marty! We are so sorry . . ."

Chad is at a loss for words and is thinking about two things. One is that he is sad to hear the news about Carrie—he thought she was all right, not shot dead in some mob war. But more importantly, the second thing is that he and Cindy are now stuck with a ton of weed, and Mazoli, their now-dead employer, is no longer around. What are they going to do with all this weed? His mind continues to run different scenarios as he haphazardly attempts to be engaged in the conversation. He truly is sorry to hear about everyone shot and killed last week, but his current priority is to protect him and Cindy.

"You say you saved Nunzio's life? That's great. He must be most appreciative of your services. Did he hire you on the spot?"

"Funny you mention that. I now work for Nunzio. He offered me a job this morning, as a matter of fact."

"Huh. You don't say. Well, damn."

Chad, Cindy, and Marty take a moment and remain silent as they think about and continue to mourn their fallen comrades and friends. After a while, Marty then turns to depart, citing some reason he has to leave town for a bit, saying he will try to come by and see them when he returns. He also makes a special request that they send flowers to Carrie's funeral as well to those of the other two. He doesn't know any details about funeral arrangements, but he figures they are florists, so it wouldn't look suspicious for them to be calling around for details about the three people gunned down last week. He tries to hand them a couple of hundred-dollar bills, but they both refuse his money, telling him they will take care of it—no questions asked and no money accepted from him.

They all share one more embrace, and then the two of them watch Marty leave through the front door. Chad then turns to Cindy and takes her into his arms. That is a sign that he has something serious to tell her, she recalls as she moves closer to his body, for both warmth and security.

"What is it dear?" She knows he always will protect her and their interest, no matter what the costs.

He begs the question. "What are we going to do with all this weed?"

"You mean who is going to pay us back for it. You better call Nunzio right away and make some arrangement. Fast. Like get on the phone right now."

"I'm telling you. We should get paid out for these outstanding orders and deliveries. After that, I dunno. Maybe just close down the shop. Hell, quickly sell the place and move somewhere else. Setup shop in a few months. Maybe in time for the next floral holiday." He chuckles.

Cindy is still glazing out the front window. "I completely agree with you. Let's move out west. Let's get outta here, like now."

"Absolutely." Chad agrees completely. "The store is closed. Permanently. Say, you wanna go to dinner tonight. Something different?"

"It's about time you said that, dear." She breaks from the embrace and turns the sign on the door to the SORRY, WE'RE CLOSED side and locks the door.

Policing the situation

Amanda Goodfry firmly waits until the automatic doors open and then steps forward, impatiently, as the doors swing open. Her long dark hair, with a tinge of gray, flows back in the breeze generated by the opening of the doors. She glances over to the desk sergeant, who is staring at her as she walks through the front office. He eyes her one more time, this time looking specifically for a particular item. Amanda holds up her detective badge, and the desk sergeant hits the button to open the main door into the police station.

Amanda thinks, *Honestly. Bill sees me every day but won't hit the buzzer until he sees the badge. Really? So much for comradery in this place.* She passes a conciliatory wave to him as she passes through the secured door and heads down the hall to the detective's office.

She arrives at her desk a little earlier than most detectives on her shift, which gives her time to make a fresh pot of coffee. She can smell the stench from the pot of coffee left over from the night shift, and it's absolutely vile. She would never just heat it back up, but she knows there are some police officers who are too lazy to make a fresh pot. It's the same ones who never wash out their coffee or tea mugs either. In her mind, it doesn't matter as she unlocks her desk drawer, the second one down, to retrieve her personal and, more importantly, clean coffee mug.

After making the pot of coffee and pouring herself a mug of joe, she sits back down at her desk, relaxing and taking in the aroma of the coffee. Opening her eyes, she then returns to reality. She looks over to see her current caseload sitting off to the right on her desk, and she glances over to the left side with the case folders marked "Unsolved—pending." She doesn't reach for either pile; rather, she bends over to reach down to the third drawer in her desk and unlocks it. In this drawer are the files she doesn't want prying eyes looking at. She digs through the pile before finding the right one and pulls out the manila folder marked "Amy."

Opening it up, her memory jogs back, reminding her of the details of this particular case. Well, it's not really a case but more of an ongoing investigation of various incidents that she is trying to piece together to make a case. There is a sticky note annotating the meeting she has today with Amy and her grandfather, Mr. Robinson, the owner of the newsstand store.

Interesting. Let's see what this Amy has to say. She remembers a brief phone conversation with the woman in regard to a male, named Marty, who was up to no good. Going through the folder, there is a log dated months ago about a chance meeting the detective had with this Marty fellow in the store. Reading the rest of the log, she sees she made an annotation at the time that Marty has possible connections to organized crime, specifically the Mazoli gang, as the newsstand is in their territory. She thinks for a moment, vaguely remembering meeting this fellow, but it was a brief encounter.

Blindly reaching over for her mug, she nearly knocks it over but grabs it quickly and secures it firmly in her grasp. With its warmth still generating from within, she inhales the aroma as she takes a deeper sip of the strong Colombian blend. Satisfied for the moment, she flips back to the most current item in the folder, a copy of the police report involving the shooting of three suspected members of Mazoli gang along with the main shooter, suspected of having ties to the Asian Crime Syndicate.

I wonder if this Marty fellow was there that night. If so, why isn't he lying in the morgue like the others?

"Hmm. Maybe Amy will give me some new insights about this man," Amanda says to herself, hastening to put the folder away because her fellow detectives have started to enter the office.

"Good morning, Amanda. Is the coffee fresh?" Another detective, Frank, puts down his coat and glances over to the coffee pot. It must have been the first thing he smelled when he entered the office.

"Of course it is. I wouldn't be drinking it otherwise." She raises her mug toward his direction as a good-morning acknowledgment.

"Yeah. You're right about that." Frank moves over to Amanda's desk and leans against her half-partitioned wall. "So, when do you want to start working on the Guigi's shooting case, Amanda? I have collected some more witness statements since the shooting last week."

What's the summation, Frank? I will read all the statements, but is there anything that sticks out? Did any of witnesses actually provide something useful we can use?"

"As a matter of fact, yes."

Amanda stares at him. "Well, what have you got? Tell me!"

"Oh. Yes. Everyone's story collaborates the shooter on the victims' side." The detective taps his head as if trying to jar his memory. When he suddenly remembers what he wanted to say, he exclaims, "*Yes*! They all described the same guy who shot back and killed the shooter."

Amanda reaches over and beings to dig through a couple of folders on her desk as if searching for something. She finds it and hands a photo of Marty to the nonchalant detective, who is standing there, drinking his coffee. The detective looks at the photo and shakes his head up and down. "Yep, this matches their description of the guy. Do you know him?"

"I am about to meet with someone who knows him well." She cracks a half smile. "A former business partner, from what I hear, and he attempted to go on a date with his granddaughter."

"Who in the hell is that?" Frank acts surprised, as he doesn't know the connection.

"Mr. Robinson. The newsstand store owner, downtown. Although it seems his granddaughter is more keen on wanting to talk to me than the old guy is. Imagine that!"

The other detective retorts, "Probably because he's wrapped up in doing something illegal with this Marty fellow. Well, good luck. Let me know what you find out. I've still got two more people to interview, and then I'll be done." Frank then turns around and walks back to his desk, chatting up another detective who has just arrived at work.

Pre-trip packing

Sitting in the bedroom, Marty is deciding what exactly to pack for this road trip he has been ordered to take with Bruce, someone whom he barely knows yet who is picking him up in under thirty minutes.

Marty thinks, *Am I to assume there will be time to launder my clothes, or do I need to bring enough clothing for each day? Am I supposed to look like a mobster, with pinstripe suits, or should I go business casual? Bruce didn't exactly give me specific instructions on what to bring or what we will be doing.*

Marty has stacks of clothes and a few pairs of shoes lying about on the bed. He also plans on bringing two handguns, a pair of brass knuckles, and a reliable knife that fits snugly into an ankle wrap. He figures Bruce will be armed most of the time, and he should be prepared to provide ample backup. Both Nunzio and Bruce provided very little background information on this assignment. He gets it that he and Bruce probably need to get out of town sooner versus later because the police are conducting their investigation of the shooting last week, and he and Bruce are likely persons of interest. Well, they are murderers, actually, as they both shot at the ACS shooter. Marty still contends it was his bullets, and not Bruce's, that killed the shooter. He swears he saw Bruce firing wildly that night, and it would be best to never mention that fact to anyone, ever.

Marty unzips the oversize, yet lightweight, black suitcase and begins to stuff as many clothes and other items as he can possibly fit into it. That way, he should be covered for just about any type of situation and weather forecast. He even packs gym clothes and swimming trunks because there has to be some downtime, at some point, over the next few weeks.

He really doesn't know how long they will be on the road, but at least he has paid his rent in advance, and the utilities are under automatic-withdrawal plans. Some things ought to be easy in one's life, and automatic payments have greatly simplified his bill-paying process. He wants to ask a neighbor to check on his place and get the mail, but he realizes that he doesn't know any of the neighbors at all. He thinks there is a woman next door and a couple on the other side. He recalls maybe even waving to one of them at some point months ago. *Wow, I really wouldn't be missed if I never returned. At least the utilities will be paid until my bank account is depleted. Maybe when I get back, I should make a point to introduce myself to a few people in the building.*

Taking a break from packing, he reaches across the bed to grab his laptop and signs in. He does a quick internet search and fills out the form for the postal service to have his mail put on hold for two weeks. He logs out and shuts down the computer, only to hear a knock at the door.

"Oh, great. The taxi service is here, and I ain't done yet." Looking back at the suitcase, he figures he better go answer the door and let Bruce into the apartment. Then he can prepare to get heckled by Bruce.

Marty opens the door cautiously. He sees Bruce standing there in a beach hat and sporting a tacky-colored Hawaiian shirt. Bursting out laughing, he eventually controls the giggles for a second. "I didn't know we were going on a cruise. Come on in, skipper. Do you want a margarita or piña colada?"

Bruce is not deterred by the immature laughter from Marty and simply pushes past him, entering the apartment and making himself at home by heading over to the bar. "Those drinks take too long to make, and we are short on time." He then selects a bottle and dispenses a straight pour of tequila. He walks past the bedroom and studies the packing stage that Marty is currently in and sighs, resigning himself to wait on the sofa until Marty's done.

"Go ahead. Make yourself comfortable," Marty says with a sarcastic tone.

After taking a big gulp from the glass, Bruce says, "I might as well, judging from the packing you haven't finished yet. Where's the TV remote?" He searches around the coffee table for it.

"For your information, I am almost done."

"Should I remind you that this is a road trip? We ain't moving off to college for a year." Finding the remote, he clicks on the TV and searches for something interesting to watch.

Marty gives up and retreats back to the bedroom to finish the packing task. He removes a few clothes based on Bruce's clue and hurries along to pack up a toiletry bag—he doesn't want to have to share with old Bruce.

Finishing up, he wheels the large suitcase into the living room near the front door. He grabs a few things and stuffs them in a backpack. Bruce is still glued to the TV, actively engaged in some nature show about Antarctica and the few animals that live there. Marty also notices that the glass has been refilled and thinks, *I guess that means I'm driving first.*

"OK. All set. Are you ready?" Marty announces.

"Oh, come on. I was really getting into this. We'll go in about ten minutes."

"Seriously?"

"Ha-ha. No." He clicks the TV off and chugs the remaining bit left in the glass. He motions with the glass as if asking where to put it. Marty snatches it and drops it in the sink, rinsing it out.

Bruce heads toward the door. "Are you sure you got everything?" He stares down at the large suitcase. "By the looks of it, you must have brought everything. Fair enough. Let's get this show on the road." He opens the door and steps out into the hallway, not bothering to hold the door.

Marty attempts to follow along as he slings the backpack on his shoulders. He then performs the balancing act of opening the door, dragging the suitcase while holding the door, and then pushing it to the side as he locks up his apartment. While he is doing this, he begins to hear voices. He recognizes Bruce's, but he doesn't recognize a feminine voice.

Finishing locking the door, Marty turns and grabs the pull handle on the suitcase, only to see Bruce chatting up, presumably, his neighbor. He slows his pace and stops next to Bruce, waiting until they have a break in their conversation.

"And then I said, 'I don't have a wife,'" Bruce says, delivering what sounds like a punchline. Both of them laugh.

The neighbor does a double take at Marty as he gets caught gazing. She reaches out her hand and introduces herself. "Hello. We finally get to meet. I'm Marissa and just moved in about three weeks ago."

Marty appears transfixed by the stunning, mid-twenties blonde in tight, neon orange, workout clothes talking to him. He takes her hand and introduces himself. "Hi, I'm Marty, and I live right there." He immediately feels like a doofus, but he is all too nervous meeting her. Smitten at first sight.

"I know, silly. Your friend Bruce has been most entertaining. He was telling me you two are going to a stag party for the week at a dude ranch out west. That sounds so exciting. You will have to come over for dinner when you return. I like to think I can cook pretty good, but bring a bottle of wine, and I'm sure it will taste great!" Bruce starts the laughter, with Marty joining in. Marissa smiles at Marty and goes inside her own apartment.

The men pause to take a deep breath and then walk down the hallway to the elevator. The doors open, and both enter the empty space. The elevator descends as Bruce punches Marty in the arm.

"What the hell was that for?" he exclaims.

"She moved in and you never introduced yourself? What are you, a hermit or something?"

"Yeah. I was just thinking earlier that I should get to know my neighbors a little bit better."

"Well, it seems she definitely wants to get to know you a little bit better. Ha-ha!" Bruce teases him.

"Really great timing on this stag party of ours," Marty says, maintaining the cover story that Bruce told Marissa. "Now I have to learn to ride a horse and shoot guns. At least I can shoot guns!"

"Maybe she is more interested in riding the broncos than you shooting your gun." He then roars with uncontrollable hilarity at his own joke.

Marty's face turns beet red just in time for the elevator doors to open. Bruce is still chuckling away, and Marty simply grabs his suitcase and walks toward the exit. Bruce hastens to catch up and grabs him by the shoulder, handing a set of car keys over to him. "You get to drive first."

"I'm glad I've been the source of your amusement."

"Let's see if your driving is better than your joke telling."

"I'm still waiting for you to tell me something worth laughing at."

Bruce doesn't need a second to think and instantly replies, "You finally get to meet your neighbor, and now you have to leave for two weeks. Now that's funny."

Marty grins. "Yeah. It kinda is." They find the car and load up the suitcase. It's a tight squeeze because Bruce has his own suitcase in the trunk, and there are several sealed boxes taking up residence in the trunk as well.

"What are these?" he asks, but Bruce simply brushes the question off.

"Don't worry about it. For now." Bruce leaves it at that and gets in on the passenger side. Marty decides not to worry about it, throws his backpack in the back, and climbs in behind the driver's wheel. He makes a few quick adjustments and starts the engine, readying himself for their road trip.

"Hey. Thanks for not bringing the Delta 88."

"No sweat. This car is less suspicious-looking anyway. Now hit the gas and let's get outta here. Get on the expressway and head west."

Marty pulls into traffic and makes his way down the road. "What's our first stop? You gonna tell me?"

"Nope. Now drive. I'm gonna take a nap, so don't be blaring the radio too loud."

Marty swerves the car a bit and taps the brakes, but it doesn't faze Bruce at all, or at least he doesn't allow it to bother him. Marty decides to let the guy sleep while he drives in a westward direction.

Meeting at the newsstand

Amanda signs out an undercover car from the motor pool and heads over to the east side of town. Her meeting is in thirty minutes, and it should take her about fifteen minutes to get there, twenty minutes tops. She couldn't care less if she was late, anyway, because she could cite her delay as being due to other police matters. However, she doesn't want to postpone this meeting with Amy because she feels she could glean a lot of information on this Marty guy. It seems he has been popping up on her radar recently, and she wants to know why, and more importantly, she wants to know how much of a disruptive person he could potentially be—especially to the secret agenda she has with her other partners.

She drives within five blocks of the newsstand and then quickly parks the car after spying a readily available spot on the street. She gets out and pays the meter with some loose change, putting in enough to secure her spot for two hours. The last thing she wants is a parking ticket, but the meter readers have been decent about not ticketing unmarked police cars. Still, it might be the one day a parking attendant has a vendetta against the police and is ever so eager to ticket anyone and everyone, including the police.

She walks down the sidewalk, trying to blend in rather than appearing to be an undercover detective. She looks at the time and figures she still has about eight minutes to kill, and she's only two blocks away. She sees a small park and finds an empty bench, taking out her phone to make a call.

"Yeah. What do you want?" the other caller responds right away, in a blunt voice.

Amanda replies, "Aren't you rude."

"You know the rules. No names. You never know who's listening. So I guess I don't have to be polite either." He snorts and then pauses before continuing with a louder voice, "And if someone is listening, then up yours, asshole!"

"All right, funny guy. Can you be serious for a minute?" Amanda says, attempting to steer the conversation toward the topic she wants to discuss.

"Sure. I can be serious. Or Fred or Drake or anyone else." He starts to laugh, obviously more of an amusement to himself versus others.

Sighing, Amanda replies, "Would you just listen for a sec? I'm seeing a potential problem for our plan. There seems to be a new player in town. This Marty guy is making quite a name for himself recently. Showing up with Mazoli and now Nunzio. You know anything about that?"

The unknown caller retorts, "I will have to inquire about that with my girl, although she hasn't mentioned anything. And she would be the one to know, hearing it straight from her uncle."

"Maybe she's holding out on you. I'm telling you, I still think she's on to you. You might find yourself digging your own grave."

"Nonsense. She doesn't suspect jack shit. The only thing I'm worried about is if you're gonna hold out on me tonight?"

Amanda blushes. "Why on earth would I do that?"

"Excellent. Meet you at the same place tonight, then?" the caller asks.

"Of course. Although do come up with better cover names this time. I think the hotel receptionist is onto us."

"Good lord, you are suspicious of everyone, dear."

"That's why I do the job I do."

"Fair enough. Goodbye, love."

"Love you too." Amanda hangs up the call and puts the phone back in her purse, next to her gun. She sits on the bench for a few more minutes, thinking about the recent phone call. She knows she's involved with a guy who is engaged to another woman, but she knows, deep down, that he really loves her and not the other woman. Besides, if this major operation of theirs goes down like they have planned, then afterward, they can be together, someday really soon. Until then, she has to maintain her cover, and she actually has a real job, being a police detective, to do. And that job helps her investigate potential problems that could throw their operation all to shit—exactly what she is trying to prevent at the moment. She stands up and walks the remaining couple of blocks to the newsstand for her meeting.

She reaches the newsstand and rechecks her phone for the time. *Precisely on time, as always.* Smiling, she enters the newsstand and walks around the small store, surveying it for future reference. She then heads to the register area and waits patiently in line; Mr. Robinson is behind the counter waiting on a customer.

"Good day, sir. What do you need?" Mr. Robinson asks the man, who is wearing a suit and talking on his phone, making what sounds like a business deal.

"Oh, a newspaper and pack of smokes." He points over to a popular brand of cigarettes.

Mr. Robinson reaches for a pack, but the customer corrects him. "No. That brand, to your right." He then goes back to his conversation on the phone.

Amanda is standing behind the rude man and thinks about grabbing the phone and slamming it down on the ground.

However, she must maintain her decorum and remains silent. She does catch Mr. Robinson's eye as he announces the total cost.

"That's six eighty-eight with tax."

The man throws down a ten-dollar bill and grabs his items. Mr. Robinson hands him his change, and the man throws the coins into a charity container on the counter and stuffs the bills into his pocket, walking out while still talking away on the phone.

"Thank you and come again," Mr. Robinson says to deaf ears. He watches the man leave the store and turns to his next customer in line. She is smiling at him, and he smiles at her. "How can I help you, madam?"

Meanwhile, Amy is in the back room, going over the latest delivery and trying her darnedest to account for every piece of merchandise for sale in the store. Armed corresponding box of merchandise sitting in the back room. She seems satisfied that everything they recently ordered is accounted for and begins loading up a cart to restock the store shelves.

Talking to herself, she argues, "Should I feel guilty squealing to the police about him? Him being Marty." She gets a chill even saying his name, let alone thinking about him. The fact that she almost went out with him months ago boils her blood. But she can't stop thinking about him.

"He has taken advantage of Grandpa, and he ran his illegal mob activity, the numbers game, out of our store for quite a while. Yeah, I know Grandpa never complained about the extra cash coming in, and lots of those people bought stuff—or probably stole stuff." She cracks a smile. "Still, we felt like we were under his control." She finishes loading up the cart but is still talking to herself, her voice getting a little louder and angrier.

"Grandpa kept telling me we didn't have to pay the protection money, either, but that's a separate issue. God, why are there people like that on this planet? Always trying to take advantage of everyone and anyone. Somebody's got to do something about people like that. But the biggest thing is the fact that he ditched me on what was supposed to be our first date. What kind of man does that to a woman? Seriously, I'm so thankful we never went out at all." She acts as if she is shaking dirt from her hands and pretends to brush dirt off her body. She then is distracted, as she thinks she hears her name being called. It is silent once more, and then she does hear her name being called, coming from the front of the store. She puts the tablet down on the cart of merchandise and heads out front, where she sees a woman standing at the counter.

As Amy is in the back talking to herself, Amanda is talking to Mr. Robinson at the counter. She asks him to go get his granddaughter. In response, he simply screams her name at the top of his lungs. When Amy doesn't appear, she impatiently stares at him, wondering why he doesn't just walk to the back of the store and fetch her. Hell, she is starting to wonder if she should just walk back there herself. The old man screams for Amy a second time, and the young woman steps out from the back of the store.

With her badge in her hand, as she just had to display it for Mr. Robinson, she holds it out for Amy to inspect. She senses the woman appears nervous or is having second thoughts about speaking to the police. Amanda sees the opportunity to take control of the situation.

"Amy, I'm Detective Amanda Goodfry. We have met before, a while ago, when I was in this store. It is great to see you again." The woman warms up to Amanda a little bit, cracking a semblance of a smile. "Say, do you want to go get a cup of coffee? Maybe take a break from the newsstand for a bit?"

"You know, I would love to, but there is a lot of work that needs to be done. Why don't we just talk in the back of the store? Is that OK?"

"Whatever makes you feel comfortable."

Amy grabs a cola from the cooler and asks if Amanda wants one as well. She declines the offer. Amanda follows Amy to the back of the store, where Amy leads her to a small office past the cart of merchandise and closes the door.

There is a small sofa, a table, and a folded cot in the room, Amanda notices as she looks around, more out of curiosity than anything else. She remarks to Amy that she must stay in there and never leave the store because it looks like this room could double as a studio apartment. Amy ignores the comment, cracks open her cola, and plops down on the sofa. Amanda assumes she should take the table so that she has something to write on. She wastes no time in the questioning.

"So, Amy, what is troubling you?" She smiles, and for a second, she sounds like she is leading a counseling session, not an informal police interview. If that was the case, then she would direct the woman to lie on the couch.

Not wasting any time, Amy begins to spill out everything, sometimes even too fast for Amanda to take notes on what she is saying.

"It's that asshole, Marty. He's the source of all our problems. I just want him out of our lives."

258

"Were you two going out?"

"*No!*" Amy stops, realizing she didn't need to scream. She recomposes herself. "No. He tried to ask me out, and we were supposed to go on a date, but he ditched me hours before."

"And that's why you're mad at him? What does this have to do with the police, dear?" Amanda stops writing and wonders if she is wasting her time with this woman because it sounds more like a bad relationship. Unless there was domestic violence involved, she starts to wonder why she was even called in the first place.

"Because he is controlling Grandpa out there." Amy reaches for the can and takes a gulp, quenching her thirst. She takes a breath then says, "Marty was running a numbers game through this store, as a front. We would take the orders, and he organized the odds and payouts. We collected the money from the customers and paid them when they won. It was bringing in a decent amount of cash every week."

Amanda writes down a few more notes. "And you are confessing to be a part of this numbers game. Is it still going on?"

"No, no. He stopped it last week after he was here. And . . . and . . . he used to use this room as a safe house." Amy continues to come clean on everything.

"Interesting. What else?" Amanda is now more curious as to what else this woman has to say, as she is confessing a lot.

"Well, it all started when the local mobsters were demanding protection money from us business owners. Grandpa started refusing to pay, and Marty made a deal that he would cover the fee if he ran the numbers game here. Also, he really fancied me and wanted Grandpa to introduce us to one another.

At the time, he said he was a business partner of my grandpa. Is that a load of shit or what?"

"But you two never went out? Interesting. Do you think he might try to exert some type of revenge on either of you or this store?"

"No, I think he's over me. Grandpa said Marty's girlfriend was killed in that shootout at Guigi's the other week. I don't think Marty will be coming by here anymore. He hasn't collected his final cut, though."

Amanda drops her pen upon hearing this interesting tidbit, but she maintains her poker face, as she does so often when people just blab away to a police officer and actually say something worthwhile. She thinks, *So the woman killed in the car outside the restaurant was Marty's girlfriend. That means he must have been there, especially if he used this room as a safe house after fleeing the scene. I bet he is now working for the Nunzio mob.*

Amy waits as Amanda appears lost in thought and then watches her quickly scribble a few more notes. She gathers up her things, as though preparing to leave.

"Do you have any other questions because I need to get that stuff out on the shelves?" Amy impatiently asks the detective.

"Oh, sorry, dear. No. I think I have everything. I do appreciate your time and your willingness to share this information with me. If there is anything else you think of or remember, don't hesitate to contact me. Especially if you see Marty again. I will give you my personal phone number; just text me the location where you see him. OK?"

Amy takes the business card with the detective's phone number written on the back. She stares at it for some time, flipping it against her hand. "Hey, I don't want to sound bitchy or jilted or something. It's just that I'm worried about Grandpa out there. These people come in and demand money from us hardworking people. It seems so unfair, and somebody has to do something about it. Right?"

"We try our best, but the mob is so connected in every facet of life. If we take this group out, another will just take its place. That shooting at the restaurant was a mob war between two different groups. It's all about greed. That's all it is." Amanda turns to head out of the back room and into the store.

"I just wish there was something more I could do," Amy says, making one last pitch.

Trying to reassure her, Amanda puts a hand on her shoulder while showing her the logbook. "You have done a great deal. What you said will help the police out a lot. Remember, if you think of anything else you might have forgotten about or if you see him, text me right away. Don't confront him either."

Amy escorts Amanda to the door, and Amanda waves goodbye to the newsstand owners. The door closes, and Mr. Robinson turns to his granddaughter, telling her she did a good thing. Amy shakes her head, not really believing it will make a difference.

"Have faith, girl. It will all work out in the end."

Amy smiles as she hears this and heads back to the cart and her restocking duties. All the while, she thinks, *What else can I do to stop these people and to stop him—Marty?* She hates hearing that name almost as much as thinking about him.

"You know, you could have just told me from the beginning that we wouldn't be taking the most direct route to our first stop," Marty says in a tough-guy voice to the guy sitting in the driver's seat.

"Seriously? Let me ask you this, then. Are you the kind of guy who reads the last page of a book first? No?"

Marty shakes his head.

"Good. Thought so. There are no spoilers, man, that's my mantra. Just let the road take you down the path."

"Piss off."

Bruce laughs. "Wow, three days and you're starting to get sick of me. Maybe you should contact my ex, as you seem to have a lot in common. Let me ask you this, then? What's going happen on day ten or day twenty? Should I bring out the dueling swords?"

"Nah. Dueling pistols so that I can shoot your ass. Is your ex good-looking and available? Obviously, if she had to put up with your ass, then I should have no problems getting along with her."

"Maybe that's enough caffeine for you today, funny guy." He halfheartedly attempts to take the cola can out of Marty's hand with a feeble grab. Marty moves it away quickly to the right, near the passenger window, but spills some as Bruce swerves the car.

"Damn it, man. Keep the wheel steady. I just spilled it all over."

Bruce gets the car steady again. "What did I say? Yeah. No more caffeine for you. It makes you all edgy and crazy. Hardy-har-har."

"Would you just turn on the radio and drive? Where are we stopping off tonight anyway? Did you already plan this out?"

"I sure as hell hope you like music because we are stopping in Cleveland. Reckon we'll go visit the Rock & Roll Hall of Fame. Is that cool or what? You can thank me later."

"I'll thank you when you find us a craft brewpub in Cleveland to eat and drink. I feel like you're trying to starve me."

Bruce points in the direction of Marty's phone. "You know the rules. You're in the passenger seat. You find the place to eat. Now find us a brewpub in downtown Cleveland. Chop-chop. Time's a wasting, and we are less than two hours out."

"Fine. But you can't dog me on the place I find just because that last one was, well, not so good." Marty brings out his phone and searches for a better place to eat as he grabs his stomach, remembering the unpleasant effects from the restaurant he picked the other day.

He conducts a quick search on Google and comes up with a promising choice—a brewpub called Great Lakes Brewing Company. Hell, they will probably arrive too late for the brewery tour, but at least, judging by the menu, it looks to be all right, and it has a lot of beer.

"I got it. When you get closer to Cleveland, I'll guide you in."

"This damn well better be better than the last one," Bruce shouts. He is maintaining his focus on the road and hits the accelerator as he passes on the left, maintaining the speed.

Marty thinks that the brewpub can't possibly be any worse. In due course, they hit the outer metro area of Cleveland. Bruce informs Marty that he needs to direct him to this brewpub. Marty gives the directions, and Bruce, who is already driving crazy, steps up his driving skills and narrowly avoids causing a few major pile-ups. He then cuts in at the last second and drives toward the exit per Marty's detailed directions and previous multiple warnings to get over a half-mile back. Bruce turns a few corners and finally parks in the brewpub parking lot.

"See? I got us here in one piece," he says as he turns off the engine.

"In a manner of speaking." Marty takes a moment to let the shock of his system subside as he steps out of the car.

"Have a beer or two but remember, it's your turn to drive."

"Oh. Or we leave the car here and Uber to the hotel for the night. Well, I'll remember where we parked, then." Smirking back, Marty moves to open the front door to the place and walks inside the brewpub. There, he is met by a smiling, decently cute hostess who looks to be about half his age.

"How many in your party?" the hostess inquires.

"Just me and Pops." Marty points a thumb back to Bruce.

The hostess lets out a giggle and then leads them to a table with a window view. There's not much to look at out the window besides the parking lot, but at least it's a booth. They both sit down on opposite sides, and Marty immediately reaches for the bar menu.

"Come on—we gotta try one of the local brews."

"What did you think I was gonna order? A Bud Light or PBR? Seriously, man. And don't forget the whisky chaser," Bruce adds.

Marty studies the menu and then hands it over to Bruce. He peruses the food menu and makes his selection in less than thirty seconds. He glares over at Bruce, who is still studying the bar menu. A waitress shows up and takes their order; minutes later, she drops off four glasses, two shot glasses and two tallboy beers. Both reach for the shot and toss it back, without a toast or cheers. They then reach for the twenty-two-ounce glasses, each attempting to drain it faster or more so than the other. Marty's glass is slightly lower than Bruce's.

Bruce comments, "I'm pacing myself. And did you forget that you have to drive next?"

"That's all right. If you can't hang, I understand," Marty goads him. "You're old and all. Probably don't have much competition left in ya. If you can't hang, then you can't hang . . ." He trails off on the last smartass comment.

Pissed off, Bruce reaches for his gun. Marty reaches for his beer and chugs it again, and now more than half is gone. He slams the beer glass down on the table. Bruce looks at him and reaches for his beer instead of the gun, chugging it all down in five seconds and flipping the glass upside down on the table.

"How about that, sonny?" Bruce says after a belch .

"So you were thirsty—big freakin' deal." Marty continues to slowly sip his own beer.

The waitress comes by to check on them, and Bruce orders another beer, this time a different one based on the waitress's advice. She is much more friendly toward Bruce than Marty, probably because she is closer to Bruce's age, and Marty can tell that she has taken a liking to Bruce. She departs to fetch the beer for Bruce.

Marty blurts out, "You know, I think she actually fancies you."

Without missing a beat, Bruce says, "Yeah, yeah. I have this problem wherever I go. All women seem to fall in love with me." He then leans back in the booth, going for more of a swagger pose.

"Except your ex," Marty says, trying for the next punchline.

"Well, that's not true. My ex is still stalking me. Every day."

Marty stares across the table. He then shakes his head, laughing. "Bullshit."

The waitress quickly returns and drops off the beer for Bruce. She comments, "It's nice to see a real man in here. I only work until seven if you're interested."

Marty is drinking his beer but starts choking on it, nearly spraying it out, upon hearing the bravado of the waitress hitting on Bruce. Bruce only glances back across the table.

"Seven, you say. Well, that should give me enough time to ditch his ugly ass." Bruce points across the table at Marty. They both have a laugh, and the waitress leaves, sliding her hand across Bruce's shoulder as she departs.

Smirking and laid-back, Bruce says passively, "You know I still got it. One day you will learn from all of the this."

"And now we have to wait for seven o'clock."

"You don't have to wait. She's interested in me, not you. I'm still thinking about it."

"You couldn't possibly leave your maiden waiting for you. That's cruel. Ask her if she has a daughter my age, will ya?"

Bruce sends the bird across the table, flipping Marty off. He takes a pull from his freshly arrived beer. "Jealousy will get you nowhere in life, son." They both have a laugh as the food begins to arrive.

The plates are licked clean, and the drinking glasses start to pile up on the table; it's time to cash out and head to their next destination. Bruce offers to pay the tab, throwing a credit card down on the bill.

"What? Old Nunzio didn't give you prepaid cash cards?"

"No. Why would he? I'm using my own credit card and get travel points on top of it. Sure, the old man will reimburse for all reasonable expenses. Did Mazoli run it differently? Because those points add up to free stuff."

"Well, shit. I should have ordered more drinks," Marty exclaims.

"I said Nunzio will reimburse expenses that he deems reasonable," Bruce counters. "Sometimes, his cheap ass doesn't always pay me back, like when I racked up a hundred-and-fifty-dollar bar tab. Bastard."

"A hundred and fifty bucks? I hope you got a lap dance as part of that tab!"

"Well, some of those drinks were for a certain lady friend I happened to meet up with later that evening."

Marty puts up a hand. "Stop. I don't want to hear any more."

Bruce waves off the hand. "No, wait. You might want to hear this one."

"Does it involve you sleeping with the woman in the end?"

"Well, of course. But it gets even funnier when her husband shows up because he left his evening shift earlier than expected. Damn, I never planned for that scenario!"

Marty readjusts in his seat and reaches for the remaining part of his beer. "So . . . all right. I gotta know what happens now. Was the husband pissed off at you being there?"

"That's an understatement. I think shocked and fucking out of his mind is a better way to say it. Not to mention the guy couldn't shoot a gun to save his life."

"No way! You dodged a bullet, so to speak. Twice!"

"Let me say that was the fastest I have ever run in my life. And for good measure, as I have no bullet holes from that night!"

The waitress comes by to collect the bill and the credit card to process the payment. She sees Bruce sticking his chest out from the previous conversation, and she is even more flirtatious with him.

Marty stands up and motions to leave, peering at her name badge. "Hey, Emma. I need to go to the bathroom. Where is the men's room?"

"Head over past the bar and make a right," Emma quickly replies as a means to get rid of the third wheel. Marty leaves the table. The waitress turns back to Bruce and leans in closer to him.

"Well, are you going to wait for me or not, honey?"

"Name a bar, and we'll be there, Emma."

"There's a bar called Thom's Dive over on Eighth Street. Can you be there, say, oh, around nine o'clock?"

Bruce takes her hand, the one not holding his credit card and the bill. "Of course, sweetie. I will be expecting to see you there. Bring a friend for old sonny boy so we can ditch his ass, the sooner, the better."

She takes a step back. "We'll see, love. We'll see." She leaves the table to process the payment. Marty then returns to the table.

"Do you have a date for this evening? I guess I need to leave, then. Figure out what to do on my own."

"Naw. Stick around, as you may have a date tonight. I need you to keep me busy until nine anyway. Besides, we can hustle some pool until then. I heard you were pretty decent."

"How much money do you want to lose tonight?"

"I was figuring we'd take some locals' money tonight."

"Whatever, man. Money is money to me. I don't care who it used to belong to, as long as it ends up in my pocket by the end of the night."

"That's the spirit." Bruce stands up and leaves the table as the waitress returns with the processed bill. She hands him the receipt and an additional piece of paper with her phone number on it. He takes the paper and blows her a kiss. She blushes but then retreats to her job, brushing her hand across his once more.

Bruce and Marty leave the brewpub. Marty reflects, "Dude. You're playing a dangerous game. She looks likes the type of woman who would stab you if something goes wrong."

"Shit. You don't know what you're talking about." Bruce takes another look at the waitress and thinks about Marty's comment. He shakes his head, figuring Marty is just messing with him.

"Trust me on this one. I know the type. I've been with one. Don't say I didn't warn ya."

"Doesn't matter. Let's go get the car and check in at the hotel. At least we'll have that part down. Because our evenings may go in a different direction."

"We should make a deal. If one of us ends up in jail or in need of help, then the other must step up and help. No matter what."

"You have no idea what you just signed up for, but hell yeah, it's a deal." He shakes Marty's hand as they depart the brewpub.

One night in Cleveland

Before the real drinking commences, Marty and Bruce find their hotel, which was booked earlier, and check in, leaving the car in the lot and taking an Uber to the dive bar Emma suggested for meeting up. Marty asks Bruce if Emma is going to bring a friend or not, based on Bruce texting her on the Uber ride. Bruce finally informs Marty that his date for the evening is named Sara.

"Sara's an all right name. It doesn't sound too hickish or trashy." Marty actually is nervous about meeting a woman after losing Carrie so recently, but he feels more influenced by the alcohol and decides to go with the flow.

"Sure, man. Whatever you say. So how do you want to do the hustle? The classic nine-ball out? How about the scratch on the eight?" Bruce continues to list various types of pool hustles. Marty thinks half of them sound like bullshit but is uncertain if these are real hustle games. It's not like he's going to google how to hustle at pool.

"It doesn't matter. I just win. You know. Clear all the pool balls first before the other guy does."

"But have you ever played against a woman?"

"What are you talking about?" Marty is thrown off by the last comment. The Uber driver announces they have arrived at the destination.

"Have a good night. Maybe even see you later on tonight," the Uber driver says as they exit. He waits until both are out and zooms off to his next pickup.

They both stare at the enormous sign, THOM'S DIVE BAR, as this place is huge, not a dive bar like they were assuming.

"What the hell?" Bruce opens the door and walks in. Marty follows closely behind. Once inside, they both are surprised by how big this bar really is. To the right are about a dozen pool tables and some video games in the back. To the left is the dance floor and a stage, where a band is currently setting up. The oval-shaped bar is located in the center. Without much hesitation, they both head toward the bar and order a cheap draft beer and then immediately separate, heading to different pool tables to start their own hustle games.

Marty lands a game in less than ten minutes. He throws the first game but challenges the victor, best two out of three. He barely wins the second game and then starts not missing the shots in the third game to win some token beer money. He is racking up the pool balls when a bigger whale comes by with serious money, two hundred a game, best of five games. Marty plays the nervous role to a T and finally accepts, provided they each show the cash. He takes a second to see Bruce holding his own at another table and orders another draft beer.

The mark is pretty decent at pool and wins the first game with ease. He plays too cocky, though, missing on one ball before going for the eight. Marty takes his time to step up and then clears the table, knocking in the eight ball and calling the bank shot for the eight ball. The score is 1-1. Marty breaks the third game and completely runs it without missing a shot. Marty is now up 2-1. Bruce finishes his game and heads over to the table, where a crowd is developing. Bruce makes a couple of sides bets. Marty gets a tough break and nails the next two balls but has no shot following and decides to play a safety shot. The mark clears the table, and the game is tied 2-2, with the mark breaking the fifth and final game. If Marty loses, he is out four hundred bucks, but if he wins, he walks away with six hundred. It would be a decent hour's worth of work.

The mark breaks and nails the next four balls; he appears to be well on his way to winning the game and the match. However, he cuts the cue too much and scratches, almost losing it among the crowd. He sends Marty a dirty look as if to dare him to run the table. Marty does it with ease, sinking the eight ball on an easy straight shot. Literally, a novice could have sunk it, and he almost wagered a bet to sink it with his eyes closed. The crowd cheers the victor and quickly disappears after the eight ball falls. Marty throws his cue on the table and walks cautiously over to the guy to collect his winnings. The mark, now supported by three of his buddies, is sitting there nursing his beer and remaining silent.

"All right, man. Time to pay up," Marty commands.

"Fuck you," the mark replies. "You were hustling me. Get the hell outta here."

"I believe it is pay me six hundred bucks and you get the hell outta here. Obviously, I need to play better pool players, next time," Marty says, never losing his stance.

That elicits a response from the mark, and he and his entourage stand up in unison, moving closer to Marty.

Marty sees Bruce hanging back in his peripheral and realizes it is getting closer to nine o'clock, and he wants to meet his blind date. So he grabs a cue and cracks it in half, shouting toward the four of them, "I may be outnumbered, but it doesn't help your side if one of ya can't walk outta here." Marty doesn't even blink while finishing speaking as he cracks one half of the cue on the knee of the unlucky guy closest to him. That guy whelps in pain. Bruce steps forward with a gun drawn on the main mark. One of the guys begins to draw his gun at the same time as Marty swings the other half of the cue down on another man's hand, breaking it and knocking the gun he was holding to the floor. Marty then steps on the gun.

"Are you going to pay my collection agent or what?"

The mark and the remaining uninjured guy collectively gather up six hundred bucks and toss it toward Marty. Marty scoops it up and sees the bouncer heading in their direction. Marty shakes his head, and Bruce quickly puts the gun away. The mark and the other guy help up the two others, and they quickly leave the pool table area and exit through the front doors. Marty grabs the gun lying on the floor and pockets it.

The bouncer arrives and declares, "Is there a problem here?"

Bruce answers first. "Naw. They all left, and they broke a cue."

The bouncer, who doesn't seem too upset, just tells them to leave the pool area, so Bruce and Marty decide to head over to see the band, grabbing a table while the band is taking a break. The waitress comes by and drops two drinks off in front of them.

"Sorry, dear. We didn't order anything," Marty confesses.

Emma walks up, along with a female friend. "No, you didn't. We ordered them for you. Once you finally finished playing pool." Emma goes over to Bruce as he stands up to hug her.

Marty stands up, smiling at the pretty woman standing nervously in front of him. "Hello, I'm Marty."

Emma's friend, Sara, greets him back. "Hiya. We were watching you play pool. I assume you won." She smiles at him. Marty is still pumped up from the earlier altercation and grabs her hand.

"Why don't we walk over there?" Marty points to the bar on the other side. "Be back in a minute," he announces to Bruce and Emma, but they seem pretty engaged with one other at the moment. He pulls her along to the other side of the bar and claims two seats so that they can sit down. The bartender comes by and takes their order, and they begin to enjoy their first drink together.

"So how do you know Emma?" Marty asks Sara directly, trying to make conversation.

She replies, "Oh, I met her in a college class last year when we started our nursing program." She takes a drink from the glass in front of her. "How do you know Bruce. Is that his name?"

Marty leans back, causing him to feel the stashed gun at his waistband from the pool table incident, which he had momentarily forgotten about. "Oh, we work together. I only met him just recently. Oddly enough."

"So . . . I must confess, we were watching you two handle Jack and his gang of thugs. We come here all the time, and you kicked his ass in pool. They busted up one of the bouncers pretty bad last year, in case you were wondering why the bouncers didn't throw you two out. How much did you make them pay?" She brushes his arm up and down.

"Six hundred cool ones."

"That's so awesome. We made thirty bucks on a side bet." Sara leans forward to get closer to him. Speaking in a soft yet sultry voice, she says, "Do you want to leave and go somewhere else?"

Marty hears her whispering in his ear and then sees Bruce and Emma standing right beside them. Suddenly, the night got more interesting.

Both women let out a cheer and collectively go to the bathroom. Marty squares up with the bartender, throwing down a twenty for the two drinks. Bruce puts his hand on Marty's shoulder but not saying anything, yet.

"Aw, shit."

"What is it now, Bruce?"

"You know, you got to start trusting me at some point." Bruce looks at him.

"What the hell are you going on about?" Marty exclaims, still watching for the girls to return.

"They are going to scam us."

"You're outta your mind."

"Walk away, my friend. Trust me," Bruce says as he heads toward the door.

Marty is unsure of what is happening or why Bruce decided to pick this moment to be righteous. But trusting his instinct, he follows Bruce's advice, and they turn around, walk out the door, get into a taxi, and head away from the establishment. Staring out the taxi window, he wonders what would have happened if they had stayed.

Either way, he is still richer—by six hundred bucks and a gun. What a night to remember in Cleveland. And he is starting to trust Bruce. As he looks out the window, he sees the distinctive pyramid of the Rock & Roll Hall of Fame in the distance.

Bag it, tag it at the property office

Sitting on the desk is the case folder marked "Carrie" in red letters across the cover. When the name is in red letters, it means the person is deceased. Some police captain thought a color-coding system would help the officers remember details about the person. Or maybe the captain just wanted to know right away if the person was dead or not without having to look inside. Whatever the reason, the system is still in place, if only because that is what everyone is used to.

Amanda decides to work a little more on the investigation with the restaurant murder case. Even though they have a suspect, because he was killed at the scene, she still has a lot of unanswered questions. Like, for instance, was it Marty who shot and killed the shooter who killed three mob members?

"Hey, I'll be down in the property room." She announces to anyone who's listening, mostly for politeness and formality. She takes the case folder and opens a drawer, grabbing a bag of items recovered from the forensics search of the car at the scene. She starts to head out of the office but turns around to grab her phone, just in case Amy texts with something that might help her out.

Walking down the stairs, she is reminded that the property office is probably located in the farthest place from the Criminal Investigative Department (CID), the area where the detectives' offices are. And of course, it's the detectives from the CID who make the most inquiries regarding the property recovered and booked in, so the placement makes no sense. The beat officers may book in property after an incident, but it is Amy and her colleagues who most often have to book the property out and then back in for interviews, investigations, and court cases. She

276

remembers how her life sometimes seemed easier when she was just a beat officer. But she loves the investigative part of her job so much that she wouldn't trade it for anything. Except maybe the thing she and her two accomplices are planning on the side.

After a long walk, she arrives at the property office and opens the door. A male police officer, a little young-looking in Amanda's opinion, is finishing up booking in some property from a domestic violence incident he attended the other night.

"Hello," the young rookie squeaks out. He then bolts out of the office, likely due to the intimidating effect detectives often have on both laypeople and police rookies.

"Hello. Or is it goodbye?" she says as she watches the rookie leave quickly, the office doors closing behind him.

Tess, the property manager, laughs. "Ha, Amanda. You put the fear into him. You'll just have to stop tormenting these young officers. He looked sooo scared of you—he ran for his life."

"Would you stop it?" she jokingly requests. Tess is known for teasing and pranks. Amanda remembers one particular incident in which Tess put a fake hand in a property bag, added some fake blood, and left it in the police common room, then asked which officer was working the case. Many of the officers fell for the prank, flipping the bag over to get a glimpse of the contents through the clear part of the bag—a real-looking hand covered with blood. It is a rite of passage for most rookies to succumb to a property-office prank, often within their first few months of starting the job.

"What brings you in here?" Tess is finished scanning the property and ready to shelve it in one of the many property-office storage rooms. Amanda looks down the long passageway, wondering how anyone could possibly work in this office.

"I need to book this in, and I need to see a list of all the property booked in under this case." She opens the folder to look up the case number, ready to recite it to the property manager.

Tess puts the property bag down. "You have no idea how many times I have to ask what the case number is, and either they don't have it or have to look it up. Do they think I've got every piece of property and every case number memorized?"

Amanda shakes her head. She's heard this speech many times in the past and will probably hear it many more in the future.

"Well, I actually do have it all memorized. I just like to watch the officer having to go find it." She chuckles at her own lame joke before continuing on. "But you, Amanda, I don't even have to ask you. You are one the few who actually has the case number ready before I even ask!"

"Just trying to make the process faster and more efficient." She hopes the process will go even faster—the sooner she gets out of this office, the better. She never could figure out why just being in this office gives her the creeps.

"Thank heaven for officers like you. Now, what's the case number?" She sits down at the computer and inputs the number, generating a new bar code for the item Amanda is booking in. With the case number still up on the monitor, she runs the other request and generates a printout of all the property for the case.

"Oh, I do remember this case—it's the Mazoli mob hit, except the hit was on him." She hands Amanda the paper and a small property bag, applying the bar-code sticker on it.

Amanda fills out the required details on the bag and places the items she brought with her into the bag. Tess then seals the bag and puts it in the holding area, ready to be shelved.

"Say, can I book this property bag out?" She points to one about two-thirds of the way down the list. It is simply marked "DECEASED FEMALE PERSONAL ITEMS."

"Sure, give me a minute." She runs off to one of the many rooms in property land and comes back a few minutes later holding the bag. She scans it in, and Amanda signs her name, electronically, on the pad, verifying she has booked the property out.

"All righty, then. That's all I needed. Thanks for your help, Tess, as always." She grabs the property bag and turns to leave.

"Sure. Anytime. Don't be a stranger. But do keep in intimidating those young rookies. Ha-ha." Tess's weird laugh dies down, and she then returns to her duties. She heads for the temporary hold and grabs two bags, efficiently keeping her office well organized and the police property properly shelved.

Meanwhile, Amanda returns to the CID office and announces her return, again more as a formality. She plops down at her desk and throws the property on top of the coffee-stained desk calendar. Noticing the red blinking light on her antiquated desktop phone, she follows the common policy of ignoring the stacks of voice mail. She glares at the property bag for a moment, wondering what she will discover inside.

Without any delay, she opens the property bag by removing the numerous staples that Tess or somebody attempted to use to seal it up. After that, she dumps the contents onto her desk while reading, silently, the inventory of the property bag.

One necklace—gold color. One set of keys. One piece of paper—a receipt from a local sandwich place. A note is attached denoting money and loose change that was booked into the property office safe. A small purse containing basic items—credit card, driver's license, and a photo.

Amanda finishes reading the list and looks down at the items scattered about on her desk. She holds the gold necklace for a few seconds and then puts it down and selects another item, picking up the purse this time. She opens it, and although still feeling awkward for going through a dead person's personal effects, she has gotten used to it after working CID for so many years.

Taking a hard look at the license, she mentally notes nothing of importance, except Carrie was an organ donor. The home address has been verified and checked out. It was an apartment, and she had forensics and some beat officers go through the place.

However, what escaped the interest of the initial police officer and others on this case is the photo. She carefully picks up the photo and then realizes the connection she has been seeking. The photo is of Carrie and Marty in each other's arms. It is a nice photo, but she now has evidence that the two of them were romantically involved. She smirks, thinking to herself that no woman is posed in a photo like this if she is not going out with the other person.

The supervisor detective, being nosy, slides on by her desk. "Whatcha working on, Amanda?" He says when he sees the photo in her hand.

"Oh, trying to build a case against Marty in the Guigi's triple homicide." She shows the supervisor detective the photo while thinking that she's found a new lead in this investigation.

"I really just wanted to know what you were doing for lunch. But good job on that. I need to read up on this case some more, apparently." He takes the photo out of her hand to study it in more in detail.

"Yup. I think this Marty fella is the guy who shot the ACS guy dead and fled the scene. I've been working on tracking his movements after the incident. I'll finish my findings and give you the report by close of business tomorrow."

"Excellent, Amanda. Then we need to discuss how to bring out this Marty fellow, as Fred over there just mentioned to me that Marty has disappeared from our radar."

"Yes, yes. Fred and I were discussing that earlier. He must have gotten wind of us looking for him, and he most likely fled town. Another person of interest, Bruce, who has ties to the Nunzio mob, is also nowhere to be found. And the mob boss, Nunzio, is not very cooperative."

"The mob bosses never are," the supervisor agrees. "Still, we believe that he will be making some kind of move. A retribution, if you want to call it that. Based on what we've been hearing on the streets from our informants, we suspect that Nunzio may be doing so quite soon."

Amanda stands up. "Well, hell. Count me in. Whatever operation is going on, I think we have an opportune time to take down both mob organizations. Or hurt them in the very least."

"Good. I'll add your name to the list. Now, I need that report by tomorrow." The supervisor leaves to head back to his office.

Amanda throws all the items back in the property bag and locks it up in her desk. She then receives a phone call and answers it. "Yes," she whispers. "I hear you, but I told you never to call me when I'm at work. Ironically, I need to talk to you right away. Meet me tonight at the hotel bar if you can get away."

The male voice on the other end of the phone replies, "Of course, dear. I see we need to share notes, as I have new information as well to update you with."

"I hope you have something else to share with me, more than just information," she says in a low voice.

"We may have to find another hotel for that," the caller jokes. "But until then, the usual time." He hangs up.

She hangs up the corded phone and smiles inside, already getting warmer and forgetting what she was working on.

"We're supposed to meet this guy here?" Marty asks, looking around and surveying the area, as they are on an island in the middle of a river.

"Pierre, you mean, and yes. On this island in the middle of the Detroit River. Belle Isle is what it's actually called." Bruce looks around as well. "Yeah. It's kinda cool when you think about it." His mind wanders, wondering why there are no homes on the island.

"Think about what?" Marty mocks.

"We are literally standing in the middle of the river, and I can see Canada, like, half a mile away. I bet we could swim to that shoreline. There's a park right there." He points to a park on the other side with the Windsor Casino and hotel in the background.

"That's Canada? Well, damn. The border is really close."

"Why didn't we just drive across the border and pick up whatever it is and drive back?"

"One, you need a passport to cross into Canada. And two, why risk it? Let him take the risk and deal with border patrol. My ass ain't going to jail on a smuggling charge. If I'm gonna do hard time, it damn well better be for something badass. You understanding me?"

"I hear ya."

"Locals talk about a time in the late 1920s -early 1930s during the Prohibition era when people would drive across the river when it froze over in the winter to smuggle bootleg whisky into the US," Bruce says, changing the topic. "Is that crazy or what? Driving across a frozen river carrying whisky, illegally."

"Holy shit. That's nuts. I guess this river doesn't look that deep." Marty looks over the railing and spits in it.

"No. It's about twenty feet deep on the average," Bruce says, continuing to quote facts as though he just read a plaque at a museum.

"Huh. Twenty feet. Like three-and-a-half times my height. Still, the water's got to be a foot frozen before I would think about driving on it."

"I hear ya. I sure as shit wouldn't do it." Bruce gazes across the river, looking toward Canada, thinking and wondering about gambling at the casino. He also thinks about how awful it would have been to live during Prohibition, but then he hears Marty chattering away.

"So how are we supposed to recognize this Pierre fella?"

"He's Canadian, for starters."

"That doesn't help," Marty replies.

"OK. He will speak with a French accent," Bruce says, trying again.

"Still not helping."

Bruce looks over Marty's shoulder. "Fine. How about he's the guy who is coming up behind you, then? Does that freakin' help you?"

"Sure," Marty says. Then he realizes Bruce is not joking around. He turns around and sees that a man has just gotten out of a car. A car with an Ontario license plate. The man studies the two in front of him before smiling and laughing. He immediately walks up to Bruce and gives him a hug.

"Bruce. What say you? Are you doing fine, eh?"

"I am doing well." Bruce smiles back at the friendly Canadian, Pierre, then acknowledges the other in their group.

Pierre lets the hug cease and turns to Marty while extending a hand in friendliness. "And who might you be, sir?"

"I be Marty!" Marty says, reflecting the friendliness back toward the Canadian chap.

"Marty. I'll remember that. There was a famous hockey player named Martin. Well, close enough." Pierre continues to shake Marty's hand and then lets it go. He then moves back toward Bruce, who is waiting patiently for the formalities to be done with.

"Did you bring it?" Bruce asks, wasting no time in going strictly business. "You want to hand it over?"

"Oh, I brought it. And I even brought a gift this time as well."

"A gift?"

Pierre retreats to his car and pulls out two items from the boot. The first is a normal-looking backpack, black in color. The second item is wrapped in a brown paper bag. He brings both items to the two men.

Pierre hands the backpack over to Bruce, who lifts it as though he is mentally weighing it. "Feels about right." Pierre is a little irate to think Bruce is assuming the weight is off, meaning he is short-changing them on what is supposed to be delivered. He turns to his left and hands the package to Marty, feeling he should give the gift to the new guy.

Marty takes the package in hand and is unsure what to do next. Holding the package, he has a good inclination as to what it is without asking and simply removes the item from the brown bag. He lifts a glass bottle from the bag and studies it. Bruce and Pierre smile.

"Well, this is mighty nice of you," Marty says, gazing at the bottle of fine Canadian whisky.

"That bottle will be gone before you even make it back over the border," Bruce laments.

"What makes you think I heading back over right now? I'm hitting the casinos over here and going over to Mexican Village. There's a lot of good places to eat over here. You all should go exploring."

"You know, that's not a bad idea. What do ya say, Marty? We're in no rush." Bruce doesn't bother waiting for a reply or opinion from Marty. "Aw, hell. We'll let the Canuck show us around here in Detroit. Now that's funny." Everyone shares in the jovial laughter, and then Bruce add, "Let's go secure this, and then we'll be up for a throwdown in the Motor City." He slaps Marty on the back, nearly causing him to drop the whisky bottle.

"Where do you reckon we should stay?" Marty asks Pierre.

Pierre laughs at Marty's not-from-around-here accent. "You've got three big casinos with hotels to stay at, but I tend to favor the Greektown casino and hotel. There are a lot of bars and restaurants in that area."

"It's sorted, then," Bruce declares. "We'll go get situated and meet back at the casino bar in two hours."

Pierre nods his head in agreement. "Save that bottle, Marty, as we may need that in the morning." He laughs at his own joke and hops in the car, driving off.

Marty turns to Bruce, who is still holding the backpack. "You know where this Greektown casino is located?"

"Yeah. It's somewhere downtown." He points over Marty's shoulder to the area where all the tall buildings are. "Don't sweat it, man. We aren't under any clock."

"You're the boss."

"Don't you forget that. Now start looking up directions to the casino so that we can start drinking some of the stuff your holding." Bruce gets into the car, tossing the backpack on the back seat. Marty does the same with the whisky bottle but then readjusts it so that it doesn't roll around in the back. He brings out his phone and googles the directions.

"Oh shit. We are really close. Go back over the bridge and turn left."

Bruce takes it all in, smiling, thinking that Marty is becoming a good fella. He probably won't mention that Pierre is a crazy ass when he has too much to drink. What would be the fun if he gave away spoilers to Marty? He also decides not to tell Marty what's really in the backpack or why they are driving around the country. Marty probably wouldn't really want to know anyway.

"You know, you're all right, Marty," Bruce says, showing a softer side for once.

"You'll be all right if you turn right up here where the light is and you buy the first couple of rounds. I hate gambling when I'm sober."

"Because you suck at it, generally speaking?"

Marty is quick to respond. "Dude, you don't want to go there."

"Ah yes, you are Mr. Numbers around the office," Bruce replies sarcastically. "I keep forgetting about that. The one who never helps his friends out."

"I didn't know we were friends. Aw, Bruce!" Marty jeers.

Bruce tells Marty to piss off.

"Well, if you think you can win more money than me tonight, Mr. Tough Guy, you wanna bet on it?" Marty says, trying to goad him into taking the bet.

"Would you just get us to the hotel to check in? Be useful and find out where the valet is."

"It's right up there." Marty points for the place to turn, where a man is waving at them, ready to park the car.

Amanda sits at her desk, doing her due diligence in the realm of police investigations. What she is actually working on, aside from the usual caseload of the regular, often simple investigative crimes from the weekend, like affray, domestic violence, and criminal property damage, is the other, more thorough and time-consuming cases. There is one in particular that holds her interest, being an important case that could especially make her career or perhaps benefit her in other ways.

She happens to gaze at the clock and decides to leave her desk to go outside and talk to her informants out on the streets. She announces to no one in particular that she is going downtown for some shopping, a police code or euphemism meaning that she is attempting to make contact and gather intel from one or some of her informants. All CID detectives have their own street informants; it's just that nobody talks about them in detail. It is assumed that confidentiality is better protected when fewer fellow detectives know about the informants. There is always the standing joke that some detectives have the same informants, but nobody wants to share names lest they lose a potential source of street intel.

"Bring us back some donuts," Joe calls out, and the rest of the detectives join in, adding to the jovial banter.

"Joe, you don't need any more donuts," Amanda says, zinging her fellow detective with a cheap shot. The other detectives continue to add other smartass replies as she closes the office door and heads out of the police station. She turns right at the corner and heads a few blocks up, toward a park where she likes to sit and relax and, more importantly, make contact with one of her informants.

She meanders down the street, trying not to give the appearance of an undercover detective. She thinks she has perfected the move of scoping the area and observing without it looking like that's what she's doing. She's even tried pulling out her phone and pretending to make a phone call, conversing with herself for five minutes—until her phone actually rang with an incoming call. Whoops.

Crossing the street, she makes a mental note regarding the few people in the downtown city park. Casually, she searches for a park bench and locates one, then sits down. Now comes the hardest part. The wait. Waiting to see if the informant comes by or signals to her that he or she has something to share or simply needs money and will tell her anything, hoping she buys it. Amanda has learned over the years that this particular informant is one of the smarter ones. In fact, prior to his substance abuse problems, he was a highly regarded professor at the local university. He is most clever, but sometimes she gets the feeling he is just playing with her with word trickery.

She recalls meeting her informant, Peyton, who also goes by the street name Crossout, many years ago when there was a VIP visit and she was assigned the downtown beat as a plainclothes officer. Peyton made contact with her and began to speak vociferously about the ills of society and how she was a pawn in the whole totality of things. She blew it off and told him to walk away, but he persisted. At the time, she didn't want to blow her cover, so she listened to what he had to say. When he finished, he added the one line she would never forget.

"OK, OK, fella, I listened, and I don't agree with you, so I'm walking away," Amanda had replied to Peyton.

Peyton said back to her, "I appreciate you listening to me, and I promise I won't tell the other thugs you're an undercover cop."

Taken aback, she shouted, "Why would you say such a thing? I ain't no police."

"Then why are you so quick to defend yourself? Think about it, and then come find me when you are truthful to yourself." With that, Peyton walked away.

She stood there for several seconds, realizing he had bested her and she simply had no further reply. Although angry at first, she soon realized he might be useful and eventually found him on the streets a few months later.

He still possesses a way with words, but she has learned to appreciate it and rather enjoys listening to him rattle on about current topics. Sometimes, it actually sounds like he knows what he's going on about. But at other times, he sounds like a complete looney.

Amanda wakes up from her trip down memory lane and quickly moves her head side to side, seeking out Peyton. When she looks left and sees nothing in her general vicinity, she then checks right and sees he's standing close to the end of the bench.

After jumping from being startled, Amanda regains her equanimity and acts as though she is meeting a friend.

"Hello, stranger."

"Why, Mandy, me dear, I hardly consider us as strangers," Crossout says with a hint of smugness. She can smell the odor of stale alcohol and a lack of personal hygiene emanating from him but continues to press on.

"Fine, Crossout. What brings you to the park on this fine day?" She spreads her hands as if demonstrating the beauty of the day.

"Money. Drugs. Booze. Engaging conversation. Sadly, my fellow bums do not provide as enlightening chats as you do." He smiles at her. She tries not to notice the missing teeth, possibly due to the years of meth and lack of visits to a dentist.

"Well, I just so happen to be taking a break and wanted the same thing." He laughs, and she quickly corrects herself. "No. Not the drugs or booze. I am searching for interesting conversation. Shall I start with the topic, say, what the ACS is doing these days?"

"A bit trite and boring. Let's discuss the global repercussions of the actions of first-world countries and their harangue effects on the third world. Now that's engaging." He leans back to stretch, and she hears a bone or two crack.

"No, no. Something a little closer to home. Like what is causing this gang war among the old Italian mobs and the new Asian syndicate."

"Huh. If you would like that topic, then we can debate the causes and effects." He pauses to reflect on how to answer her question. Amanda beams inside, knowing that it is all a game to him and that she has to play it correctly. If that means rewording points for his amusement, then so be it. It doesn't matter how they get to the point, as long as he shares what he knows, as she deems him to be a somewhat trustworthy source.

"You were starting to say something?" she says, prodding him on.

Crossout closes his eyes and reopens them. He seems a little disoriented but then regains his mental state and presses on. "Ah-ha. Yes. The Asian group is moving in, and the Italians don't like it. So what do they do in their master strategy? They take out one of the Italian leaders. Kind of a brilliant move, wouldn't you say? Reduce your competition as a means of gaining their businesses. An unusual business strategy but proven quite effective. Except I don't buy it. I think there is another group playing the two sides."

She ignores his theory, although it's correct, and instead questions him further. "Are you saying the Italians want a war, then?"

"No. Quite the opposite. They are trying their hardest to prevent one. For reasons I cannot fathom, as I think they actually have the advantage. I heard they are going to offer the Asians a token of appreciation." He stops and gazes at her as if assuming she didn't understand him before continuing. "Dear, they are going to bribe them with a deal happening next week."

Amanda is racking her brain to remember everything Crossout has said. Luckily, she has a decent memory and begins to think of different outcomes if she were to intervene on the bribe exchange. "Now what would happen if someone messed it up for them?" she whispers under her breath. She observes Crossout waiting for her, waiting for something to happen. She remembers what that is and fishes a hundred-dollar bill out of her back pocket.

Crossout takes the money and stuffs it in his own pocket but laments, "I see the city council budget cuts are affecting us all."

"Well, that can be increased."

"Tell me more." He perks up as though she just offered him a free hit of meth or something.

"If you can tell me when and where this meeting is going down, then I will double the amount for your efforts."

"My dear, triple would be a fairer price, but I will see you, nevertheless, in two days' time here in the park. Please bring a sandwich for a tired old man next time. It would surely be appreciated. You know, from the fancy deli on Twelfth Street." He tips his hand and turns around to walk away, leaving the park and her.

Amanda laughs at the gall of the old man and brings out a private notebook, not her police logbook, to jot down some notes. She then pulls out her police logbook and writes down a couple of entries, sanitized, of course, for the sake of legal documentation. As she readies herself, a homeless person stumbles by and asks her for any spare change. Snorting out loud, she asks, "What are you going to do with the spare change?"

"What do ya think, lady, I'm gonna by drugs." He gets in her face, trying to intimidate her.

She shows her badge and asks him if he wants to rethink his actions or response, to which he replies more calmly.

"It's all cool, police lady. I was just lookin' for some money to feed my belly. No disrespect meant, police lady."

"What's your name?" She stands up as he slowly steps back.

"It's all cool." He flashes his hands to show he is not a threat.

"Yes, yes." As he steps back, she steps forward. "I still didn't catch your name. Are you gonna tell me?"

"Elijah. Like the dude in the Bible."

"Well, Elijah. Nice to meet you. And what is your other name?"

"I told ya my name." He continues to walk backward as though readying himself to flee at a second's notice.

"No, no. Maybe you didn't understand me. What is the name you go by?" She smirks at him and asks again, "What's your street name?"

"Oh. Oh. Gotcha, lady. My street . . ." He pauses as though he just fell into a trap he can't get out of. He debates whether to make a run for it, but sizing the police lady up, he sees that might not be advantageous.

Instead, he changes his voice, slightly, to a more normal tone and inflection. "It's Icebreaker."

Amanda is stunned by the change in vocal tone. She starts to formulate a question for him but decides to let this play out.

"So, Mr. Icebreaker, what's your game? It's not drugs, so you must be out here for some other reason."

"Aren't you the clever one." He continues to talk in more normal tones and not his initial gangster voice.

"I'm just making an honest living. Nothing more. Are you really a cop? Let me see that badge again."

She shows it to him, and he acknowledges it. "Listen. You appear clean, so I'm not looking to bust you for drugs or some shit like that. However, you do seem like an opportunist, so I am willing to pay if you can deliver."

"Say that again, police lady." Icebreaker's thoughts are all over the place, and he needs clarification on what she is asking of him.

"Icebreaker, I need information on what's happening out and about on the streets. You know, stuff that isn't reported on the evening news. I need someone to tell me these things on, you know, specific stuff. Are you catching my drift? You know what I'm saying?"

"Oh. I hear you. You want me to be a squeal. It's just that I haven't heard of any amounts from ya. You know what I'm sayin'? Mucho dinero?"

"Name a price, then."

Icebreaker chooses his words carefully because he's trying to get the best deal for himself. "Depends on what's it worth to you."

"Why don't we see what you have, and once we verify it's true, then we can negotiate amounts." Amanda demands valid information and not disinformation. "I'm not going to cheat you, but I need stuff I can use. You give me bullshit, and I guarantee your life will get most complicated. You understand me?"

"I hear ya." Icebreaker tells her a few things even she was surprised to hear from him and certainly things that Crossout didn't even mention. She listens intently and brings out the notebook to make additional notes. She congratulates herself on potentially scoring another useful informant. Of course, she has to pay him, and she brings out her purse.

"How's two hundred for starters?" She counts out four crisp fifty-dollar bills and hands the bills over to him, with a slight grip before finally releasing them into his eager hands.

"Fine by me." Icebreaker takes the money, raises his head to look at her once more, and then bolts from the scene.

Amanda debates if she was conned or stumbled upon a gold mine of information really cheap. She was ready to offer up to five hundred and decides the two hundred was equally agreed upon because Icebreaker, or Elijah, doesn't seem too keen on his negotiation skills. She thinks to herself that he could have demanded more, especially if half of the stuff he stated is proven to be true. She has to make a few calls to some people not tied to the police and certainly not legal in regard to her job. But if she plays her cards right, then she may be quitting her day job sooner than she thinks. Now, if her side partner can leave his woman, then all of this will be worth something to her.

The rules of the road

Two days later on a remote highway in the middle of the country, Marty adjusts himself in the driver's seat, something he has been doing every thirty minutes due to the long, boring stretches of endless highway and endless wheat fields.

"Oh, look. This exit coming up has exactly the same fast food and hotels as the previous exit about twenty back. It's like it's the same town, repeated over and over." Marty slams the wheel with his hands as he zooms past the exit.

"Nah. You got to do some research to find the mom-and-pop places. I have to admit, there are decent places once you go a few miles past all the chain stuff located at the exit," Bruce comments as he stares out the window, gazing at another fast-food burger place.

"I dunno where. You never see them advertised on billboards along the highway."

"Of course they ain't gonna advertise. Why should they? The locals have known about them for years. Seriously, you need to venture out sometime. Get outta your comfort zone, Marty."

Marty stares down at the speedometer and then rechecks the cruise control. They are good on gas, having topped up when they last switched. He calculates he has approximately another seventy miles to go before having to switch the driving duties. He thought about it for a while yesterday and finally has the courage to ask Bruce the question.

"Yo, man," Marty blurts out.

"What?"

"I was gonna ask you at some point, and now's as good a time as any." Marty coughs as he struggles to formulate the question.

Bruce never raises his head due to playing a game on his phone, some card game like solitaire, to occupy the time. "Ask me anything except why we didn't just fly out to Albuquerque."

Marty remains mute, having been called out.

"Seriously?" Bruce asks, going in the for the kill. "Was that the question you been meaning to ask me? Fine. I'll share a few things with you."

Marty raises his eyebrows as though surprised. "What the hell do you mean by that?"

Leaning over, Bruce declares, "Well, for starters, we needed to leave town. Get outta sight—the police are looking for us. We are now persons of interest. Nunzio got word some hotshot female detective has your number."

Racking his brain, the only detective that comes to mind is the woman he saw at the newsstand a while back. Marty thinks to himself, wondering if old man Robinson dimed him out to the police.

Chatting away, Bruce keeps spewing out words. "And then Nunzio and I thought it would be fun for me and you to get some bonding time together, and you looked like you needed a vacation."

"*What?*"

Bruce has a chuckle. "No, jackass. I'm bullshitting you. We needed to pick up a few items on the road. The kind of things one can't use the post office for. But I am not shitting you that you and I are wanted by the police for the shooting weeks ago."

"Can't Nunzio get that buried? Surely he has bought a few judges and police officers by now?"

"Having them in one's pocket is one thing. Having them make cases disappear is another thing. And it's tougher to pretend it didn't happen when a formidable mob boss is gunned down along with three other people found dead at the scene. Hence, why we are a thousand miles away in the middle of nowhere."

"No. In the middle of wheat fields is what you meant to say."

"Whatever."

The conversation in the car comes to a complete halt, and they both remain silent for the next few miles. Marty concentrates on maintaining the wheel to keep within the lines as Bruce continues his marathon run of solitaire. Bruce wins the latest card game and then puts his phone down, deciding to speak about something he feels he must share at this point in time.

Bruce starts talking and only assumes Marty is listening to him. During these long stretches of driving through central Americana—vast stretches of farmland, basically—there is really nothing else to keep one from falling asleep at the wheel. Thus, Bruce decides to share some mob wisdom with the current driver—although Marty still has not been told why they couldn't just fly; it would have been much easier and quicker. He is starting to wonder if wasting a lot of time was the game plan all along, just to get them out of town.

"Let me tell you about the rules of the road. Something you will need to know at some point," Bruce says, beginning his speech.

"What are you going on about this time?" Marty protests, half waking up, as he felt like he was in a trance for the last ten miles.

"Just shut the hell up and listen. Got it?"

"Fine. You're the boss."

"At least we agree on something."

Marty attempts a passive-aggressive move by swerving the car, causing Bruce to be shifted slightly in his seat from the jerking motion. Bruce ignores the juvenile gesture. Marty wonders how long of a drive it is to Albuquerque and starts to wonder where they will be driving off to after that. He also wonders what Bruce is going to be yakking away about, but it may actually be interesting, and it most certainly will help pass the time until his driving shift is over. From all this driving, at least he and Bruce are starting to be pals of some sort, despite constantly annoying the crap out of one another.

"OK. Let's hear what you gotta say this time," Marty says, yielding the floor to Bruce. I'm sure it will be enlightening or, at the very least, entertaining."

"Finally, I got you interested in something I might never have revealed to you otherwise as long as I live."

"That's not true. Your story about your ex was amusing if not the funniest as all hell. Probably the best story from you yet."

"Well, I wish I could share your laughter, but then again, you weren't married to her. But listen up. You're digressing, and you may learn a thing or two from this."

"I'm all ears, like the cornfields to either side of us." Marty rechecks the cruise control and opens up his mind, ready for Bruce to bestow some ancient mob advice.

"So. Let me pose this question for you to think about. What do you think is the top way we would get caught by the police doing what we're doing?" Bruce asks, turning off the radio and beginning his lesson. Marty remains silent, understanding the question but not really sure what it is that they are doing.

"OK. Let me rephrase the question. This is for real. Cross my heart and all that shit. You and I, we're smuggling and transferring hot merchandise, drugs, and cash illegally and across state lines. I know there's faster ways to do it, but it's one of the ways to do it, and it is the oldest way of doing this business."

"Yeah. I get it now," Marty interrupts. "I'm a drug courier."

"We are," Bruce corrects him. "Yes. Anyway, back to the original question: What do you think is the number-one way we would get caught?"

"Aw, I dunno . . . doing something stupid, I reckon."

"What? You mean like write 'Drug Runners' on the side of the car? You mean something obvious like that?" Bruce exhales a sigh of disbelief as he starts to wonder if Marty is ever going to get the message.

"No, jackass. That's not what I meant. I mean overlooking something simple that we forget to check, causing the police to have a reason to stop us." He reaches for a bottled water from the back.

"Well, well. Somebody's a clever ass today. OK, Mr. Smart Guy, give me some examples of what you mean."

"That's easy. For one, we ain't driving an expensive car. Nothing fancy or super high end. Just a normal-looking car so as not to be suspicious. And not a POS car either. It doesn't appear to be stolen, ditched, abandoned, or wanting to be set on fire at a moment's notice."

"Yup."

"We aren't driving a car that looks outta place," Marty continues after taking a hit from the water bottle. "We don't have a bumper falling off or missing. We just don't look suspicious. Except we are driving a car through the cornfields, and the last four vehicles I have seen have all been pickup trucks." He cracks a smile.

"Bingo," Bruce exclaims. "You wouldn't believe how many drug runners we have employed who show up in a car that screams, 'I'm carrying drugs in here!' Oh, and this is a personal favorite, getting back to your point about something wrong with the vehicle—for instance, maybe a burned-out brake light or their freakin' tags expired months ago."

Shaking his head, Marty replies, "Sheesh. It was the first thing I was looking at when we got in this car. The tags."

"Good job. I did tell Nunzio you are a smart one."

"A smartass, maybe." Marty laughs.

"Yeah, yeah. At least you know how to appear normal, although your style in clothes leaves a lot to be desired. Still, we should be looking like two guys driving across the country on a road trip." Bruce checks his phone for an incoming message and types a reply as Marty starts talking, not noticing Bruce replying to a text.

"A good ole road trip. Like we are back in our twenties, it's the weekend, and we are taking a break from our university studies. And we are—"

"I get it," Bruce quickly interrupts, attempting to stop Marty from going any further. "You got a hell of an imagination, buddy."

"About another forty miles before it's your turn to take over. What else you got?"

He slides the phone back into his pocket. "We covered the art of looking normal while driving a normal-looking car."

"Yeah."

"Oh, let me tell you this. This one time, me and this other dude were wearing matching sports shirts to appear like we were going to a big college football game. We even got pulled over, randomly, I reckon, and once the police saw us wearing the university jerseys, he just smiled and waved us off."

"No shit? You lucky bastards."

"No luck. Just the forethought to preplan for any potentialities." With that, Bruce taps the side of his forehead to refer to his knowledge of street smarts. Marty only smirks, disagreeing on this point.

Mockingly, Marty says, "And here I thought you were going to reveal a trove of out-of-state license plates and make me switch them out every time we crossed a state line. You know, so that we appear to be local."

"That's a good idea, actually. I may submit it at the next monthly mobster meeting!"

Marty wonders just how long his driving shift is going to last. He peers down at the odometer, and it has only increased by another fifteen miles, twenty tops, since the last time he checked. He snickers to himself, having thought of something to kill some more time.

"OK, Bruce. We're drug runners. Or drug couriers. Or consignment courier specialists. Whatever. I reckon you have done this many times and, judging by the fact that you're sitting next to me and not in prison, haven't been caught."

"Yeah. I'm pretty good. One of the best in the business. I've been referred for jobs in other mobs because I'm that good. What point, if any, are you trying to make?" Bruce boastfully declares his accomplishments, not really thinking of what Marty is trying to ask.

Ignoring the goading attempts, instead Marty says, "You have done this running for a while, with much success. My question is more related to the ones who haven't been so successful. Has there been a time when someone failed on their own account and not because of the police?"

"Say what? No, I told you I have never been caught. We already established that point. What the hell are you asking?"

"Bruce, I was wondering about *someone*. I don't mean one of us, the good guys. Has there been a time when a courier, or drug runner, actually has done a runner?"

Stretching out as much as he can in the passenger seat, Bruce begins to reflect on a time when somebody actually tried to make off with a monthly delivery and honestly thought they could get away with it. Of course, the mob always employs various tracking devices, some that are told and known by the courier and others that are not—because there is always a chance that one guy thinks he is smarter and can escape clean and free.

Bruce moves his head to the left to face the driver. "Funny you should mention that because there is a guy who comes to mind."

"I assume he wasn't successful?"

"You assume correctly. Wanna hear about it? Just in case you were having thoughts of doing your own running?"

"Let's hear it. This should be entertaining, judging by your buildup. Oh, and I will be stopping at the next rest area so you can take over."

"What's the gas level at?"

"Yeah. Good point." Marty observes the gas indicator below the halfway mark. "I will just find a gas station in about fifteen minutes. We can fill up and switch as well."

"Sure. But don't you want to hear what happened to Fred?"

"Why haven't I ever heard of Fred?" Marty jokingly asks.

"Why do you think?"

"Uh . . . Fred's dead?"

"No. But he probably wishes he was. Now shut the fuck the up and let me tell the story about Fred's really terrible life choice."

"Here we go again. Storytime," Marty enthusiastically cheers on.

Bruce gives him the eye before starting the story about Fred.

"Fred was a young guy with a lot of potential. You know the type because he was a lot like you. Hell, buddy, we were both like that, were we not?" Pausing, Bruce reflects on his own personal decisions and where he is at now.

"Are you telling me that we all have a little Fred in each of us?"

"Only if you really hate your goddamn life." He waits for that to sink in before going forward with the story. "Like I was saying, Fred is in each of us when we assume and make the wrong fuckin' decision."

"How so?"

"Stop interrupting and let me tell ya!"

"Then get on with it because I'm starting to look for a place to switch and fill up the gas tank."

"Fine. Fred was the typical guy who wanted to make an impression in the mob world. Yes, he could shoot rather well, but that was probably due to his army training. Yes, he had street smarts, but he also grew up on the mean streets of Chicago. Now, where he had the balls to think he could rip off the mob and get away with it, I have no idea where that came from."

"Just how much did he try to abscond with?" Marty asks, stopping him for a moment. "Was it worth his while?"

Bruce has to think for a second, then replies, "Oh, I would reckon a cool quarter million."

"Well, hot damn. And he didn't think somebody would notice a quarter of a million dollars missing?"

"Fred apparently did not think so."

"I'm afraid to ask what happened to him."

"I'm getting to that."

Bruce continues his monologue regarding Fred's backstory and his failed attempt to rip off the mob. He goes into great detail of the events leading up to Fred nearly absconding with the money and finally getting caught.

"Old Freddie thought he was too slick for us. We assigned him to transport money from out west back to our place on the eastern seaboard. It was a simple job to transport the goods, in this case, the cash, and follow the specific guidelines we talked about earlier."

"I assume the almighty greed part in him took over," Marty says.

"You bet your ass it did," Bruce comments. "Fred tried—and failed—to walk away with over a quarter mil."

"So what you're saying is that I probably don't want to know what we are hauling around the country in the trunk, then, do I?"

"As long as you don't want to steal it and attempt to flee, I'm fine with telling you if you really want to know. It is—"

Marty stops him by raising his hand. "*No* . . . I really don't want to know what we are transporting."

"Fine. Suit yourself. Knowledge is power, but if you don't want to know . . . Well, at any rate, let me finish up with Fred."

"Yes. What happened when you finally caught up with him trying to run off with a quarter million?"

"We applied mob justice, naturally."

Marty laughs. "OK, then. What is mob justice?"

Bruce cracks his knuckles. "It's like this. We eventually tracked him down and then demanded he hand over the money plus interest."

"Oh, come on, that's all?"

"Let me finish. We started by breaking one of his legs. And yes, even after he paid us."

"And then we waited four weeks and broke one of his arms."

"The opposite one to the broken leg?" Marty questions.

"See? You understand how it works."

"So let me guess," Marty says. "You waited another two weeks and then broke his other leg or arm?"

"Nope. The next time we visited him, we grabbed him, threw him in a truck, drove to a bridge, and then threw him over the bridge," Bruce says nonchalantly, as though he was describing a night out.

"WTF! You literally threw the guy, Fred, over the bridge after you spent weeks breaking his arm and his leg?"

Bruce shakes his head. "No, no. You've got it all wrong. It's true, we broke his leg one week and then broke his arm another week. We eventually chucked him over the bridge only because he stole from us and deserved appropriate justice for his crimes against us."

"I'm afraid to guess." Tensing up, Marty prepares himself for what Bruce is about to explain in detail.

"It only cost Fred an arm and a leg. We figured if the bastard lives after all that, then he is absolved of his with us. You see? Karma at its finest." Bruce slaps his knee and continues to smirk in defiance.

Marty is not amused at all. He reflects on the methodology his cohort employs in normal business dealings with problems and is trying to decide if this job is the right fit for him. He reflects on Carrie and wonders what they would have done if they had been able to pursue their relationship even longer. Marty searches to find resolve in all of this, but he starts to unwittingly trust Bruce, the crazy mobster next to him, as a brother and confidant in his current predicament. Maybe this lifestyle isn't so bad after all. Granted, there was a lesson to be learned from Fred. And that is, don't cross the line. No matter what. You will live longer if you stay the course in this business, Marty reflects—easy enough to follow these simple rules.

"Well, hot damn. Fred should be dead for his ultimate betrayal. Yet you guys kept him alive. How noble of you." Marty has been reflecting on his current assignment but gives a standard answer, one to Bruce's liking.

"You act as though you disapprove of the means to the end. So let me ask you, given the choice, would you rather feed him to the gators?"

"Ha-ha. I can only make that decision if the scene takes place in Florida."

"We'll hold you to that, then, should you ever be sent to Florida. Now turn off at the next exit. There's a gas station. We can switch then and stock up on water and snacks."

"Absolutely," Marty replies, reflecting on Bruce's last words. He sees the exit sign up ahead and begins to prepare for a hard-earned break.

What is really going on?

Before Amanda talks on her cell phone, she peers over her shoulder to ensure no one is listening in. And why would anyone be, as she is just someone sitting in a random city park? Still, it is better to be safe than sorry, and she doesn't trust anybody these days. She continually searches her surroundings to make sure she was not or currently is not being followed before answering the call from a mystery caller.

"And you're sure this alleged meeting between the ACS and Nunzio's gang is to take place? What's your source?" Amanda questions the voice on the other end of the phone.

"Of course I am," the caller responses defensively. "Who do you think was the one who arranged the meeting with the Asian Crime Syndicate? You think Nunzio did all of this? That lazy ass? Hell no, he didn't. I did."

"No . . . but—"

"Of course you don't," the caller interrupts. "That's one of the reasons why our plan is gonna work. Nunzio never suspects me at all." His enthusiastic voice gives the impression of victory before anything has happened.

"No," Amanda says, trying again to have a turn in the conversation. "What I was going to say was how certain are you that this meeting will actually take place? I'm not talking about your ability to set it up. I'm more concerned about both parties' willingness to actually show up."

"Damn, woman. You demand a lot," the caller callously retorts. "You act as though you are seriously doubting my abilities."

"No. It's not that," she says reluctantly.

"The hell it is. Just be honest, dear."

"The word I'm hearing on the streets conflicts with what you are telling me. That's all."

"So you always question the firsthand source? What the hell, Amanda? Maybe I should start to question our relationship."

"No," Amanda cries. "That's not what I mean. Come on, Brad!"

"Then what precisely do you mean? Please inform me, then, of what exactly you mean. I got a lot riding on this. If Nunzio ever finds out, then you and I might as well start digging our own graves, if you know what I'm saying!"

"And you don't think my police reputation is on the line, partner?" Amanda fires back, defending herself. "You know what happens to bad police officers when they get sent to the slammer? No? Well, it's not pretty, I'm telling you. So think about it next time before you question my loyalty to our scheme."

"Fine," the caller halfheartedly says.

"Then are you setting things up, from your end, according to what we discussed earlier?" Amanda asks, changing her tone.

"Yes," the caller replies. "I had to make a few modifications. But otherwise, it should go down the way we want it to."

"It better. For all of us." Amanda sighs.

"Oh, let me be clear on one point. Don't think for one moment that if I am going down, you and Chuck won't be going down with me. We're all in this thing together. We are all going down, Amanda, together." Brad wants to add, "Or we kill each other before the pigs get us."

"Hey, you know better to mention names on an unsecure line!" Amanda shouts into the phone.

"And so do you, lass," Brad says, referring to her violating the protocol just as much as he has.

"Oops. Shit. Dammit."

"So have you figured out how to handle that pain in the ass? And here, I will damn well say his name: Marty. He has been a thorn in our side from the beginning. He's onto us. Well, to you. I just feel it. It was a stroke of luck his girl got whacked when the ACS planned their attack because I was going to do it myself. Well, I thought about it, at least," Brad confesses.

"I hear ya. Marty has been an issue from the get-go," Amanda says, voicing her concern. "Cutting in on our profits from the numbers racket is one thing, but I closed that issue and even voided the safe house he had at the newsstand. Unless he is slick enough to avoid this trap, I dare say me or my agreeable second shooter should eliminate any further issues from him."

"Are you so sure?"

"Yes, I am. What do you think of me? Seriously? I am a detective with the police. Cut me some slack." Upset and offended by such accusations emanating from the caller, she protests the allegations and defends herself.

"I hear things. And besides, you aren't the only one in this group who has a lot to lose should our identities be exposed."

Amanda laughs out loud, maybe too much for the other caller. "Oh yes. Once they figure you out, you are good as dead. From your fiancée's hand or otherwise. Like you said earlier. Although I was thinking of buying you a new shiny shovel if events turn unfortunate for you."

"Thanks for the reassurance. Just remember your status—being a cop and being sent to prison. Remember, at least I'm a lifelong criminal. We know how they just love bad cops in prison." The caller laughs maniacally.

"Well, neither of us wants to go to prison or, quite frankly, even think about that," she says, attempting to steer the conversation. "So instead, can we focus on what we need to do to avoid that possibility?"

"Sure. Let me share with you what I do know about what Nunzio wants to do with the ACS, specifically, at next Thursday's meeting."

"I presume this is the meeting I need to intervene in?" She ponders the implications and visualizes the outcome.

"If you can do your thing, this would be the perfect time to implement the plan. Or some part of it."

"Oh, I think this is the opportunity we all have been waiting for, and Nunzio's gang will never see it coming," Amanda says, but internally, she hopes Marty, the great oddsmaker, hasn't anticipated it.

"Then stop yakking on the phone with me and let's just do it. You know, do your part of the plan, and then pass it along to me and Chuck so we can do what we need to do at the right time. Try to get it right the first time—or something close to that."

Amanda thinks long and hard about all that is about to happen before formulating her response. "Sure. I have the plan coming together in my head."

"Good. Just keep us updated, then, will ya?"

"I just have to go visit an old friend first to finalize it all. I'll get back to you within two hours. Fair enough?"

"Sure. Stop blubbering on about it. Just do what you need to do. That's all I need to hear from you. Later, dear." The caller hangs up.

Amanda hangs up her cell phone and pockets it. She then stands up, having one last thought before deciding where to head next. It isn't much of a decision, as the logical choice is most obvious, and it all goes back to the original source, the newsstand. Although her second choice is the Italian deli up the street in the other direction, as she recalls that make some tasty sandwiches. Going against her internal needs, she heads in the other direction, and accordingly, in her mind, she thinks about what to say to old Mr. Robinson.

Walking through the front doors, she immediately sees the old man about to greet her, but then his facial expression reveals apprehension on his part. He is not so happy to see her in his store and knows she is going to demand something of him. However, he continues his facade, sporting a fake smile and displaying a humble attitude as he provides his exceptional customer service skills to the next customer standing in the queue.

"Thank you. That will be seven dollars and twenty-three cents, madam." He smiles at the customer in front of him while seeing, in his peripheral vision, Amanda at the front of the store. He already is starting to sweat, knowing that she wants him for something and that he can't refuse her directly. At least when he was under the control of Marty and the Mazoli gang, he had some bargaining power over Marty because of his ability to bait him with his granddaughter. Even though everyone knew Amy would never go out with his type. Man, that guy was so lovestruck about Amy, but he knew she would make a good decision in how to handle it. That's why he loves his granddaughter so much—she's always had a good head on her shoulders and can sense when something or, in this case, someone, isn't right. He can't say the same for himself, as he keeps cutting deals with the devil, be it the mob or crooked cops. In the end, he'd had a go-around with the devil twice and ended up losing both times. *As long as I keep Amy safe, that's all that really matters,* he reasons. The last customer leaves with her purchases, and Amanda then steps up to the counter.

"Hello, old friend. Is it time for your break so that we can talk?"

"Hardy-har-har. I never take breaks; you must know that. I work here to the bone from open to close. I even—"

Amanda cuts him off midsentence. "Amy. Are you back there?" she belts out with her bossy voice, still looking at him directly. "Come up here, will ya?"

Mr. Robinson now displays the face of a man who has been outwitted, but with a hint of a willingness to raises the stakes and bet again in the next round. Amanda grins, thinking she outplayed him and won this round, which she confirms by seeing Amy marching toward them from the back room.

"I hear my name being called. What is it, Grandpa?" She notices the detective standing at the counter and sees that her grandfather appears to be nervous.

"Your grandpa and I need to have a chat, in private," Amanda says right away. "Mind watching the store while we go talk in the back?" She smiles with an evil twist in the corner of her mouth, and Amy suspects something is afoot. She steps up to the register as Mr. Robinson and Amanda retreat to the room in the back—formerly known as Marty's safe house.

Silently and under her breath, Amy whispers, "Be careful, Grandpa, as I have a bad feeling." She is then distracted by a customer who walks through the door, demanding her attention.

Amanda walks toward the infamous secret room, the very room that once served as a safe house for Marty. She wonders how many other safe houses Marty has around town. Come to think of it, she wonders how many safe houses are actually in existence and used by the criminal element. Maybe she should submit a report to the higher-ups on how to find and then shut down these possible safe houses.

Mr. Robinson cautiously walks to the panel and moves the boxes that were placed for disguise. He opens the door to the room and enters, with Amanda following close behind. He is quick to grab the sofa first and plops down on it, momentarily causing confusion for his guest before she finally pulls up a chair and sits down next to him.

"Well, if you are expecting coffee or something, you can forget about it. I ain't in the serving business," Mr. Robinson says gruffly to his female guest, declaring that he is not going to cater to her beyond what is required.

"No worries. I'm not here to have tea and crumpets with you." She stands up and starts to pace around the room and back and forth in front of him—possibly to intimidate him or simply a ruse or just for the pure hell of it. It doesn't matter, as she has an agenda to adhere to.

"Aw, hell, lass, get on with it," he says.

Amanda stares back at him. "All in due time, Mr. Robinson."

"Are you gonna kill me?" the old man asks fretfully.

"No. Quite the opposite. I want to kill someone, just not you. Sorry. I will tell you some information, and I want you to listen up and decide how to handle it. I trust you will make the best decision for yourself. Or should I say for your lovely granddaughter out there, Amy." She points to the front of the store.

"Well, if it's gonna be like that, then I guess I am at your disposal. What do you need me to do? It must be something, or else why would you be here?"

"For starters, are you good with a rifle?"

His own pride begins to take over. "Hell yeah. I served in the US Army. Was an expert with the rifle, I must confess. What is it you're asking, then? You want me to shoot somebody? Is this even legal? Will I go to prison for it?"

"Old man, you talk too much, you know that? Now, shut up."

He ignores her and keeps right on jibber-jabbering away. "I was a talker in my day, my wife, the love of my life, used to say. God bless her soul." He stares upward, thinking of his beautiful wife, who passed away so many years ago he has lost track of the exact number. He maintains his silence, offering a prayer for his wife of so many years.

Amanda breaks his silence. "Are you even listening to me? I want you to be somewhere, at a particular place and at a certain time, with your rifle. It's as easy as that. You decide what you need to do, but I will give you one additional clue. Your old friend, Marty, will be there. But he won't know it's you. I don't think he would even suspect you either." She then turns to grab him, pulling him closer to her and reciting those memorable words: "I am telling you where you need to be. You make the choice and do what you have to do. But choose wisely, old man."

"I get what you are saying," Mr. Robinson says. "I just want to be clear on what happens if I decide otherwise."

"That's easy. Your granddaughter will be brought in on trumped-up charges. Everything from racketeering to drugs to whatever I think up at the time. She will probably go to prison, maybe for a couple of years. You never know how these things work. You know, she is quite pretty—I'm sure she will make a lot of friends in prison. So does that answer your question? Does that calm your fears?"

"You drive a hard bargain, Detective," he responds somberly, wondering if this is going to get any worse. He takes a second, thinking of his lovely granddaughter and how sad it is that she is the real victim in all of this. The thought that he should raise the rifle and point it at Amanda versus Marty crosses his mind. But all he has to do is do her bidding this one time and take out Marty. Easy enough. If it makes his life and Amy's life a little less stressful, it's worth it. It's too bad, though, he thinks. He actually doesn't mind Marty and thinks he is an OK guy. His mind continues to wander as he thinks about how the detective will then have leverage and can blackmail him again and again, forcing him to do some other task.

"Lass, I'm waiting for you to tell me where I need to be."

"Are you certain you can do what I ask? Are you crystal clear on what is required?"

"Sure as I could ever be." He acts like he is holding a rifle, then aims and pretends to fire. "Old skills never go away."

"Then I will hold you to your word. For Amy's sake, I hope you won't disappoint me."

"You've got your shooter. Now just leave this store, if you'd be so kind, madam."

Amanda stands up and takes one last look at Mr. Robinson, judging him to be one who will keep to his promise. Still, she needs to know that he understands who is calling the shots and who is the boss. She brushes his arm before moving her hand down to his hand and shaking it. "I believe we have a deal."

"Whatever you say; you're the new boss," Mr. Robinson regretfully replies. He's thinking, though, that at the very least, Marty wasn't so bad after all.

That's what friends are for

Marty sits behind the wheel, driving the car like it is not his, pushing the boundaries of the federally mandated speed limits. It's the high plains of New Mexico, and he figures doing 90+ mph is respectable if not demanded on this sparsely populated highway. He begins to have deep thoughts about this whole road trip and decides to question the guy sitting in the passenger seat about all of it.

"So," Marty says to Bruce, who is otherwise engaged with his phone on personal business.

"Yo. Just stay on this road. Head east. It's as easy as that. When you hit the ocean, let me know." Bruce continues to stare down at his phone, never looking up or toward the driver as he is answering emails and text messages emanating from the organization.

Not satisfied with the typical bullshit response and the fact that Bruce is not giving his full attention to the situation, Marty throws another question at him.

"Hey. We made this pickup back in Albuquerque, but what is all this for? Is this something you want to share, or is it hush-hush, top secret, not for the lowly peons like me?" He says it with sarcasm and a little passive-aggressiveness to make his point clear.

Not taking any offense or seeming to be bothered by what the driver is saying, Bruce pauses from his messaging in order to reply to Marty.

"Oh, so you want to be let in on all of it?"

"Rightly so."

"You think?"

"I deserve it, don't you think?"

Bruce chuckles. "Maybe. OK, fine. I'll let you in on some of it, but you gotta keep it under wraps. Otherwise, I will know who squealed, and don't think I will hesitate to knock you off. No offense."

Soberly, Marty states, "None taken." He secretly wonders if he really wants to know it all or not. Bruce seems to be forthright in spilling the beans on top-secret mob stuff. Unless he's been bullshitting him all along. It doesn't matter, really, and Marty thinks Bruce is never totally honest with him anyway.

Bruce leans back after putting his phone down on the console. "Fine. The shipment we just picked up will be used as payment. A bribe, you might call it. It is to pay off the ACS." He hesitates and then adds, "To maintain the peace."

"Get outta here. You're lying."

"God's honest truth. If I'm lying, then I'm dying." He shifts his head upward, as if checking the sky to see if a lightning bolt will suddenly rain down and strike him dead. Marty even wonders, too, and stares upward for a split second before returning to his driving duties.

Marty rethinks his response. "You're lying. You could have shipped the package FedEx or something. We didn't have to drive across the country to pick up a simple package."

Bruce laughs, shaking his head. "No, no. You've got it all wrong, Marty. How else could we have this quality time together and become the good friends we are now?" He smiles. "I feel like I know your entire life history, and you know half of mine." He cracks a grin.

Confirming the same, Marty has to agree with the previous statement, as he knows a lot about Bruce. Maybe way too much and definitely some parts he'd rather not think about, ever, lest it would give him nightmares. He smiles, thinking of some of the rather unusual stories Bruce has recited, running the gamut from some fictional to some being believable but all nevertheless entertaining.

Chiming back in, Bruce reiterates, "Why, how else could we become the good friends we are now? In fact, I may boldly declare that I feel you are like a little brother I never had."

"Gee, thanks. I'm not sure if that's a compliment or an insult or if it just plain creeps me out."

"It is what it is."

"That clears things up. I think. Thanks, pal. Or I should say brother. Ha-ha, older brother!" Marty rebukes.

"Good. Because I have some serious business to discuss. Do I need to be driving, or can you handle the heavy stuff while driving? I don't want you too distracted, as I really would like to arrive alive in a couple of days."

Marty takes a look at their surroundings. He realizes that theirs is one of a handful of cars on the expressway heading east and that they're in the middle of nowhere—some part of northern Texas. He thinks so, anyway, as he recently noticed a sign that they had crossed the state line and were now in Texas. Not that it made any difference, as it is still flat and plain in every direction, with nothing noteworthy to comment on. Rather desolate land, perhaps good for drilling oil or cattle ranching, but that's about it. How Marty yearns for his small apartment on the east side of town, complete with the street noise and the concrete and tarmac of big-city living. It's kind of sad, but right now he actually wants to hear gunfire in the middle of the night in order to feel like he is back in his own proper environment. He jolts himself out of his thoughts.

"Sorry. Is there something you wish to discuss?" Marty asks.

"Don't let me disturb your private waking dream there, buddy. I hope she was beautiful and worth it," Bruce says, referring to what he assumes Marty was daydreaming about. "Although may I plead for caution, as you are the one driving and daydreaming . . ." Bruce begins the attempt at a lame joke before deciding to give up on it.

Meanwhile, Marty goes down the path of his own comic routine, not really listening to Bruce as he babbles about something. "But, Bruce, are you sure the car is not bugged? I don't want to hear something so secretive if somebody else knows about it. Then it's not so hush-hush."

Bruce smirks, in a weird sort of way. "No. The car is not bugged. I guarantee it. Honestly. Who is gonna do some petty shit like bug a car? What are they gonna glean from listening in on us?"

"For one, your cousin is extremely hot and extremely easy." Marty slaps his thigh in laughter at his own joke.

"Can you not focus on her for a sec? Granted, I understand that's hard to do." Bruce smiles mischievously, remembering the story he had recited earlier in the day.

"See? It's tougher than you think!"

"Anyway," Bruce begins, attempting for a second time to be serious with Marty. "Yeah, yeah. So what I am about to tell you, well, there are only two other people that know it. So what I'm saying is if word gets out, then I know who the leak is. And what do we do to leaks? We plug them. Catch my drift?"

"What happens to me, then?" Marty baits him. "Are you gonna throw me off a bridge like the last guy?"

Bruce waves his hand in negation. "Nah. I would simply tie you to a railway track so you'd get run over."

"Seriously? Do people still do that in this day and age?" Marty exclaims.

"Absolutely. Just think about it for a second. You are tied in ropes, struggling to get free, and the train approaches. You hear it first. You then feel the vibration on the track, and there's nothing you can do. Hell, you probably even smell the scent of death, your own, as the train fast approaches, yet you feel helpless, bound by the ropes as the train continues to come closer and closer. You see the lights, blinded by them for sure by now, and hear the high pitch of the whistle trying to warn you. Yet, you are still bound and gagged and seconds away from being run over," Bruce says, lamenting on how it would be a terrible predicament to be in.

"And just how many times have you tied some dude or even some woman up in ropes and positioned them on the train tracks?" Marty questions Bruce. "Your explanation is too perfect to just be making it up."

Bruce laughs. "For starters, you don't see Chris around the office anymore. Or ever, for that matter. Think about that."

"Then I should probably just drop it," Marty declares and instead focuses back on his driving.

Bruce gives Marty a hard stare and then retreats back to his phone, replying back to the messages that have popped up from various people, some from the mob and some not from the mob. Bruce has a wide network of people he communicates with, not always for business and not always for pleasure. Sometimes, though, the two cross paths, but he strives to maintain the boundaries in the conversation with whomever he is chatting with. A most difficult task, at times.

Marty decides to change tack and go down a different conversation track. He wants to ask for more details about all the loot they have been picking up throughout this road trip.

"Yo, Bruce."

"Now what?"

"What's with all the stuff we have in the trunk?"

"Why do you ask?" Bruce says quizzically, giving more of a response than a typical reply to one of Marty's questions.

"Well, I was just thinking. We have acquired a fair amount of stuff. God knows I probably don't want to know what exactly some of the stuff really is."

"A good observation on your part."

Marty stares at Bruce, wondering what he means by that. Be that as it may, Marty still continues ahead. "Yeah. I was kinda wondering, what are we going to do with it?" He gestures to the boxes in the trunk.

Without hesitation, Bruce replies, "All the loot in the back will be part of the bribe we are using toward the ACS."

"Serious?"

"Yup."

"Then are we switching sides or something? What are you not telling me?" Marty asks.

Bruce ignores the insinuation from Marty and instead attempts to explain it in terms of the totality of the situation. "You know, you can call it a bribe. You can call it a peace offering. Hell. You can call it whatever the fuck you want. I don't give a shit. But, I personally think of it as a peace offering for a truce. A calm period after the storm." Bruce hits the button, and the window goes down, letting in a breeze for added effect.

Reflecting on the latest development, Marty thinks about his reply and asks, "So . . . do we get anything in return?"

"Yes. As a matter of fact, we do. We get most of Mazoli's old territory."

"And you think it's fair?"

"What is fair? Honestly? But yeah, I reckon so."

Marty shakes his head. "Why do I need to know any of this? I mean, I just work for the boss. Of what importance am I?"

Bruce gives the look—the look that changes from laughing and joking to one of seriousness and malevolence. It changes the dynamics in the car, demanding the utmost attention of both men. "You think you have no role in all of this? Is that what I'm hearing?"

"Again, why am I being a party to all of this? I'm just the guy who collects the protection money, delivers drugs, and makes the odds."

"Well, me and Nunzio thought about it, and we have the perfect job for you. I wouldn't ask if you are interested because there is no choice in the matter," Bruce declares without much emotion.

"Oh, wow. No choice. I guess I have to accept, then."

"It is most wise of you."

"Then, do I at least get to hear what I have to do?"

"You are going to be the backup shooter," Bruce divulges. "We will be deploying you to a rooftop, and you will be taking out—only if necessary, of course—the ACS person. It's an easy shot and an easy gig. With all your alleged shooting skills you boost of, you should have no worries."

"I didn't say I was trained sniper."

"That's beside the point. You have fired a rifle, and you'll have a target within three hundred meters. Hell, if I can do it, then it should be a piece of cake for you," Bruce says, reiterating his confidence.

Without thinking it through, Marty says, "Then should I start watching some sniper movies? Can I borrow your Netflix account?"

"No. You cannot. But if things go bad, then just shoot everyone and leave. Easy enough. Can you handle that?"

"What could go wrong?" Marty fires back. "I assume our guys are meeting with the ACS representatives, and they hand over the bribe. It should be easy as pie. Right?"

Bruce laughs. "Yeah. That all sounds good, but these things never go as planned. Hence why we need you on the rooftop for that just-in-case scenario. Besides, me and old Nunzio have a standing bet. I think this will go down poorly, but I'm a pessimist. So you're the oddsmaker. What are the odds? How are you calling this one, Marty?"

"Not good," Marty says, blurting out his first instinct, which is usually right. "Especially if you are counting on me to save the day." He snickers before fully comprehending the whole plan and his role in it.

"You will be getting a briefing package within twenty-four hours after we get back. Assuming you speed it up and don't go sixty miles per hour." He points to the speedometer. "In the meantime, you've got to come up with something else to talk about for the next thousand miles or so."

"Actually, it's closer to one thousand and five hundred miles. Not that it matters, though. Still, I'm sure there's plenty of topics to cover we haven't even breached yet." Somberly, Marty ups the cruise control a couple of additional miles per

327

hour in the hopes of lessening the time he has to spend with Bruce. He racks his brain for other topics and decides to switch to sports. Not just one sport but all of them. Heck, if they could talk about the four professional sports plus the two major college sports, football and basketball, then that should kill at least an hour or two. He only hopes and prays this trip ends eventually.

The showdown

Amanda sits in her unmarked car parked on the street near where the meeting is supposed to go down tonight. She is worried about doing this all undercover without radioing it in, although her detective partner is sort of aware of where she is and what she will be doing. Based on the latest intelligence she has read, the ACS is supposed to send a representative to meet with the Nunzio gang. The Nunzio representative is then to hand over a briefcase, full of uncut diamonds of some decent value, which is basically a bribe to have the ACS back off and not start a gang war. In exchange, the Nunzio gang is to have full territory rights to the former Mazoli territory for a period of at least two years. After that, the ACS can start their marketing campaign, and future negotiations regarding the territory rights can commence later on down the road.

As she ponders this, she sees that it kind of makes sense for both sides. However, what if there is another side that has decided to make a play at this, possibly disrupting the balance, that no one accounted for in the grand scheme of things? And it's not the police, although that would be the logical choice. No, it started with a chance meeting of two people, with one in the inner circle of Nunzio's gang. In addition to her, there was another guy, a former, now dead, member of the ACS. Too bad, she thinks, as her own little group of four, now three, could use some intel on the latest movements of the ACS. Now she and the other two have to wing it and make the best guess on future operations.

Like the one tonight, as she is sitting in her car waiting for the ACS representative to show up. Had her ACS partner stayed alive, this part would have been much easier, as nobody would have to die. But with things as they are now, the three of them had concluded that the ACS representative and the two Nunzio members all had to die tonight. And meanwhile, the three of them got to abscond with the diamonds and, in essence, spark a war between the ACS and Nunzio gangs.

She peers out the windshield to witness the ACS representative getting out of the car and walking toward the meeting space, exactly seven minutes too early. She has to hand it to this guy for being punctual—except this time, which will be the ultimate reason for his untimely demise. She steps out of the car and follows him, pausing to shoot the two ACS henchmen sitting in the car, as they are lazily watching their fellow ACS member and not their surroundings. She sneaks up on the unsuspecting car and, without hesitation, shoots four rounds with a silencer, two for each person sitting in the car. Obviously, they were expecting a simple meeting and a handover of the briefcase, nothing more. Too bad for their error in judgment. Amanda opens the car door and quickly pats down the driver, taking his phone and a switchblade but nothing else.

"Seriously, people," she says to no one in particular. She grimaces, thinking about how this gang can possibly compete against the Nunzio gang, then remembers that rival gang members killing other rival gang members will benefit both her own group's interests and the police interests as well—which are, incidentally, not quite the same thing. But she is not bothered by any of it. It's still funny to her to think that one of Nunzio's own is partnered with her and her other associate in bringing down all the gangs, only for her own group to eventually take control—and they're not even a gang. Or at least, their plan B, make a better deal with the ACS for control if the ACS wins outright. Nobody wants this old-school Italian mob stuff that is so dated. She will be the new sheriff in town, and she won't stand for this old-world crap anymore.

She wonders, as she is walking to where the representatives from the Nunzio gang are to meet the ACS rep tonight, if this Marty fellow is an outdated kind of guy or if he would be willing to join her and her crew in the new order. It suddenly occurs to her that her own group has never discussed the possibility of making an offer to Marty. After all, everyone has a price, as there are no honest criminals.

"Things happen for a reason," she whispers as she emerges from the alley after disposing of the third body and then crosses the street, where she sees two men waiting in the alleyway off Fortieth Street. She notes that one of the guys is holding a briefcase, exactly what she is expecting he would be doing. *He might as well hand over my retirement case, as I should warn him, he is not going to survive this night.*

Amanda saunters up to the two men, who stare at her quizzically. She senses their hesitation and notes their defensive posture but decides to play this out, as they have no idea what is about to happen. She knows she has to catch them off guard if her scheme is going work.

"Hey, boys." She smiles and winks at them, trying to act innocent and playful.

Unsure what is going on, one guy replies, in a questioning tone, "Hey."

Amanda continues the facade. "So, boys, I'm looking for a party tonight. Are you two interested in partying with me?" She brushes the man closest to her, up and down his arm in a playful tease.

"Uhhh. Sure. Whatever," both of the men squawk back.

Amanda continues to stare and smile, holding the attention of the men, meanwhile using her hand to slowly withdraw her silencer, pulling it out from behind her. Still maintaining eye contact, she bats her eyes once more and then begins to play her hand.

"Well, well, babe." The male on the right is transfixed by this mysterious woman, never thinking it might be a trap.

"Oh, honey. It's too late." The man is surprised, unable to comprehend her last remark. That split second of uncertainty allows Amanda to take one last look at the man as she unleashes hell upon him before he even has a chance to comprehend the situation. She fires consecutive shots into the first man and immediately, without hesitation, turns a few degrees and fires two rounds into the second man. At least he started to reach for a gun, but it was too late. Both men lie dead in front of her, without even having a chance to fire back.

Satisfied with her actions, she begins to reach for the briefcase but then reacts as she hears a rifle shot ring out. She automatically assumes it is headed for her and drops for cover, her silencer drawn. She scans the area, up and down and all around. She sees nothing and is about to stand up until she hears another rifle shot, this time from a distance, and it doesn't sound as if it's headed in her general vicinity. She still reacts and ducks down again, wondering who is shooting and, more importantly, who are they shooting at? She chuckles as she remembers the conversation with Mr. Robinson, and she now applauds him for actually being a man and understanding what she demanded of him. Although that also means Marty is in the vicinity. She brings out her phone and calls the emergency number first to report shots fired and then phones her partner for additional backup.

***

Marty reviews the briefing packet twice in his head as he takes up his position in the abandoned building across the alleyway from where the meeting is supposed to go down. His head is spinning from all that Bruce has told him over the last few weeks in the car, particularly in the last twelve hours prior to returning home on Tuesday. He swears he needed a day, yesterday being Wednesday, to digest all that was hypothetically supposed to happen and all that will probably happen. Right now, the only thing that is happening is he is sitting in a drafty, abandoned building and is the point man just in case a meeting doesn't go down like it should.

He attaches the plug to his phone and then places the other end in his ear. He clicks on the app from his phone and hears the other person in this two-way conversation.

He begins his callsign authentication. "Dragon Seven. This is Dragon Ass." He waits for the recipient on the other end to get the joke.

"Ha-ha. Dragon Ass. Draggin' ass," Bruce repeats. "Now wise up, will ya, Marty?"

"It's Dragon Ass."

"Whatever. Shut up and listen. Our boys should be moving into position momentarily," Bruce responds over the phone.

Marty peers through the scope in the alley for any additional people entering the vicinity and sees none. He then checks other parts of the field of view, including some windows in other buildings near his position.

"Are you sure? 'Cus I don't see anyone in the alley. It's empty."

"I swear you should be seeing them any second now," Bruce says in a normal, conversational voice. "Keep checking."

"I am." Marty rechecks the alley and then scans around to other parts of the neighborhood, including some open windows. He spots one that might prove its worth and waits it out. Sure enough, as he called it, a woman appears in the window, obviously exiting from a shower and draped in only a towel. Marty continues to watch the woman through the scope as she goes about her business.

"Stand by. I am reacquiring the target area." Marty is transfixed by the woman with the towel and losing sight of the people now occupying the alleyway that he is supposed to be watching.

"Are you seeing any of this, Marty?" Bruce asks on the open mic. "Hello? Earth to Marty?"

Marty watches the towel-draped woman in the building, nowhere near what he is supposed to be looking at. She is oblivious to anyone watching her and is confident in her own privacy, unaware that Marty is tracking her every move with a high degree of creepiness.

"Are you getting any of this?" Bruce screams on the private network.

"What?" Marty exclaims as the woman begins to undo the towel. *Really, Bruce, you picked this time of all times to divert my attention?*

Marty shifts his focus away from woman and back to the alleyway, where three people are now standing. Except two of the three start to fall as the third person, a woman, fires a gun at the other two.

"Oh shit. Bruce!" he shouts as he attempts to realign the rifle. It is at that moment, although briefly, that he spots a police badge on a lanyard around the neck of the shooter. Or he should correctly say, the murderer of two of his comrades. Marty gasps, realizing that the woman who shot his fellow associates, known as Freddie and Pauley, in cold blood is some sort of cop. He aligns his shot and is ready to take it, but then he shanks the shot, possibly due to the shock of the assailant being a woman and a cop.

Although he missed the first shot at the policewoman, Marty automatically reloads and paces himself for the next shot. He will not miss the next one. Except he then realizes, after the fact, that someone else has taken a shot at him. It hit him in the right shoulder, and the pain begins to grow in intensity—it hurts like a SOB. Marty starts to lower the rifle as he is experiencing some serious throbbing pain.

"Bruce. I've been shot. Need pickup immediately. Over."

"Confirm. Did you bag her?"

"No. I fuckin' did not. Somebody bagged my ass, though. Or my shoulder, to be more exact. We need to talk about this."

"Car en route to your position. You better haul ass down the stairs. Now."

"I hear ya." Marty grabs his gun with his left hand. He then runs down the stairs despite the intense pain and burning sensation in his right shoulder. He stumbles down the last flight of stairs and exits the building, spotting the car waiting for him and diving into the back seat before it peels off.

Marty in the getaway car

"Holy shit. What the hell just happened?" Marty shouts, suffering intensely from the pain in his shoulder but still hyped up from all that has happened in the last twenty minutes.

Bruce is behind the wheel of an unmarked car, driving across town toward a destination only he knows. "Shit, Marty! What the fuck just happened?" He continues to turn corners every couple of blocks as though he is trying to shake anyone from following him.

Marty reels in pain. "Shit. I don't fuckin' know. One minute I'm watching some woman in a towel, and the next I'm watching two guys getting gunned down, and then I'm getting shot." He reaches back toward the wound as if trying to alleviate the pain.

"You weren't supposed to be shot," Bruce shouts.

"Well, I did," Marty yells from the back seat. "And I've got a sneaking suspicion on who pulled the trigger. I just know it." He reaches back toward his shoulder, still howling in pain.

Bruce looks to the back seat in the rearview mirror. "So, Marty," he says softly. "Want to tell me what the hell just happened?" He then slams hard on the brakes.

There is an awkward moment of silence in the car. Marty doesn't understand what Bruce is asking of him. He has the errant thought that Bruce is going to pull out a gun and shoot him in cold blood, push his body out the car door, and then go to a drive-through to order a burger and fries. Of course, that would be the second time somebody shot him this evening. What are the odds?

Bruce shifts the car into park. He hits the steering column once or twice before turning around to the back seat. He stares at Marty before deciding to make a confession of his own.

"OK, Marty. You ready for this?"

"What are you going on about?" Marty declares, half of him still waiting to see the gun pointing at his head. He then slowly shifts his body as he tries to reach for his own gun.

Bruce tenses up and then finally says to his friend, "Oh, I guess I didn't tell you everything, did I?"

"What part did you miss, then?" Marty is irate. But now he's more suspicious and less feeling like his life is going to end in minutes.

"Ha-ha," Bruce chides. "Maybe an important part."

"Then enlighten me."

"Of course."

"Why are you hesitating, then?"

"I'm not."

"I disagree." Marty smirks as though he called Bruce's bluff.

"Fine. I'll tell ya."

"Told ya—you're stalling."

Bruce readies himself as though making a confession. "We knew it was all a setup, so the briefcase the woman grabbed contains fake diamonds."

"Say what?" Marty gasps upon hearing this startling revelation.

"Just wait until she realizes that part!" Bruce then calmly explains the whole situation. He tells Marty that they suspected the ACS meeting was going to go astray, so they planted a briefcase filled with fake diamonds in case the meeting was all a sham.

"So it was all a hoax? Wait a minute—then who are we trying to flush out?" Marty asks, wondering who the mole might be.

Bruce responds right away. "The one Nunzio and I think is double-crossing us."

"And you know who that person is?"

"We know who it isn't," Bruce replies. "Still, we knew this was all a setup. We just confirmed somebody is betraying us." He states it boldly and with total confidence. He looks back to Marty, who still is sporting a confused look. "Listen. We always suspected there was a mole in our organization. This now has proved it and reveals who it might be," Bruce declares.

"How so?"

"Well, I can say with certainty that it ain't you."

"That's a relief. By the way, my shoulder is really freakin' hurting. You think you can speed this up? Huh, there, buddy?"

Bruce ignores Marty's comment and presses onward. "Yeah. So we planted the story and the briefcase with the fake diamonds to give to the ACS. Imagine that. The one who just shot Freddie and Pauley will eventually realize the diamonds are fake. But, more importantly, they now know their cover is blown. We set them all up, and it's going to be the reveal time soon enough."

Bruce stops at the mob-approved after-hours medical center. They enter the building, and Bruce speaks first. "Hey, my buddy has just been shot in the shoulder. You think you can patch him up?" He then produces a wad of cash.

The receptionist scoops up the cash as though dealing with normal clientele. "Sure, your money is as good as anyone else's." She pauses as if reflecting on what to call him.

Without missing a beat, Bruce matter-of-factly states, "Why, I'm Mr. X, and he is Mr. Y." He points to Marty, the patient who has been shot.

"Of course—we understand and can accommodate your needs. For the right price." She laughs, not bothering to hand him any forms to fill out and instead ushering them into a room.

"Well, I threw down enough cash to pay for a semester of college. Will that suffice?" Bruce asks the receptionist.

"No worries." She continues to lead them through a set of doors and down a hallway. "You have may just jumped to the head of the line."

Marty, still in pain from being shot in the shoulder, turns to Bruce, declaring, "You know, you're all right. Sometimes."

"Yeah. I feel we got a lot more adventures together, so get healed up. Quick."

"Sure thing, buddy."

"I just hope you can take a joke or two," Bruce responds. "The last guy had no senses of humor. A joke every now and then. But get yourself fixed up first. We will setup a meeting with the boss in a couple of weeks."

"That's what I love about this job—it never bores me," Marty jokes as he reaches for his shoulder, wincing in pain.

"Laugh it up now. You never know when the joke's on you." Bruce slaps Marty's non-injured arm and then leaves the building.

Marty is unsure how to take all of this. Should he still count Bruce as a friend and ally? Will Bruce shoot him at a moment's notice? It doesn't matter, as Marty begins to realize that there are people to trust and some people you don't. Just like he knows what teams are expected to win and which ones won't. And he is certain most of the time. He is directed to remove his shirt and lie on a table by a normal-looking nurse. She attaches an IV line to him and starts it up.

His last thoughts shift to how he is going to repay the person he suspects of shooting him—or should he just let it go? This is one of those moments when it would be a good time to start a new life, with a new job and new location, and go forth from there, once he is all healed up. He could just walk away and never return. Maybe head out west or move to another country. Going with a safer bet, he discards all those irrational thoughts and vows to stick it out with Bruce and the Nunzio mob. The doctor enters the room and surveys the rifle bullet wound. Marty closes his eyes and thinks, *I only pray it may be better than anything else before. What do I have to lose? I think it's a bet I would wager on.*

Don't forget to catch up with Jim and Selma's latest adventures as they travel on the Tequila Highway! In this third book in the series, they journey from their home in the Bahamas to England as they continue to be tracked by an international mob syndicate.

Enjoy this short excerpt on the British Mob from:

TEQUILA HIGHWAY: ACROSS THE POND

Magnus is hanging about at the local pub to where he had lived for many years prior to moving to London for fame and glory. Granted, the fame and glory consisted of running guns to illegal factions in Scotland and Northern England, but he has proved himself over the years as an enforcer and hired muscle. Now that he has drawn the attention of one of the crime bosses in the UK, Sir Owen, Magnus feels he has elevated his status in this tight circle of the crime underworld.

Magnus recalls the first time he met Sir Owen. It was an incident in Manchester that he will never forget. A local crime boss had sent him to enforce a business that had decided not to pay their tribute. Now, Magnus never had an issue with collecting funds from local businesses, but this place was a mainstay in downtown Manchester, a local fish-and-chips shop that happened to make a lovely curry sauce for their signature curry chips. The dish was well known in these parts, and folks from as far as Birmingham even would pay a visit.

Magnus was ordered to do a collection on this particular day when he was also hungry himself. He remembers going to the business during lunchtime and demanding to speak to Amon, the proprietor. Now, Amon immediately recognized Magnus as a regular customer and gave him a curry chips order on the house. Magnus responded in kind by stalling the collection for weeks until Sir Owen intervened.

Sir Owen is a just and fair crime boss, even if he has a liking for killing a person for no other reason than, rumor has it, a bloke sneezing too loud. Whether the rumor is true or not, Sir Owen has a reputation of not taking any gruff whatsoever. Now, this was the time that Sir Owen decided to audit the books, and he looked at why a particular business had not paid their tribute for many weeks. Sir Owen called Magnus to his office. Magnus thought ahead of time to bring in a curry chips meal especially for Sir Owen.

Sir Owen asked Magnus as he entered his office, "Can you give me a reason why I should not put several bullets in your chest? Why have you defied me and my order to collect from this business?"

Magnus remembers his unorthodox response: "Have a taste of the curry chips, and then you can kill me, if you feel compelled to do so."

Sir Owen was taken aback. Surely this bloke wasn't risking everything for a proprietor's signature dish? Why was Magnus so confident that he would like it so much that it would change his view? Sir Owen was flabbergasted and could only stare at Magnus, pointing his .44-caliber gun at Magnus's chest. Magnus never flinched.

He could not take any more of this farce. Sir Owen looked down in the container that housed the curry chips. He opened it up and grabbed a spork in the bag and resolved to taste this dish. Sir Owen took two bites of the curry chips. The savory taste of curry would linger in his mouth for days to come. He has been to curry houses high and low but has never encountered such a taste as this curry. The sauce blended so well with the hand-cut chips that soon he forgot where he was or why Magnus was standing in front of him, silent and without emotion.

Sir Owen composed himself, grabbed the gun, and shot Magnus in the left thigh. A shock and confused expression overcame Magnus's face as he crumbled to the ground in agony and pain.

Sir Owen called for his lackeys to attend to Magnus and take him to the A&E as quickly as possible to tend to the gunshot in Magnus's thigh.

Magnus was straining to understand why the crime boss had shot him. Sir Owen leaned over and stuffed his pocket with a handful of pound notes and said to Magnus, "Your only crime is not telling me of this place sooner. Pray you never fail me again."

And that is the only time Magnus has ever been shot.

About the Author

R.J. Matthews grew up in the Downriver area, south of Detroit, Michigan. He served in the U.S. Army for over 10 years and worked with the British Police Force for 5 years before moving to the beautiful mountains of Western North Carolina. R.J. Matthews and his wife are on a quest to visit all NHL arenas and are close to halfway. He has several writing projects in the works including a screenplay for Tequila Highway: Last Exit and a TV script for Mobster For Hire.